D1124425

THE THIRTEENTH AMENDMENT
AND AMERICAN FREEDOM

The
Thirteenth Amendment
and American Freedom

A LEGAL HISTORY

Alexander Tsesis

NEW YORK UNIVERSITY PRESS
New York and London

NEW YORK UNIVERSITY PRESS
New York and London
www.nyupress.org

© 2004 by New York University
All rights reserved

Library of Congress Cataloging-in-Publication Data
Tsesis, Alexander.
The Thirteenth Amendment and American freedom : a legal history /
Alexander Tsesis.
p. cm.
Includes bibliographical references and index.
ISBN 0-8147-8276-0 (cloth : alk. paper)
1. Slavery—Law and legislation—United States—History.
2. United States—Constitution—13th Amendment—History.
I. Title.
KF4545.S5T74   2004
342.7308'7—dc22   2004010882

New York University Press books are printed on acid-free paper,
and their binding materials are chosen for strength and durability.

Manufactured in the United States of America

10 9 8 7 6 5 4 3 2 1

For my parents,
   Vladimir and Marina Tsesis

Contents

Acknowledgments

Contacts I made with friends and acquaintances during the writing of this book made for a delightful process. Their ideas elevated my understanding, and only time constraints and my shortcomings prevent a better integration of their suggestions. I am deeply grateful for the generosity with which collocutors shared their precious time discussing a subject so important to me and giving feedback at various stages of writing.

Even before I put fingers to keyboard, several outstanding scholars helped with the project's proposed organization. And even though I kept tinkering with the structure until the very end, the advice I received from them was critical. Most encouraging were the recommendations of David Brion Davis, Eric Foner, James M. McPherson, and David M. Oshinsky.

Once the manuscript was complete, Andrew E. Taslitz's multi-page critique, which spoke volumes on how the Reconstruction altered the Constitution, was very helpful. G. Sidney Buchanan and William M. Wiecek aided me with their rich comprehension of legal history that came from decades of research into the Thirteenth Amendment. Both of them provided tremendous insights on an earlier draft and raised my spirits with their support. Segments of the text profited from the excellent editing of Howard S. Erlanger and Richard Warner. I also owe gratitude to the anonymous readers whom the New York University Press solicited. At various points, Daniel Bordoni, Kenneth Obel, Shannon Verner, and Amy Wolff provided helpful stylistic remarks.

Among the many others who offered invaluable advice were Richard Delgado, William E. Forbath, Bruce Goldstein, Emma Coleman Jordan, and Jonathan Lurie. Conversations with Robert J. Cottrol on aspects of slavery helped to put the United States experience into better perspective. The comments of Harold J. Krent, Stewart Macaulay, Sheldon H. Nahmod, Mark D. Rosen, Richard J. Ross, Margaret G. Stewart, and Michael J. Zimmer, who participated in faculty workshops at the University of

Wisconsin-Law School and the Chicago-Kent College of Law, helped to hone the discussion. Gloria Sanders's and Cassondra Mehlum's administrative assistance made the writing process more efficient.

My best advisor and confidant has been my wife, Alexandra Roginsky Tsesis. While her area of specialty, surgery, is quit different from mine, her work ethic and achievements are inspirational. Watching our baby daughter, Ruth, has given me further meaning in life and a deeper understanding of the human condition.

Preface

The Thirteenth Amendment abolished slavery in the United States. Moreover, the amendment's contemporary relevance extends well beyond the abolition of slavery: Its two sections grant the federal government authority to prevent many private and state civil rights abuses. Congress can pass any laws preventing intrusions on liberty that it finds to be rationally related to slavery.

The amendment ended all aspects of the South's peculiar institution, which spread far beyond plantation husbandry into interstate commerce, government fiscal policy, and private sales transactions.[1] Only some of the exploitations associated with slavery were related to forced labor. Slavery emaciated blacks' civil rights and created an aristocratic class that also disassociated itself from the welfare of white laborers. Slavery spread a tangled web that covered many essential aspects of U.S. society, devaluing individuals' humanity and denying them the opportunity to live a good life. Powerful forces in the United States, who imprinted the Constitution with their views, placed a greater value on property rights than on the civil rights of a large segment of the population. Property qualifications throughout the Union silenced blacks and unpropertied whites and prevented them from resorting to political alternatives for ending this hierarchy of privilege. Slave ownership became not only a means of plowing a plantation and caring for a household; it was also the way for whites to assert their supposed dominance both as individuals and as members of Southern society.

The control that masters had over their slaves did not only involve economic oppression. American society viewed slaves in commodification terms; thereby, the spurious right to own human chattel eclipsed slaves' rights to live free, unmolested lives. Owners' property interests trumped their slaves' basic interests of receiving wages, making parental decisions, choosing spouses, or traveling off plantations. The reach of the Thirteenth

Amendment's prohibition against the incidents of involuntary servitude extends to all of these oppressions.

The amendment changed the fundamental structure of U.S. law. Before states ratified the Thirteenth Amendment, the Constitution protected slaveholding interests. The delegates to the Philadelphia Constitutional Convention of 1787 decided that the Three-Fifths Clause, the Fugitive Slave Clause, and the twenty-year protection on slave importation were more important to drafting an acceptable Constitution than including a Bill of Rights.[2] Thus, from the founding of this country, slavery's protagonists held a decisive share of power in the highest echelons of national decision making.

The Thirteenth Amendment abolished the political structure that was linked to slavery. The amendment also changed the dynamic between state and federal sovereignty, granting Congress the authority to protect civil rights. In fact, I argue that the amendment requires the federal government to protect individuals' liberty rights, both from arbitrary private and arbitrary state infringements. The Thirteenth Amendment's idealistic roots lie in the Declaration of Independence, which left the task of fleshing out national civil rights protections to later generations.

The Civil War Congress fashioned the Thirteenth Amendment in the midst of blazing events that almost produced a very different amendment, one that would have explicitly guaranteed states the right to maintain the institution of slavery. Just before the Civil War, on March 2, 1861, Congressman Thomas Corwin from the Seventh District of Ohio proposed an amendment in a vain attempt to appease secessionists, reading: "No amendment shall be made to the Constitution which will authorize or give to Congress the power to abolish or interfere, within any state, with the domestic institutions thereof, including that of persons held to labor or service by the laws of said state." The Corwin Amendment, as it came to be known, mustered the necessary two-thirds majority of Congress required by Article V. The vote in the House of Representatives was 133 in favor of passage and 65 against; 24 senators voted for and 12 against. After President James Buchanan took the unusual step of signing the Corwin Amendment, three states ratified it, and only the onset of the Civil War stopped it from gaining further momentum.[3]

The Thirteenth Amendment began on the road to success about two years later, on December 14, 1863, during the 38th Congress, by which time Corwin was U.S. Minister to Mexico. A different Ohio representative, James M. Ashley, introduced the proposed amendment as one of that congressional session's first bills. He announced his intent to submit an amendment "prohibiting slavery, or involuntary servitude, in all of the States and Territories now owned or which may be hereafter acquired by the United States." In the Senate, John Henderson of Missouri introduced the proposal on January 13, 1864.[4] The Senate Committee of the Judiciary reported the final language for the amendment's first section, which the committee had appropriated from the Northwest Ordinance of 1787. The decision to use readily identifiable model language made the first section's wording ambiguous enough to retain the support of Radical Republicans and conservative enough to gain the votes of several War Democrats.[5]

The proposed amendment then ground its way through Congress until its ratification in 1865. The Senate had passed the proposed amendment in 1864, but because of Democratic congressional gains in the 1862 election the proposal initially had failed to muster sufficient votes in the House. However, after President Abraham Lincoln was reelected in 1864, his support for the amendment helped sway the House, which adopted the proposal on January 31, 1865.[6] After states ratified the Thirteenth Amendment, the Reconstruction Congress relied upon it to pass several laws that were primarily aimed at protecting newly freed people.

After Reconstruction, however, a series of Supreme Court decisions substantially diminished the amendment's significance in achieving genuine liberation. The Court did not revisit the amendment's meaning until 1968, during the heyday of the Civil Rights movement. In *Jones v. Alfred H. Mayer*, the Court found that the Thirteenth Amendment not only ended unrecompensed, forced labor but that its second section also empowered Congress to develop legislation that is "rationally" related to ending any remaining "badges and incidents of servitude." The Court's holding in *Jones* enables Congress to pass statutes against present-day human rights violations, such as the trafficking of foreign workers as sex slaves and the exploitation of migrant agricultural workers as peons. To pass constitutional scrutiny, such laws must be historically related to institutionalized slavery. The judiciary's role is to evaluate whether Congress overstepped its section 2 authority. Unlike the Fourteenth Amendment, which the Court has limited to state-sponsored discrimination, *Jones* iterated that the Thirteenth Amendment prohibits private and public deprivations of constitutional freedom. It is this dual capacity that makes the Thirteenth Amendment a powerful complement among the

Reconstruction amendments, providing liberty rights protections in cases the Fourteenth Amendment does not reach.[7]

Literature on the Thirteenth Amendment is relatively sparse, and only recently have scholars begun parsing its expansive meaning. Akhil Amar has left an imprint on the scholarship with a series of articles. For instance, he has argued that child abuse is analogous to slavery and that hate speech is a badge of servitude. The congressional debates preceding ratification and the congressional powers arising from the amendment's second section were the subjects of Douglas Colbert's work. Both Amar and Colbert drew extensively from the seminal article on the subject, which Jacobus tenBroek wrote in 1951.[8]

Nor has the Thirteenth Amendment received much in the way of book-length treatment. In 2001, Michael Vorenberg published *Final Freedom: The Civil War, the Abolition of Slavery, and the Thirteenth Amendment.* Vorenberg provided a noteworthy historical account of the years preceding ratification and those immediately following it, but his book contains little about the amendment's significance to modern legal theory. G. Sidney Buchanan wrote another excellent book on the subject, *The Quest for Freedom: A Legal History of the Thirteenth Amendment.* Buchanan's book, however, gained a limited readership because the *Houston Law Review* published it only serially in 1974. Further, Buchanan's treatment is not current with recent Thirteenth Amendment scholarship. I draw upon these and a host of historical, legal, and philosophical studies to construct a coherent theory of the amendment's relevance.

My analysis of the Thirteenth Amendment begins in chapter 1 by looking at the degree to which slavery was entrenched in the antebellum United States. Its intrusion into political and social events was so pervasive that virtually all the cataclysmic events of the nineteenth century were conflicts over whether slavery should spread westward or eventually be abolished. I reflect not only on the political events leading up to the Civil War but also on slavery as an institution, for a key to understanding the Abolition Amendment is first to comprehend the workings of the institution that it ended. Such a contextual analysis brings to life events that gripped the country and led it to adopt an amendment that, ultimately, provided a substantive assurance of freedom. Just as the intellectual and historical context of the revolutionary period enlightens the study of the U.S. Constitution, a similarly in-depth evaluation is critical for understanding the Thirteenth Amendment.[9]

The second chapter involves the incremental steps taken toward the amendment's ratification. While the Civil War raged in the divided country, the Thirteenth Amendment's framers argued the desirability and the reach of the proposed constitutional alteration. The congressional debates contain precious nuggets of wisdom that are helpful for understanding the profound change the Reconstruction Congress intended to achieve. Many Radical Republicans, such as Senator John B. Henderson of Missouri, recognized that slavery had "curse[d] the country" and brought "untold miseries."[10] The 1864 and 1865 congressional debates on the proposed amendment indicate that many of the amendment's proponents were not only committed to setting slaves free but, more generally, to protecting civil liberties. Even those congressmen who opposed the proposed amendment foresaw its potential to end many discriminatory practices. Thus, at its inception, Congress viewed the Thirteenth Amendment as a definitive blow to slavery and its vestiges. But a series of emasculating Supreme Court decisions, which I analyze in the third chapter, thwarted the hopes born in the wake of the amendment's ratification. Only in 1968, when it decided *Jones*, did the court reinstate the amendment as the bastion of viable sources for civil rights reforms.

Next, I examine the concept of freedom. That concept is so central to the entire book that I think it best to explain my basic meaning up front and then provide more detail in the fifth chapter. Individuals within a free and equal society have the right to pursue self-defined goals, so long as they do not arbitrarily infringe on the fundamental rights of others. Restrictions on autonomy that are predicated on arbitrary characteristics, such as race, ethnicity, gender, or sexual preference, encroach upon the victims' dignitary rights and harm overall welfare. Within the context of a constitutional republic, by which I mean a representative polity established on fundamental law, each person has the right to pursue and fulfill his or her unobtrusive vision of the good life. In such a society, the common good is the cumulative product of free and equal individuals who pursue meaningful personal aims. Where people are uncoerced by obtrusive laws and private prejudices, they are more likely to creatively contribute to the pool of talents that can be tapped to further community contentment. My account of the Thirteenth Amendment asserts that a society that safeguards the rights to self-determination and self-realization is more likely to achieve a common good. Thus, the Thirteenth Amendment is both deontological, because it protects individual autonomy, and consequentialist, because it aims to achieve a better society.

This concept involves freedom *from* unjust and arbitrary treatment; freedom *to* define one's purposes in life; and freedom *for* choosing from a variety of civic and social opportunities. National protections of civil liberties should facilitate people's pursuit of meaningful lives and conduce to social welfare. Emancipation is only meaningful where persons are left free to fulfill their potential, unfettered by the "idiosyncratic judgments" of others.[11] The Thirteenth Amendment grants the U.S. government power to secure the autonomy of emancipated, equal citizens. That power is profoundly tied to this country's collective passion for liberty. Throughout its history, the nation has often fallen woefully short of its self-image as a free republic of equals, particularly when slavery was so endemic that even presidents like James Polk, senators like John Calhoun, and representatives like Henry Wise owned slaves and acted in the political realm to spread the institution. The Thirteenth Amendment reflects the legal triumph, after the Civil War, of abolitionist aspirations. Each generation is left to reconsider the amendment's pertinence against any remaining injustices that resemble slavery or involuntary servitude.

After a theoretical analysis, I conclude the work by explaining, both in chapters 6 and 7, why the amendment is a potential wellspring for federal civil rights reform. This point of view aims to refine the typical approach to civil rights law. Congress and the Supreme Court have rarely relied on the Thirteenth Amendment for protecting the fundamental right to liberty. They have preferred to locate a variety of liberty rights in the Due Process and Commerce Clauses.

Part of my contention in chapter 6 is that the Fourteenth and Thirteenth Amendments are complementary. While the former only provides guarantees against discriminatory state actions, the Thirteenth Amendment enables Congress to pass nationwide legislation against any state or private vestiges of servitude. This distinction is significant for choosing legislative and litigation strategies. I disagree with scholars who regard only the Fourteenth Amendment to be currently relevant while virtually relegating the Thirteenth Amendment to the past. For instance, David A. J. Richards correctly thinks that both amendments concern the equal respect for persons, but he mistakenly confines the Thirteenth Amendment to a prohibition against slavery while maintaining that the Fourteenth Amendment is an "affirmative principle of justice" that grants "enforceable guarantees applicable against the states of equal protection, privileges or immunities, and due process of law." Richards seems to only credit the Thirteenth Amendment with ending coerced labor, thereby rendering the amendment irrelevant to cases of other civil rights abuses. Similarly, I disagree with George H. Hoemann's view that although the Thirteenth Amendment was to be "the crowning achievement of antislavery, [it] became instead the most modest of ornaments." While for years the amendment's potentials have largely gone untapped, it remains one of the principal achievements of abolitionists and Radical Republicans.[12]

Further in chapter 6, I compare the civil rights value of the Thirteenth Amendment to the Commerce Clause. Congress has enacted civil rights legislation, such as the Civil Rights Act of 1964, pursuant to its authority to regulate interstate commerce. However, the Supreme Court has recently significantly diminished this congressional power, which has further elevated the relevance of a Thirteenth Amendment litigation strategy.[13] Moreover, I show that the Thirteenth Amendment has two advantages over the Commerce Clause: First, Congress can pass laws prohibiting acts resembling involuntary servitude even when they occur only within one state; on the other hand, the Commerce Clause relates to interstate activities. Second, statutes that rest on the Thirteenth Amendment are clearly related to human rights, while those that were enacted under the Commerce Clause place an emphasis on economic interests. Relying on an amendment passed for the express purpose of ending oppression has an important communicative value that commercial regulations do not.

In conclusion, I touch upon several current issues. First, I argue that the federal legislature can prohibit states from adopting Confederate symbols into their official logos since such displays amount to badges of servitude. Then, I claim that the second section of the amendment authorizes Congress to pass a national hate crimes law that would prohibit certain acts not currently covered under any federal statute. Finally, I discuss the Thirteenth Amendment's significance to the labor movement, a subject about which James G. Pope and Lea S. Vandervelde have written more expansively.[14] Even though slavery officially ended in the United States in 1865 with the passage of the Thirteenth Amendment, cases of peonage, international human trafficking, and sharecropping continue to appear.

Before moving into the amendment's potential uses, we must examine the history from which it arose. The task of resurrecting the Thirteenth Amendment into an effective civil rights instrument should begin with an understanding of slavery's broad effect on U.S. society.

PART I

1

Slavery and Its Social Penetration

Study of constitutional law is most rewarding when it concerns civil rights. The chief aim of Thirteenth Amendment analysis should be understanding how to enforce the humanistic principles that lie at its core. Constitutional abolition profoundly transformed the United States from a land that tolerated racial slavery to a country whose core law protects fundamental liberties. The Thirteenth Amendment is not merely a positive prescription against slavery; it is a normative statement about the intrinsic value of freedom. It is both an excoriation of slavocracy, by which I mean all the institutional practices of hereditary servitude, and the guarantee of personal liberty.

The amendment's full effect on the Constitution can best be understood by first examining the oppressive institution it ended. This chapter traces the centrality of slavery in the sectional conflicts that played out in the decades preceding the Civil War. Understanding this history is key to constructing a present that is committed to interpreting the liberal principles of the Reconstruction generation. The discussion here is selective, using a thematic approach, trying to give sufficient context to an infinite set of causes. The aim is to provide adequate historical background, using a synthesis of facts needed for understanding the legal and political events that led to a war born from the South's desire to protect its peculiar institution and that culminated in an amendment designed to destroy it. To this end, some interpretive discussion of the practices of slavery will be helpful. For a more comprehensive overview, there are a number of excellent studies on slavery, including Leon F. Litwack's *Been in the Storm So Long* and Kenneth M. Stampp's *The Peculiar Institution*. Put simply, this institution was one of unrequited exploitation and broken family life that provided its victims with only the bare amenities and forced them into lifelong, hereditary servility. Slaveholding was the aspiration of many whites living in the South who longed for a sense of economic independence and social standing through the ownership of human capital.

A. *Slavery and the Founding Generation*

The revolutionary generation was engrossed in creating a free republic. The Sons of Liberty rallied colonists against taxation without representation, Liberty Polls were assembly places, Patrick Henry embodied the revolutionary project in his pithy statement "Give me liberty or give me death," and Thomas Paine believed America to be "the place where the principle of universal freedom could take root."[1] Revolutionary colonists typically proclaimed that they were under the British yoke of slavery. The 1774 Rhode Island law prohibiting slave importation proclaimed that among rights and liberties, "personal freedom must be considered as the greatest." Black leaders and some of their white counterparts, such as James Otis, recognized the opportunity that the Revolution offered for putting an end to slavery. A group of black New Hampshire petitioners used natural rights terminology to make the point, "[t]hat freedom is an inherent right of the human species . . . [and] [t]hat private or public tyranny and slavery are alike detestable." Similarly, on April 20, 1773, black petitioners from Massachusetts expressed their expectation of "great things from men who have made such a noble stand against the designs of their *fellow-men* to enslave them." The same year, blacks from Boston and other Massachusetts provinces demanded relief from the manifold burdens New England slavery placed on them: "We have no Property! We have no Wives! No Children! We have no City! No Country."[2]

The ideal of universal freedom, particularly as John Locke presented it, made its way into the Declaration of Independence, but it did not end slavery.[3] The Declaration adopted Locke's statement of inalienable human rights, unbeholden to positive laws and not subject to arbitrary governmental infringements.[4] The Declaration's promise of equal freedom would later serve as the starting point for Radical Republicans, who advanced the Thirteenth Amendment through Congress and, later, through state ratification. But the founding generation of American revolutionaries lived with the contradictory promises of civil freedom and property rights in human chattel. In Thomas Jefferson's original draft of the Declaration, his accusations against King George included a clause condemning the British monarch of acting "against human nature itself" by keeping open an international slave trade that violated the "rights of life and liberty in the persons of a distant people." South Carolina, which repeatedly appeared as a leader in the antebellum proslavery camp, opposed the clause, and the Continental Congress did not retain it in the final version of the Declaration.

In the decades between the passage of the country's founding documents and the Thirteenth Amendment, the Declaration's universal guarantee of freedom posed a moral dilemma to politicians and citizens who tolerated and participated in an institution that was contrary to core national commitments. Even though it excluded the antislavery passages, the Declaration of Independence nevertheless established liberty as a chief national aspiration. The Declaration's terms created a rhetorical dilemma for the nascent republic because the nation relied on eugenic theories about supposed black inferiority to justify slavery even though the Declaration proclaimed its support for the principle of universal equality.[5]

The Declaration's wording was so general, without any accompanying philosophical or policy explanation, that politicians only began to identify the Declaration with antislavery sentiments shortly before states ratified the Thirteenth Amendment. In 1844, the Liberty Party's platform asserted that the Fifth Amendment's protections for life, liberty, and property were based on the Declaration's recognition that "all men are endowed" with inalienable rights. Their 1844 platform further declared that slavery was "against natural rights" because it deprived persons of life, liberty, and property without due process of law. The Republican Party likewise understood the Fifth Amendment's commitment to natural rights as a guarantee against the spread of slavery. Accordingly, the 1860 Republican platform stated that "the normal condition of all the territory of the United States is that of freedom. That, as our Republican fathers, when they had abolished slavery in all our national territory, ordained that 'no persons should be deprived of life, liberty or property without due process of law' it becomes our duty, by legislation, whenever such legislation is necessary, to maintain this provision of the Constitution against all attempts to violate it." Even though the Republican Party had adhered to the view that "all men are endowed with inalienable rights" in its 1856 platform, it had then only committed itself to preventing the spread of slavery into the Western territories but not to its total abolition. This stance fell short of the full implications of the Republicans' perspective on the Fifth Amendment. Only in the midst of the Civil War did the

Republican Party adopt the position that slavery had to be eradicated throughout the nation and shifted from relying on the Fifth Amendment to calling for constitutional change.[6]

The Fifth Amendment had proven itself to be a two-edged sword, as proslavery forces also relied upon it. Nineteenth century apologists for the expansion of slavery developed a political philosophy that placed property at the pinnacle of personal interests and regarded its protection to be government's chief purpose. The Fifth Amendment's Just Compensation Clause provided the proslavery camp with a bastion for fortifying the peculiar institution against congressional restrictions to its spread westward. Based on this property rights-centered argument, Chief Justice Roger B. Taney, in his infamous *Dred Scott v. Sanford* (1857) decision, found the Missouri Compromise unconstitutionally violated substantive due process: "[A]n act of Congress which deprives a citizen of the United States of his liberty or property, merely because he came himself or brought his property into a particular Territory of the United States, and who had committed no offence against the laws, could hardly be dignified with the name of due process of law." Taney further equated slaves with chattel, holding that nothing in the Constitution enabled Congress to give less protection to slave property than to any other possessions.

Taney's decision was intended to undermine the Declaration of Independence's embrace of universal equality. He did not stand alone in his wish to limit Congress's power to prevent the spread of slavery, siding with the prejudices of other prominent government officials. For instance, during debates on the Kansas-Nebraska Bill, Senator Albert G. Brown declared that "negroes are not men, within the meaning of the Declaration. If they were, Madison, and Jefferson, and Washington, all of whom lived and died slaveholders, never could have made it, for they never regarded negroes as their equals."[7]

Jacobus tenBroek, a historian of the Reconstruction period, pointed out that the ability of both camps to harness the Fifth Amendment for opposite ends indicated the centrality that constitutional interpretation played in the historic struggle over slavery: "Once the constitutional starting point on either side was accepted, almost all else followed automatically." If slaves were merely property, then the Fifth Amendment protected owners' property rights, but if they were humans, and the proslavery argument was a self-interested excuse for tyrannical exploitation, then the Just Compensation Clause was inapplicable and the Due Process Clause protected African American liberty rights. The antislavery position relied on the Fifth Amendment to expound a natural rights theory against exploitation of persons and the misappropriation of their fundamental interest in life and liberty. Meanwhile, proslavery rhetoric, which the Taney Court accepted, relied on the natural or vested property rights claim that the federal government could not trump state control over private economic interests.[8] Therein lay the need for a clear constitutional pronouncement against slavery and all its manifestations; unfortunately, in the face of Supreme Court conservatism, even the language of the Thirteenth Amendment for a time turned out to be inadequate.

Ironically, the compromise on slavery that the framers of the Constitution made to secure the Union was almost its undoing. Among the framers were a number of outspoken supporters of abolition. Benjamin Franklin was well known for his antislavery sentiments, and in 1787 the Pennsylvania Society for Promoting the Abolition of Slavery, the Relief of Negroes Unlawfully Held in Bondage elected him to be its president. At the constitutional convention the same year, George Mason and Gouverneur Morris argued against continuing the slave trade. Some powerful Southerners sided with Thomas Jefferson, who was an ambassador to France during the Philadelphia Constitutional Convention, in calling for compensated, gradual manumission.[9]

Economic interests, however, proved more powerful than ethical ones. By the mid-eighteenth century, slavery was entrenched in both the North and South. Northern shippers and merchants participated in slave importation in the years preceding the Constitutional Convention until 1808, when Congress legally ended the slave trade. Northern industrialists shipped Africans into the colonies and assured Southern return on human capital by purchasing Southern goods. The North's willingness to ship Africans provided the South with enough laborers to turn a profit on what otherwise would have been fallow farm land.

The proslavery camp used its leverage at the 1787 Constitutional Convention by demanding protections for slavery in exchange for ratifying the Constitution. The willingness to sacrifice human lives for the sake of gaining the consent of South Carolinian and Georgian representatives led the country away from the universal values of the Declaration of Independence and toward an enduring factional division on the question of slavery. Those Northern and Upper Southern delegates who had sought an immediate cessation of the trade gave in to the Deep South's demands.

To their credit, the founders provided avenues for formal political change, including a method in Article V for proposing and amending the

Constitution, which Radical Republicans later used to nullify the proslavery sections. However, the founders did little to alter oligarchical social relations that existed in their own time, granting disproportionate power to slave owners, rather than immediately producing the representative democracy that the Declaration heralded.[10]

The framers' lack of concern for the human rights of slaves was reflected in numerous constitutional clauses. The constitutional concessions to slavocracy were so extensive that the Thirteenth Amendment profoundly altered U.S. laws and society. The antebellum Constitution was marked by a glaring contradiction with its protection of both liberty and slavery. In an article first published in 1850, Frederick Douglass, who had escaped from slavery in his youth and became a renowned civil rights leader, brought out this contradiction: "If we adopt the preamble, with Liberty and Justice, we must repudiate the enacting clauses, with Kidnapping and Slaveholding. . . . Every slaveholder in the land stands perjured in the sight of Heaven, when he swears his purpose to be, the establishment of justice—the providing for the general welfare, and the preservation of liberty to the people of this country; for every such slaveholder knows that his whole life gives an emphatic lie to his solemn vow." Similarly, two years earlier Douglass explained slavery's success to be grounded in "moral, constitutional, political and religious support which it receives from the people of this country." Douglass's clearest explication of his meaning came in a March 16, 1849 article in his newspaper *North Star*, which he published under the slogan, "Right is of no Sex—Truth is of no Color—God is the Father of us all, and we are all Brethren." In the article, Douglass provided a list of constitutional provisions that furthered slaveholding in spite of the Constitution's avoidance of the terms "slaves" and "slavery."[11]

The Importation Clause prohibited Congress from abolishing the international slave trade for twenty years after ratification. During that period of time, the Importation Clause limited Congress's authority to levying a ten dollar head tax for each imported slave. Even though Congress passed laws in 1818 and 1820 that severely punished participants of the slave trade, calls for reopening it continued to be heard until the Civil War. Supporters of the slave trade, particularly those from South Carolina and Louisiana, sought to depress the prices of slaves by flooding the market with them, thereby decreasing labor costs. The Three-Fifths Clause in Article I, section 2, enabled the South, Douglass's article explained, to obtain a "domineering representation" in the House of

Representatives. This provided the Southern congressmen with the power to proffer proslavery laws and the numbers to pass them. Another author has recently pointed out that the Three-Fifths Clause also had a direct effect on presidential elections. Article II, section 1, clause 2 granted each state presidential electors whose number was equal to the states' combined number of senators and representatives. The electors, who comprise the body that votes for the president, played a consequential role in both placing slaveholders, instead of principled antislavery advocates, into the executive office, as occurred in 1800 when Thomas Jefferson defeated John Adams for the presidency, and in seating Northerners willing to placate the slave South, as was the case with James Buchanan's victory in 1856. The Insurrection Clause gave Congress power to call up the militia to suppress revolts, including slave rebellions such as the Nat Turner Rebellion. The Fugitive Slave Clause, which passed without any dissenting votes at the Constitutional Convention, required fugitives to be returned "on demand" and prohibited free states from liberating them. Douglass denounced the provision for making "the whole land one vast hunting ground for men," making felons out of persons who broke the fetters of slavery. The amendment provision in Article V required two-thirds of both congressional houses to propose an amendment and three-fourths of the legislatures or conventions of states to ratify it. This made the passage of an antislavery amendment wholly impossible in the United States before the Civil War, since, in 1860, slavery was legal in fifteen of the thirty-three states in the Union.[12]

This superabundance of slaveholding compromises rendered the Thirteenth Amendment not only critical to ending the physical bondage of slaves; the Abolition Amendment liberated the entire Constitution. It rendered all clauses directly dealing with slavery null and altered the meaning of other clauses that had originally been designed to protect the institution of slavery. The Thirteenth Amendment further reinterpreted the Declaration of Independence to apply the universal declaration of human rights to blacks, whites, and any other citizens. Until the Thirteenth Amendment's ratification, abolitionists who, like Charles Sumner, argued that Fifth Amendment guarantees applied to blacks and whites held this view in the face of explicit constitutional provisions to the contrary. Antebellum constitutional efforts to restrict slavery were ingenious but limited in scope. In 1850, Congress used its Article I, section 8, clause 17 authority over the nation's capital to prohibit slave trading, but not slavery, there; however, the Constitution did not empower legislators to do the same in the slave states.

Antislavery advocates faced the dogma that states had the exclusive right to determine matters about slavery. In this regard, the proslavery camp typically grounded its assertion on the Tenth Amendment's reservation of powers to the state or Article IV's guarantee of a republican form of government. Senator John Calhoun, the leading nineteenth-century state's rights advocate, refined this proslavery concept into the doctrine of concurrent majorities. He argued that the national government lacked the authority to regulate slavery since it was unable to gain support from each state to do so.[13] The Thirteenth Amendment was Congress's response to these influential political ideologies. The amendment's second section made the right to liberty enforceable. It placed the power to protect civil rights in the hands of federal legislators, thereby shifting the balance of power from the states.

B. Slavery as a Cultural Institution

Constitutional protections of slavery coexisted with an entire culture of oppression. The peculiar institution reached many private aspects of human life, for both whites and blacks. An analysis of the Thirteenth Amendment's scope requires a discussion of slavery and its infringement on human liberty. The amendment's prohibitions against involuntary servitude and its grant of congressional enforcement power extends to any remaining vestiges that can be reasonably associated with the institution.

In a 1987 speech, Justice Thurgood Marshall attributed our current "respect for the individual freedoms and human rights" to Reconstruction and the constitutional changes that it wrought. The "momentous social transformation" to which Marshall referred began with the emancipatory power of the Thirteenth Amendment.[14] To start with, it permanently altered Southern culture. Before the amendment worked this qualitative change, the Old South built its society around racial and economic controls founded on racial subjugation. Children learned their identity within this hierarchical structure; husbands, and more rarely wives, took lovers from their slaves; and, at death, testaments were written mindful of any property interest in slaves. Southern politicians con-

cerned themselves with controlling enough slaveholding states to coun-
terbalance the power of Northern Free Soilers. And the number of Southern representatives in the House depended on the number of slaves
owned within congressional districts. Even more, the Southern socioeconomic system, which relied on slave labor for a large portion of its manual tasks, made racial inequality seem to be efficient, thereby attributing
a sense of capitalistic necessity. The means of control, as a leading scholar
has pointed out, extended far beyond slave codes. For instance, plantations, such as those in the Deep South, were established in secluded areas
to better recognize strangers who might be interested in stirring insurrection.[15]

Living under a cloud of coercion, slaves sought a modicum of nor-
malcy whereby they could assert personal and familial autonomy. The
means they used varied from passive resistance to forced work hours (for
instance, feigning illness instead of heading out to work), to independently learning to read and write, running away, and even to organized
rebellions. Their ability to mold their identities was limited by rules,
which often varied among masters and amounted to intrusions into the
most intimate aspects of their lives. Masters often chose their slaves'
spouses, decided whether to separate families through sales, regulated the
money they could earn from their private gardens, named slave children,
and chose the occupations the slaves had to pursue. Even a slave's education was at the master's behest. This broad-ranging subversion of self-as-
sertion was what the Thirteenth Amendment aimed to eradicate. Break-
ing the bonds between slaves and their masters was only the starting
point.

Slavocracy also created a landed gentry that dominated the white un-
derclass. In spite of whites' unequal political standing, racism provided
most of them with a deceptive sense of superior purpose. Although non-
slaveholders typically lacked the material comforts and educational opportunities of their affluent neighbors, race made all whites eligible for
slave ownership. Whiteness was therefore itself a vaunted social station
that conferred a sense of power. Even whites who had no slaves helped
neighbors search for runaways on slave patrols. In reality, there was a
wide disconnect between labor and capital in Southern economy. Slave
owner exploitation of black labor gave employers an unequal bargaining
position that could not be rectified without abolition. Southern white
wage earners competed against substantially cheaper slave labor. White

workers had little bargaining power for demanding increased wages in a world where employers could opt for slave labor and keep it at subsistence levels. Poor whites lacked political leverage in an agrarian system that conferred voting privileges based on wealth and land ownership. Consequently, the wages of Southern laborers tended to be lower than those of their Northern counterparts. For instance, in 1860 the annual average wage for textile workers was $205 in New England and $145 in the South. Instead of organizing to demand adequate wages and reasonable work hours, indigent whites, who could show few immediate benefits from slavery, nevertheless found common racial cause with their rich brethren in maintaining the status quo.[16]

The widely held sense of racial superiority was partly the result of Southern children's daily exposure to the tyranny of forced labor. Children who lived on plantations found slaves willing to act on their slightest whims, which made one firsthand observer of this lifestyle, in 1839, tremble to "think of learning to rule despotically your fellow creatures before the first lesson of self-government has been well spelled over!" Children raised in this environment struggled with their inner sense of empathy and the mores they learned in a culture based on exploitation and subjugation. Huck Finn's dilemma in deciding whether to expose Jim's escape or to help him flee from slavery reflects this inner conflict. Childhood development included learning about social station. Blacks were treated as less than human, unworthy of compassion. In 1840, an emancipation newspaper published a narrative of James Curry recounting what happened to his mother who, in response to a young mistress striking her, pushed the girl away. When the girl told her father what happened, "He came down, called my mother out, and, with a hickory rod, he beat her fifteen or twenty strokes, and then called his daughter and told her to take her satisfaction on her, and she did beat her."[17]

Such early exposure to enforced subordination made owners callous enough to make decisions based on their commercial interests rather than on any consideration for the slaves or their families. The reach of the Thirteenth Amendment needed to provide Congress with the power of preventing these forms of degradations. In the antebellum South, the law left slave families beholden to their masters' economic interests. Slaves could not enter into contracts, so their marriages were not legally recognized. Spouses could be separated by sale, or the master could send one of them to work on another of his plantations or lease him to another person. Even parent-child relations were not respected in this culture. At least six Southern states (Virginia, North Carolina, South Carolina, Tennessee, Arkansas, and Texas) had no law against selling parents and children separately. Masters timed slave sales on economic considerations. For instance, children who were younger than eight were typically not sold apart from their mothers because, until the child was that age, they fetched more money at the market as a duo. However, one owner asserted that "frequently . . . they sell me a mother while they keep her children. *I have often known them, to take away the infant from its mother's breast and keep it, while they sold her.*" At death, the executor could sell the families separately to satisfy the decedent's creditors, keep slave families together, or the testator might bequeath them to a variety of parties.[18] When the Thirteenth Amendment did away with any incidents of servitude, it prescribed the arbitrary interference with family life. The freedom it created ended family coercion and provided federal protection for parental privacy rights.

Blacks were turned into outsiders living in a nation they helped build. Any legal rights they had were tied to their masters' property interests, providing them with virtually no personal security nor right to self-determination. Slaves were afforded none of the rights of citizenship and were prevented from developing their talents.[19]

Even free Southern blacks lived in a world so legally constricted by racial domination that it offered only a deceptive shadow of freedom. Their movement was severely restricted. Some Southern states forbade free blacks from entering at all, coupling the prohibition with the imposition of severe fines against offenders. Louisiana, Mississippi, and Alabama did not even permit free black sailors to alight from their ships. North Carolina forbade them from traveling beyond the county where they resided. Even the paternalistic form of kindness Southerners gave their slaves was not afforded to free blacks. They lived under constant surveillance, lest they become educated and organized enough to rebel. Laws throughout the South prohibited them from assembling, not even for religious services or charitable purposes. Free blacks often worked in the most menial jobs, excluded from professions either by cultural or statutory barriers.[20]

These nominally free people suffered from many of the same burdens inflicted on slaves, and the Thirteenth Amendment sought to prevent their continued denigration. Its sweep, therefore, stretched to Northern discriminations as well since free blacks in the North were saddled with many of the same discriminations as their Southern counterparts. During his U.S. tour, Alexis de Tocqueville remarked that race prejudice was stronger in the North than it was in the South. As with free blacks in the South, the movement of Northern blacks was severely curtailed. In 1859, Oregon was the only free state to enter the Union with a constitutional prohibition against blacks residing there. In 1861, an Iowa statute prohibited any free blacks from entering the state or subjected them to fines, but in a show of faux compassion the state allowed law-abiding blacks already living there to remain. Iowa followed an established line of Northern legislation designed to keep blacks from moving about the expanding country. Ohio, from 1803, effectively limited the number free blacks who could enter because it was practically impossible for them to pay the required $500 bond of good behavior. The Illinois Constitution of 1848 prohibited entry to free blacks. An 1853 Illinois law gave this provision effect, making it a misdemeanor for blacks and "mulattos" to enter the state for the purpose of residing there and subjecting them to a fine or, if unable to pay the $100 to $500, sale to forced labor to pay off the fine and court costs. Then, just a month before President Lincoln's Emancipation Proclamation, during the state's 1862 constitutional convention, Illinois adopted a constitutional article prohibiting blacks from immigrating to the state, which passed by a majority of 100,590 popular votes. Similar exclusionary provisions were found in Indiana law.[21]

Travel restrictions were not the only burdens on Northern black freedom. The Oregon constitution further forbade blacks from owning real estate, entering into contracts, or maintaining lawsuits in the state. In Ohio, they could not testify against whites, even though they were tried before white juries. Ohio also forbade black children from enrolling in schools, although they could obtain instruction inferior to white students. As American migration moved West, it brought with it prejudices that the population wanted to formalize by law. Saddled with restrictions on their liberties, few African Americans could pursue their aspirations; instead, they were forced to live in a discriminatory society. Northern blacks needed the liberating provisions of the Thirteenth Amendment almost as much as Southern slaves.

The incidents of servitude that the Thirteenth Amendment wiped away were endemic to the entire culture. They were neither confined to plantations nor even just to the South. Constitutional protections for slavery percolated into accepted ruthlessness against blacks. They encountered barriers to freedom in their work, family life, child rearing, career pursuits, mobility, and entertainment. The Thirteenth Amendment ended all of these incidents of servitude and provided the United States Congress with the enforcement power to prevent them.

C. Centrality of Slavery in Sectional Conflicts

The history of the sectional conflicts, which ultimately convulsed into the Civil War, is a story about the meaning of freedom in the United States. The centrality of slavery in these conflicts made clear to Radical Republicans of the Thirty-eighth Congress, nearly at the end of the War, that only a constitutional amendment abolishing the institution would definitively resolve the main *casus belli* of secession.

The eighteenth-century constitutional compromises on slavery could only be temporary resolutions to the dilemma of governing a free country where persons were kept in legally recognized bondage. Slavery did not disappear on its own, and probably would not have disappeared following the Civil War without a fundamental change to the Constitution, because it was tied to a racialized worldview. Proslavery thought, which had been gaining in popularity since the 1830s, made emancipation further from the 1861 reality than it had been at the Constitutional Convention. The South feared the loss of power at a time that the United States was expanding westwardly, where slavery had little foothold. Furthermore, the South's economic and social system deprived it of a dynamic workforce since it relied on uneducated workers, both black and white, who were poorly compensated and had few financial incentives.

The Civil War pitted the conservative forces wanting to maintain the status quo against those who desired to use Lincoln's election as a first step to the logical emancipation that framers like Washington, Jefferson, and Madison had foreseen. Even the gradualism of these three founders was unacceptable to the radical opponents of human bondage, and, in pressing to increase federal authority over those Southern domestic institutions that furthered involuntary servitude, Radical Republicans hastened the Abolition Amendment's ratification.[22]

The series of appeasements made to the proponents of expanded states' rights, which favored the slave-owning states, turned out to be counterproductive to the country. In the end, the Thirteenth Amendment was the logical conclusion of a conflict derived from a lack of moral fortitude to act on the principles to which the country committed itself at independence. The very nature of these conflicts indicated that slavery was at the forefront of sectional disagreements. Beginning with the Missouri Compromise of 1820, which admitted Missouri as a slave state and prohibited slavery in the rest of the territory North of 36°30' latitude, Congress paved the way for ever greater Southern demands.[23] The Missouri Compromise attempted to offset the Southern congressional gain of admitting Missouri into the Union by admitting Maine as a free state, but the Compromise only established a temporary calm that led to later cataclysm. The *Dred Scott* decision would later intrude upon this false sense of security to show that as long as slavery remained a legally protected form of property, no compromises could end the moral antagonism extant between proslavery and antislavery forces. In fact, slavery was by 1820 so much a part of the United States' landscape that the only alternative offered to allowing Missouri into the Union would have freed no slaves at all. Representative James Tallmadge of New York, during his only term in Congress, proposed two amendments to a bill allowing Missouri to write its own constitution. The first prohibited any further introduction of slavery or involuntary servitude in Missouri, and the second provided that any children born after Missouri obtained statehood would be free by the age of twenty-five. His amendments passed the House but were not adopted in the Senate. With the entry of Missouri as a slave state, the stage was set for a series of compromises that put off the abolition of slavery until after the peculiar institution's advocates drew the country into Civil War.[24]

The South Carolina nullification crisis was the next great national conflict on this issue. It foreshadowed the later popularity of secessionism. Just as the Northwest Ordinance was Thomas Jefferson's creation, so too was nullificationism, which Jefferson first proposed in the Kentucky Resolution (1798). Writing anonymously, Jefferson posited that states have the right to nullify national laws when Congress presumes to exploit powers that states had not granted to the national government. The Palmetto State issued the 1832 Ordinance of Nullification, nullifying both the 1828 and 1832 federal protections on manufactured goods. South Carolina conceived both of them to be favorable to the North and harmful to its agricultural use of slave labor. The state refused to be moved by a growing worldwide condemnation of slavery and the newly vociferous abolitionist movement. In a September 11, 1830 letter to Virgil Maxcy, Calhoun espoused rebellion rather than the continued infringements of such tariffs on the South's "peculiar domestick [*sic*] institution." Two years later, Governor James Hamilton Jr. made ready to follow Calhoun's advice, raising a twelve thousand strong state army prepared to act against the national government. Rather than stand stalwart, President Jackson threatened reprisal but, in 1833, supported a compromise bill that offered little indication of substantive federal resolve in the face of threatened nullification. This concession, which reduced the tariff over the next nine years, emboldened nullificationists who realized the power of their threats; moreover, the crisis further cleaved the sections into camps with differing interests.[25]

While South Carolina urged nullification, a movement was afoot to immediately liberate slaves. Abolitionists, during the 1830s, had moved beyond the gradualism of their predecessors, and it was their idealism that would eventually influence leaders like Charles Sumner and Thaddeus Stevens to advocate for passage of the Thirteenth Amendment. Beginning in 1831, two wealthy philanthropists, Arthur and Lewis Tappan, began funding an antislavery movement through their dry-goods fortune. They helped establish the American Anti-Slavery Society in 1833, which began to spread abolitionist ideas throughout the country. James Birney, the son of a slave owner from Kentucky, spread the society's message through his widely circulated newspaper, the *Philanthropist*. Another of the society's founders, William Lloyd Garrison, brought an unapologetic vehemence to the movement and an uncompromising stand against gradualism, unwilling to accept anything short of total emancipation. After years of struggle, the Thirteenth Amendment would, according to Garrison, change the Constitution from "a covenant with death" to "a covenant with life." Garrison, who had long been fighting for constitutional change by 1865, when the amendment was ratified, first published his weekly journal, the *Liberator*, in 1831. He was then only twenty-six years old. Articulate ex-slaves like Frederick Douglass, who wrote an autobiography about his escape from slavery in *Narrative of the Life of Frederick Douglass, an American Slave* (1845), and William Wells Brown, who penned *Narrative of William W. Brown, an American Slave* (1849), gave firsthand accounts of the American Anti-Slavery Society's narrative. The oratory and research skill of Theodore D. Weld further promoted the liberation movement. Weld first began practicing and preaching against racial intolerance while a student at the Lane Theological Seminary and at the progressive Oberlin College. Through his influential book, *American Slavery As It Is*, he passed onto Radical Republicans the view that slavery involved "plundering the slaves of all their inalienable rights." Slaveholders robbed slaves of their "bodies and minds, their time and liberty and earnings, their free speech and rights of conscience, their right to acquire knowledge, and property, and reputation." And this view would come to buttress the Senate and House debates supporting passage of the Thirteenth Amendment. Weld's marriage with feminist abolitionist Angelina Grimké was productive, and together they advocated racial equality and spoke against Northern racism. These trailblazers faced violent mobs, who often assaulted them with stones and bricks, with uncompromising abolitionist principles, not afraid to "lie upon rack—and clasp the faggot—and tread with steady step to the scaffold," as Weld put it. The South's reaction to abolitionists was increasingly entrenched dogmatism coupled with a demand for more compromises to assure the continued vitality of slavery against abolitionist firebrands.[26]

To be sure, the compromises between North and South were not only about regulating slavery. But it was an issue that was central to them all. The Compromise of 1850 best illustrates how, among a diversity of negotiated issues, the dispute about slavery was by far the most rancorous and almost plunged the nation into Civil War eleven years before the fighting actually broke out.

Prior to forging the Compromise of 1850, the United States acquired land after the Mexican War (1846–1848). That territory had been free under Mexican law, and it remained free as the territory of New Mexico. Soon, California also declared its intent to remain free under the U.S. flag. The South, as a section wanting to preserve its economic interests and social customs, sought to gain significant compensation in exchange for free states entering the Union. Several bills began circulating in Congress to end the standoff.[27]

Senator Henry Clay, the "Great Compromiser," stepped in to create an omnibus bill from various existing proposals. Clay became involved after his disappointing loss to General Zachary Taylor in the 1848 Whig presidential convention. Clay had a passion for ending sectional conflicts by integrating Northern and Southern interests, and he took the job of leading the 1850 debates even though he had decided the year before to step out of the political limelight, when he asked not to serve even on standing committees.[28] Unfortunately, his solution, just as the Missouri Compromise, which he also brokered, was a half-measure that failed to address the fundamental constitutional conflict between freedom and slavery. Major disturbances bordering on secession, culminating in the Civil

War, continued until conflict over slavery was removed from the sectional debate by constitutional amendment.

With the support of Senator Daniel Webster, who delivered the votes of his large congressional following, Clay proposed eight related resolutions designed to gain the votes of congressmen who would have otherwise only voted for some but not all of the proposals. The provision with the widest effect on the North was the Fugitive Slave Law.[29]

At first, the political momentum favored the North because President Taylor refused to buckle to what he called the "intolerant and revolutionary" demands of Southern politicians, at the head of whom was his former son-in-law, Jefferson Davis. Taylor, himself a slaveholder, was ready to lead an army against Southern secessionists and hang all "damn traitors" rather than enter into Clay's concessions to the South. But Taylor's untimely death altered the political balance of power in favor of slavery. Upon succeeding to the presidency, Millard Fillmore signed the 1850 Compromise, not knowing that it was merely a bandage on a problem in need of constitutional resolution and not acquiescence. The best that can be said about the delay in 1850 of the inevitable conflict is that it allowed the North time to strengthen itself for war. Not only did the Republican Party come to power in the intervening years, led by abolitionists like Thaddeus Stevens and Charles Sumner, but it also elected a president, Abraham Lincoln, who eventually became willing to alter the Constitution, making future compromises with slavery unnecessary.[30] Sumner, Henry Wilson, and other congressmen who would be instrumental in passing the Thirteenth Amendment became prominent for their opposition to the 1850 Compromise. They most vociferously opposed its protection of slavers' right to recover runaways.

The Fugitive Slave Law of 1850 was designed to close the loopholes of its predecessor, the Fugitive Slave Law of 1793. The earlier law, which came into effect during George Washington's presidency, provided no federal habeas corpus protections nor right to jury trials. It prohibited purported fugitives from testifying against slave owners who typically crossed state lines to recapture runaway slaves. In response to the 1793 law, several Northern states passed personal liberty laws designed to protect wanted fugitives from being forcefully returned to slavery. For example, Vermont's act of November 1, 1843, forbade courts and citizens from seizing, arresting, or detaining anyone claimed as a fugitive slave or from aiding others in doing the same. Violators were subject to not more than five years imprisonment and a $1,000 fine. Commonly, state personal liberty laws provided fugitives with a right to jury trials, granted them *habeas corpus* guarantees, prohibited their detention in state or county jails, penalized kidnapping, and provided fugitives with free legal counsel. The Fugitive Slave Law of 1793 left to the federal government the onus of administering the necessary enforcement and adjudication mechanisms, but it did not require states to aid in the process of recapture.[31]

The frequent success of state laws to render the federal scheme ineffectual led to a Supreme Court review of the 1826 Pennsylvania Personal Liberty Law. In *Prigg v. Pennsylvania* (1842), the Court overturned Edward Prigg's conviction under the state law for kidnapping a black mother and her children in order to return them to a Maryland owner. Chief Justice Story, writing for the Court, found that the 1793 act was constitutional while the Pennsylvania statute was not. The Court extended the power of owners, giving them "the entire authority," even without state or federal legislation, to retake fugitive slaves. The case's sole redeeming quality was the Court's position that state governments were not obligated to enforce the Act; therefore, the federal government was alone responsible for recapturing runaways. Even after Story drafted the *Prigg* decision, at least eight additional states enacted personal liberty laws. In practical effect, these laws complicated the apprehension of fugitives, making pursuit more costly and less attractive.[32]

In 1850, approximately twenty thousand blacks in the North were avoiding their masters' pursuits.[33] The 1850 Fugitive Slave Law attempted to make federal efforts effective against resistant states and citizens. In order to establish title over runaways, live witnesses were no longer required, claimants needed only to swear out a written affidavit and this *ex parte* information sufficed to establish a cause of action. Pursuing owners could recapture fugitives without resorting to a formal hearing or jury trial; specially appointed federal commissioners were granted authority to determine cases "in a summary manner." At the end of this process, without due process and without giving the alleged fugitive an opportunity to offer a defense, the commissioner could issue certificates that would immediately return the respondent to a life of slavery. In what resembled a bribe, and at least indicated a preference for reenslavement, commissioners who found respondents were runaways received $10 while those who set them free were paid $5. Not only did the law require marshals and deputies to participate in recapture, and fine those who refused, but the law also required the public to participate in recapture. Anyone who knowingly or willfully obstructed the effort was subject to a $1,000 fine. Likewise, persons who hid or aided fugitives could be fined $1,000 and imprisoned for up to six months.[34]

Contemporary proponents of antislavery aimed to show that the 1850 act violated the U.S. Constitution. They based their opposition to the act on three constitutional guarantees: the Fifth Amendment's guarantee against the deprivation of life, liberty, or property without due process; the Seventh Amendment's guarantee of trial by jury; and the Article 1, section 9, clause 2 prohibition against suspension of the writ of *habeas corpus*. While these arguments were obviously well intended, their validity was questionable since courts had to balance those three constitutional guarantees against other constitutional clauses, such as the Fugitive Slave Clause, that safeguarded slavery. Only a constitutional amendment could have protected blacks in a racist environment where courts recognized owners' rights to slave property, and slaves were legally treated as if they were just another form of chattel.

The Supreme Court, in an 1858 decision drafted by Chief Justice Taney, *Ableman v. Booth*, found the Fugitive Slave Law to be constitutional. The case arose when the Wisconsin Supreme Court found the 1850 act unconstitutional and twice issued writs of *habeas corpus* to intervene on behalf of a fugitive named Booth. The U.S. Supreme Court, however, reversed the state court ruling, deciding that state judges had no jurisdictional authority to issue writs of *habeas corpus* for persons held "under the authority of the United States."[35] While, in 1864, more than three years after Confederate secession, Congress did finally repeal the Fugitive Slave Act of 1850, the Fugitive Slave Clause of the Constitution, which was the real source of the human rights infringements, was not invalidated until states ratified the Thirteenth Amendment.

Following the Compromise of 1850, abolitionists redoubled their frenetic efforts against slavery. For instance, Garrison, during a July 4, 1854, speech that he delivered in Framingham, Massachusetts, burned a copy of the Fugitive Slave Act and called for the dissolution of the Union. "So perish all compromises with tyranny," he challengingly proclaimed to his audience.[36] According to him, the Constitution was the most far-reaching compromise with slavery. He continued to maintain this point of view until the Constitution was amended in 1865.

Rather than going away as a political issue, after the Compromise of 1850, slavery continued to haunt sectional disputes. So, in 1854, what began as a sectional struggle for the location of a transcontinental railroad and the pursuit of Kansas farmland deteriorated into the same disagreement over slavery that plagued all major disputes of the era. Illinois senator Stephen A. Douglas, then head of the Committee on Territories, introduced the Kansas-Nebraska Bill. Its stated purpose was to organize the territories of Nebraska and Kansas. To achieve this, Douglas decided to curry the favor of Southern Democrats. Political forces who were both financially and ideologically zealous to spread slavery manipulated Douglas's well-known derisive views about blacks, his indifference about their plight, and his belief that slavery was a local matter. The "Little Giant" proposed that the settlers who would eventually organize these territories, both of which lay North of 36°30' within the land acquired through the Louisiana Purchase, decide whether or not they would be free or slave states. Such a grant of populist power abrogated the Missouri Compromise's prohibition against slavery anywhere in the Louisiana Purchase Territory above 36°30', with the exception of Missouri.[37]

The inclusion of this provision settled the alignment of the differing congressional camps. Senators Sumner and Chase and Representatives Giddings, Edward Wade, Gerrit Smith, and DeWitt established the tone of the debate by publishing the *Appeal of Independent Democrats* in the anti-slavery weekly, *National Era*. The Bill, they wrote, was "a gross violation of a sacred pledge; as a criminal betrayal of precious rights; as part and parcel of an atrocious plot to exclude from a vast unoccupied region immigrants from the Old World and free laborers from our own States." The existence of slavery in the territories, Whig Representative Richard Yates of Illinois argued during a House debate, would hurt white labor: "The free laborer does not wish the labor of slaves to come into competition with his labor. The effect of slave labor is always to cheapen, degrade, and exclude free labor." Once again a controversy over the Missouri Compromise, which was originally designed to exclude slavery from a territory, manifested that without a constitutional amendment politicians could depart from previous commitments against spreading the peculiar institution. "I can tell you now, as I told you in 1850," exclaimed Seward, "that it is an error, an unnecessary error, to suppose that because you exclude slavery from these Halls today, that it will not revisit them tomorrow." Sumner used an argument in the Senate to which he would return during the debates on the Thirteenth Amendment, "Slavery," he uttered, "is an infraction of the immutable law of nature, and, as such, cannot be considered a natural incident to any sovereignty, especially in a country which has solemnly declared, in its Declaration of Independence, the inalienable right of all men to life, *liberty*, and the pursuit of happiness."[38]

As the violent rupture between the North and South approached, the *Dred Scott* case exhibited the continued Supreme Court tendency to be accommodating on the issue of slavery. The Thirteenth Amendment would overturn that opinion and end the practice of compromising with slavocracy. The *Dred Scott* decision opened all states and territories to slavery because Chief Justice Taney, writing for the majority, held that a master could travel to any state in the Union and remain there with his slaves.

Dred Scott, a slave, filed a lawsuit in Missouri claiming his freedom since he had for a time resided with his master in free Illinois and in Fort Snelling, in a northern part of the Louisiana Purchase that is part of current-day Minnesota. Taney took up the issue of Dred Scott's citizenship to determine whether a federal court could have jurisdiction over the matter at bar. He found, first, that slaves could have no citizenship in the United States nor in the states where they were born. Therefore, Scott could not bring suit in an Article III court. Second, Taney held that the Missouri Compromise violated the Fifth Amendment's prohibition against depriving persons of property without due process of law.

Justice Curtis, one of the two dissenting justices, refused to recognize the majority's decision to be binding because it went beyond the issues in controversy:

> I do not consider it to be within the scope of the judicial power of the majority of the court to pass upon any question respecting the plaintiff's citizenship in Missouri, save that raised by the plea to the jurisdiction. . . . The judgment of this court is, that the case is to be dismissed for want of jurisdiction, because the plaintiff was not a citizen of Missouri, as he alleged in his declaration. Into that judgment, according to the settled course of this court, nothing appearing after a plea to the merits can enter. A great question of constitutional law, deeply affecting the peace and welfare of the country, is not, in my opinion, a fit subject to be thus reached.

Since he found that the District Court in fact had jurisdiction over this case, Curtis believed that the Court should decide in favor of Dred Scott because "it was the will of Congress that the state of involuntary servitude of a slave, coming into the Territory with his master, should cease to exist."

Dred Scott showed that as long as the Constitution contained language committing the country to both liberty and slavery, constitutional interpretation would be subject to factions who were interested in changing the dynamic of the country by making slavery a national rather than just a local institution.[39] The compromises had empowered the South to gain strength, and slavery had not gradually disappeared, as Madison and Jefferson had anticipated; in fact, it could not do so. Since the Constitution protected slavery, amending that document would have to be the first step in avoiding sectional conflict in the future.

In the aftermath of *Dred Scott*, North and South drifted farther apart and the rumbling of war grew closer. It drew the South together, making them more zealous for slavery, and it drew together the Republican Party, which gained political office on a platform of protecting free labor.

In many ways, Lincoln's 1860 victory of the presidency was a response to *Dred Scott*. The Republican Party platform called for the abolition of slavery in the territories of the United States. These were not the national abolitionist ambitions that Republicans would come to embrace in 1864, when debates on the proposed Thirteenth Amendment began, but they were a step in that direction. In 1860, Republicans had already committed themselves to arresting the national spread of slavery, at least into the Western territories. They were bent on ending what they perceived to be slave power's augmented stronghold on national politics. Indeed, slave owners held the presidency for fifty of the nation's first seventy-two years of existence. As Eric Foner, a leading Civil War historian, perceptively stated, in 1860 the Republicans nominated a man conservative enough to sweep the North, and "yet radical enough to trigger a secession crisis."[40]

For its part, the South was leery that Republicans planned to come to power and put an end to slavery altogether—whether gradually or immediately was irrelevant to them. The South's zeal for this sectional issue, however, cost Democrats Northern votes, especially because the 1860 Democratic convention failed to nominate Senator Douglas to be the party's presidential candidate.

In the wake of Lincoln's election, even before his inauguration, South Carolina published the Declaration of Causes, announcing that it was seceding from the Union. The Declaration of Causes made no mention of any economic grievances; instead, it concentrated on what the state considered to be national burdens placed on its domestic institution, slavery.[41]

Compromise legislation did not resolve sectional difference about slavery, and Southern aggression at Fort Sumter eventually provided the opportunity to pass the necessary amendment to the Constitution. The seceding South regarded the slavery provisions in the Constitution to be a license for further extending the property rights of slave owners specifically and whites generally. On the other hand, the North increasingly viewed them to be in conflict with the revolutionary principles of natural freedom on which the United States was founded. At loggerheads, Republicans realized, as the Civil War dragged on and the casualties mounted, that there could be no end to the sectional conflicts without an amendment voiding the proslavery concessions found in the Constitution. There was no other way to stop the continued extension of slavery into the territories and no other way to end the institution that repeatedly demanded more land, more political rights, and less interference in its denial of procedural and substantive rights.

2

On the Road to Ratification

The Constitution in its original form tolerated and protected the institution of slavery despite the Declaration of Independence's categorical commitment to universal freedom and equality. The opening of new lands to the West, after the Louisiana Purchase and the Mexican-American War, offered enticing locales to enterprising slave owners. The Constitution needed fundamental alteration to make a clean break with legally countenanced bondage. The Civil War provided the opportunity for ending the institution that was central to every major interstate conflict since the Missouri Compromise.

The Thirteenth Amendment was monumental because it overrode all constitutional provisions that protected and furthered the institution of slavery. Its ratification signaled the end not only of hereditary slavery but of all badges and incidents of servitude. By ratifying the Thirteenth Amendment in 1865, the United States committed itself to promoting freedom through a national mandate. This was no formulaic act; it created a constitutional obligation to preserve and further liberty rights.

A. Emancipation by Statute and Proclamation

Union generals John C. Fremont and Benjamin Butler were first to act, in 1861, on liberating slaves who streamed into their ranks. Fremont initially regarded them as free, although President Lincoln countermanded his position, and Butler considered them the contraband of war. Congress incorporated Butler's view into the First Confiscation Act, which it issued on August 6, 1861, during the first summer of battle. The Act subjected to prize or capture the property of masters who used their slaves to support the Confederacy. But the First Confiscation Act, even in its March 1862 modified form (forbidding the return of any fugitives), liberated no slaves. On the other hand, the Second Confiscation Act, passed on July 17, 1862, provided that the slaves of any rebels were "forever free of their servitude and not again held as slaves." Further, the Act called on the president to develop a colonization policy to provide for blacks who wanted to immigrate to any country willing to acknowledge their freedom. The Second Confiscation Act also fell short of abolishing slavery, leaving unaffected any slaves owned by masters who did not participate in the rebellion. However, the Militia Act, which was passed on the same day and worked in concert with the Second Confiscation Act, granted freedom to all military servicemen, even those escaping from loyal masters, and to their mothers, wives, and children. These laws answered the military's need for reenforcements and offered some slaves a way out of bondage.[1]

Outside of slave states, a liberation movement was also afoot. The congressional battle to free slaves in the District of Columbia, which John Quincy Adams first waged two decades before the War, finally ended successfully. In April 1862, Congress accepted Lincoln's plan of compensated emancipation there. The measure provided for emancipation hearings and certifications of freedom, not predicated on a master's disloyalty. The Act further provided $100,000 to encourage black emigration to Haiti or Liberia. This was a project that Lincoln had backed since his 1854 debates for the U.S. Senate seat against Senator Stephen Douglas of Illinois. Lincoln's impulse, he had told a hostile crowd who heard one of the debates, was to "free all the slaves, and send them to Liberia, to their own native land." On July 12, 1862, Lincoln met a deputation of border-state congressmen and suggested that they shorten the War by accepting his plan of gradual, compensated emancipation, suggesting South America for colonization. A month later, Lincoln met a deputation of blacks, whom he told about the colonization apportionment. He also suggested that racial friction could best be avoided by voluntary black colonization into Central America.[2] Finally, in a move that seemed to nullify the Supreme Court's authority to interpret the Constitution, Congress, in effect, statutorily overturned *Dred Scott* by abolishing slavery in the territories without providing owners with any compensation.

After the War, Gideon Welles, Lincoln's secretary of the navy, remembered how the President decided that, since the July 12 meeting was ineffective, he could no longer take the "temporizing and forbearing policy" of trying to appease the rebels. Border states had refused Lincoln's plan of compensated emancipation, and "constitutional safeguards" would need to be surmounted in removing the "insuperable obstacle to peace." Lincoln only awaited a major victory to issue a proclamation, and the Union Army's success at Antietam, on September 17, 1862, offered the opportunity to issue it from a position of power rather than retreat.[3]

Lincoln issued the Emancipation Proclamation on January 1, 1863. Its authority, as the last sentence stated, rested on the president's wartime powers as commander in chief. He had abandoned any reference to colonization, indicating the development of Lincoln's thought toward action and away from appeasement. It emancipated only those blacks who were then enslaved by states "in rebellion against the United States." Therefore, the Proclamation did not alter the legal status of slaves in Kentucky, Missouri, Maryland, and Delaware, and it exempted Tennessee and the Union-occupied parts of Louisiana and Virginia. The Proclamation also recognized African Americans' right to self-defense and allowed for their enlistment in the Union Army. Most immediately, the Proclamation affected slaves whom the Union Army liberated and those who escaped into Union lines. It also untied the hands of Union officers from having to return freed people to their former masters and turned the conflict into a liberation campaign, not merely a war to save the Union.[4]

The Proclamation has been the subject of a fair amount of criticism because it freed no slaves in areas that the Union did not occupy. Such criticism overlooks the Proclamation's significance to slaves who had lived in Confederate areas on January 1, 1863, but later greeted the conquering Union Army as freed people. Moreover, many slaves who lived within the Confederacy, like those residing in Norfolk, Virginia, simply walked off plantations after hearing of Lincoln's decision. The Proclamation offered them unbounded hope of freedom and army protection. While slaves had been steadily escaping their bondage since the beginning of the War, Lincoln's Proclamation immensely accelerated this trend. Nevertheless, Southern culture often reasserted its autocratic character whenever Union soldiers removed to a different location.

Peace Democrats soon responded in their racialist press, decrying the Proclamation as an unnecessary impediment to immediate reconciliation and a means of taking jobs from low-wage white laborers. Some abolitionists, on the other hand, regarded the measure to be inadequate, but many agreed with Garrison that it was "an important step in the right direction."

While the Proclamation may have been predicated on military expediency rather than moral considerations, Lincoln seems to have had no other alternative for antislavery action, given the constitutional guarantee of slave property. Indeed, it was only at the end of 1863 and in the winter of 1864 that abolitionist organizations like the Women's Loyal National League began circulating petitions to pass a constitutional measure securing emancipation. About 42,000 persons circulated petitions calling for Congress "to pass at the earliest practicable day an act emancipating all persons of African descent held in involuntary service or labor in the United States." When they reached Sumner's Senate desk, on February 4, 1864, the signatures numbered 100,000; of these 34,399 were signed by men and 65,601 by women.[5]

Although the Emancipation Proclamation had a limited reach, it propelled the abolition of slavery into a principal directive for the Union's war efforts. Lincoln demonstrated that the South's intransigence to his proffered terms of surrender could be exploited to free slaves. Donald E. Fehrenbacher has emphasized that historians who seek to downgrade the Proclamation's significance by pointing out that it freed no slaves fail to take its political significance into account. Such detractors could likewise argue that the Declaration of Independence did not liberate any of the British colonies. The Proclamation focused the North's war efforts on liberating slaves, not only on ending the rebellion. Replying to the charge that the Proclamation only abolished slavery in the rebel states, Frederick Douglass called it "the greatest event of our nation's history if not the greatest event of the century" because it changed the terms of government from one which was a "stupendous engine of slavery and oppression." But Douglass recognized that more needed to be done. "The world has never advanced a single inch in the right direction, when the movement could not be traced to some such small beginning," he said, and the Thirteenth Amendment would soon provide the opportunity for further progress.[6]

B. *Congressional Debates on the Thirteenth Amendment's Meaning*

Framers of the Thirteenth Amendment were like politicians in any representative government: they spoke from both conviction and political expediency. Regardless of their motives, the adoption of abolitionist ideals in congressional discourse reflected the changing character of U.S. society. The amendment signaled a new reliance on Congress to protect individual rights and legislate for the general welfare. Freedom reemerged from these debates as a central U.S. tenet, born out of the country's experience with tried and failed appeasements of slavocracy.

Radical Republicans sought to make the amendment's scope sweeping. They intended that it provide Congress with the national authority to enact laws that would assure that freedom would not be a hollow word but a national commitment vested with substantive protections. This meant nothing short of erasing vestiges of the Old South. However, to achieve this end, they needed to meet political contingencies for gaining the votes of their more moderate colleagues as well as those of a few War Democrats, without whose vote Radical Republicans could not have passed the proposed amendment. Thus, their congressional pronouncements sometime coupled ideals with political realism.

The amendment's Republican proponents gained significant Democratic support in the Senate, especially after Maryland senator Reverdy Johnson's influential speech, but in the House they ran into strong Democratic opposition. Senators and representatives expressed a variety of views about the amendment's scope. Consequently, they left little in the way of an authoritative, contemporary perspective beyond the virtually universal belief among congressmen that the amendment should accomplish much more than the mere abolition of chattel slavery. What emerged from these debates was a commitment to end the vestiges of servitude without the realization of how difficult would be the break from entrenched racist attitudes and practices.

The advocates of universal liberty would not be satisfied with the Emancipation Proclamation because it offered a solution that extended no further than the president's authority as commander in chief over the military. Congressmen sought a more effective anti-slavery measure that would last beyond the Civil War.

On December 14, 1863, Ohio representative James M. Ashley first introduced a bill to submit to the states a proposed constitutional amendment that would prohibit slavery and involuntary servitude within the United States and its territories. That same day, Iowa representative James Wilson proposed a more detailed joint resolution to submit an amendment to the states. The language Wilson introduced resembled the Northwest Ordinance, which was to be the foundation for the Thirteenth Amendment. The resolution was referred to the House Judiciary Committee in the following form: "Section 1. Slavery being incompatible with a free government is forever prohibited in the United States; and involuntary servitude shall be permitted only as a punishment for crime. Section 2. Congress shall have power to enforce the foregoing by appropriate legislation." But it was the Senate Judiciary Committee's version of the bill, which it reported on February 10, 1864, that would become the final version of the amendment:

> Section 1. Neither slavery nor involuntary servitude, except as a punishment for crime whereof the party shall have been duly convicted, shall exist in the United States, or any place subject to their jurisdiction.
> Sec. 2. Congress shall have power to enforce this article by appropriate legislation.

This joint resolution, as Senator Charles Sumner explained after it was read to the Senate, would cover "every proposition relating to slavery."[7]

The amendment was ratified in 1865, after some initial disappointment, becoming the first alteration to the Constitution in sixty-one years. The Senate passed the resolution on April 8, 1864, by a vote of thirty-eight for and six against. Delaware senator Willard Saulsbury Sr. grimly, but inaccurately, warned that this meant the end of the American Union and any chance for reconstruction. In the House, while the resolution received a majority of the votes, it fell short of the two-thirds super majority necessary to move the proposal to the states for ratification. The House returned after the 1864 election, debated the issue extensively, and then passed it. Remembering those days, former congressman Isaac N. Arnold considered the debates on the amendment to have been "the most important in American history. Indeed it would be difficult to find any others so important in the history of the world."[8]

Many of the amendment's supporters claimed that it accorded with the ideals of a republican government reflected in the general welfare provisions of the Preamble to the Constitution. James Wilson, a coauthor of the Thirteenth Amendment, saw the entire institution of slavery as "an incessant, unrelenting, aggressive warfare upon the principles of the Government." While the number of congressmen representing the slaveholding states was increased by the number of slaves, he said, Southern politicians who were thereby elected did not represent "all rights of the people."[9]

The proposal's opponents argued for the states' rights view, which had long prevented any national law from being passed to end the institution. On this view, any federal limit on slavery was an infringement of state sovereignty. Representative William S. Holman of Indiana regarded the proposal to be "fatal to the fundamental principles of the Republic, the right, the irrepressible right of the states to domestic government." Similarly, Representative Samuel J. Randall of Pennsylvania exclaimed that it "strikes at the root of all State institutions," signaling how deeply entrenched slavery was in governmental practices.[10]

The opposition found it difficult to muster enough votes to defeat the resolution partly because so many congressmen recognized that black participation in the Union Army demanded tangible gratitude. To that end, in April 1864, Sumner offered to alter the proposed amendment to include the guarantee that "all persons are equal before the law, so that no person can hold another as a slave; and the Congress may make all laws necessary and proper to carry this article into effect everywhere within the United States and the jurisdiction thereof." Some scholars have mistakenly suggested that the rejection of Sumner's proposal meant that congressmen were not yet ready to commit to the equality of rights. In fact, many Radical Republicans espoused Sumner's ideal of equality but believed the Senate Committee of the Judiciary's proposed language was sufficient for achieving that end. For example, Senator Jacob Howard of Michigan, a committed Radical Republican, thought that "[i]n a legal and technical sense that language [of Sumner's proposal] is utterly insignificant and meaningless."[11] Congressional debates, in fact, indicate that some congressmen wanted the Thirteenth Amendment to end discriminatory practices and inequitable labor practices. Along these same lines, Congressman Isaac Arnold argued that by passing the amendment Congress recognized that "*equality before the law* is to be the great cornerstone" in this country.

The overt commitment to equality would have to wait until the passage of the Equal Protection Clause of the Fourteenth Amendment.[12] Sumner's suggestion that the Thirteenth Amendment should contain a guarantee of equal legal treatment went the way of many of his anti-slavery suggestions during the course of his career. Few of his bills ever became law, but the larger picture to which he clung, the imperatives to stop slavery from expanding and to end its hold on the United States, became a reality.

Sumner's convictions against slavery were born of his experience with its unyielding practices and ideology. He had been an involved abolitionist since 1835, when he first subscribed to Garrison's *Liberator*. However, Sumner, unlike Garrison, believed the Fifth Amendment and the constitutional guarantee of a republican government were enough to end slavery. The *Dred Scott* decision put in doubt Sumner's argument that the Bill of Rights was enough to achieve freedom. By 1864, Sumner put his weight behind the amendment because he saw it reaffirming the anti-slavery principles the Constitution had embodied from the beginning. For him, the Thirteenth Amendment made explicit what he believed was implicit in the original Constitution.[13]

On the House side, Thaddeus Stevens, the leader of the Committee on the Ways and Means during the debates on the Thirteenth Amendment and, then, the Committee on Appropriations during the debates on the Civil Rights Act of 1866, maintained a tight grip on party discipline, making sure that Republican votes lined up on the side of the proposed amendment. He viewed the Constitution very differently than Sumner did. According to him, the Constitution had proven itself inadequate for uprooting slavery in the states and territories. Without the power granted under the Thirteenth Amendment, Stevens believed the Constitution protected slavery and did not grant the federal government the power to regulate it.[14]

Stevens, like Sumner, began the struggle against slavery early in his life. As a Pennsylvania attorney, he represented fugitive slaves without charge and bought the freedom of one slave. He remained a principled abolitionist, entering national politics in 1849, at age fifty-seven, in response to the agitation over slavery that arose after the cession of Mexican lands. He voted against any compromise with slavocracy, including the Fugitive Slave Law, and upbraided Northern appeasement of the South as a "cowardly breath of servility and meanness." After the outbreak of the Civil War he was one of only two persons who voted, in 1861, against the Crittenden Resolution, which asserted that the War was not being fought to subjugate the South nor to interfere with its peculiar institution. He also attacked Lincoln's hesitancy on emancipation.[15]

Stevens sought to make the Thirteenth Amendment's scope sweeping, even vociferously espousing a project to provide reparations for the freedmen, his "forty acres and a mule" plan as it came to be known. The United States, in his view, had an obligation to provide homesteads for the newly freed and to enact laws for protecting their property rights. Setting "loose four million slaves without a hut to shelter them or a cent in their pockets" was an injustice he wanted to prevent. The federal government's obligation, he believed, should have gone beyond solely emancipating slaves. The government was also obligated to act against the racist system that had supported inequality through "infernal laws . . . [which] have prevented them from acquiring an education, understanding the commonest laws of contract, or of managing the ordinary business of life." In spite of his hold on power in the House, Stevens was never able to translate this ideal into law.[16]

Legislators who sided with Sumner and Stevens wanted to end discrimination perpetrated against blacks throughout the country. Congressional proposals at the time extended to employment, housing, and educational practices in the North. Some, such as Wisconsin senator Timothy O. Howe, believed the amendment should "go further" in entitling free persons to rights such as education.[17]

The proposed amendment, even without Sumner's suggested emendation on equality, had significant civil implications for blacks, regardless of where they lived in the Union. This was a groundbreaking achievement because it implied that, along with the South, those Northern states that still denied blacks the use of public facilities and public transportation would be required to purge exclusionary provisions from their laws.

Some of the ideals expressed during the congressional debates were visionary and were not realized even after the Thirteenth Amendment's ratification. Senator James Harlan of Iowa was the first to aver that the future amendment should function as a battle axe against any "incidents of slavery." The Supreme Court later adapted Harlan's terminology into its most important holdings on the Thirteenth Amendment. Harlan listed interference with black family relationships, the prohibition against black participation on juries, and restrictions against black property ownership as examples of the incidents of slavery. Senator Henry Wilson waxed eloquent about the abolition of those incidents:

> If this amendment shall be incorporated by the will of the nation into the Constitution of the United States, it will obliterate the last lingering vestiges of the slave system; its chattelizing, degrading, and bloody codes; its dark, malignant, barbarizing spirit; all it was and is, *everything connected with it or pertaining to it*, from the face of the nation it was scarred with moral desolation, from the bosom of the country it has reddened with the blood and strewn with the graves of patriotism. The incorporation of this amendment into the organic law of the nation will make impossible forevermore the reappearing of the discarded slave system, and the returning of the despotism of the slavemasters' domination.[18]

Senator Wilson, like Sumner and Stevens, put a lifetime of conviction behind his abolitionist agenda. His hatred for slavery derived from a visit he made to Virginia when he was still young. There he witnessed slave families auctioned off separately. From then on Wilson vowed "with unalterable determination to give all that I had, and all that I hoped to have, of power, to the cause of emancipation in America." He not only empathized with the plight of slaves, his rise in life also gave him insight into the life of working people, which made him an ideal leader of the Thirteenth Amendment debates. Wilson was born on a very poor farm in New England. As a child, he was "bound-out" working for a month's winter schooling, board, clothing, and some livestock. For a time, he was even an editor of the antislavery *Boston Republican*.[19]

Without the presence in Congress of incessant abolitionists like Wilson, Sumner, and Stevens, the Thirteenth Amendment would have been doomed. Their devotion to this cause went far beyond the economic interests involved, being rooted in human rights principles that they intended the amendment to promote. The end of slavery, for them, could not come unless constitutional law protected the natural rights of all citizens.

In fact, the framers grounded the Declaration of Independence's assertion of "self-evident" truths in natural-rights philosophy. Many congressional Republicans expected that the Thirteenth Amendment would enable them to secure the rights of liberty, life, and the pursuit of happiness. The Thirty-eighth Congress's reliance on the Declaration of Independence was not new; in fact, antislavery spokesmen had used that line of argument from the early days of the Republic, pointing to the contradiction between the existence of inalienable rights and the institution of slavery.

The proslavery retort in the antebellum South had been that the Declaration of Independence and the Constitution referred only to white men, not to blacks, since only whites took part in the Continental Congress and Constitutional Convention. Therefore, the proslavery argument went, blacks were never part of the social contract that secured the rights of citizens. Further, slavers asserted that those founding fathers who were slaveholders did not intend the nation's fundamental laws to entitle the government to confiscate their property.[20]

Radical Republicans had a very different view of the Declaration of Independence and relied on it to elucidate the proposed amendment. Representative Godlove S. Orth from Indiana expected the Amendment to "be a practical application of that self-evident truth" of the Declaration "'that [all men] are endowed by their creator with certain unalienable rights; that among these, are life, liberty, and the pursuit of happiness.'" Its more progressive advocates made an "earnest effort" to remove impediments standing in the way of human rights. Francis W. Kellogg, representative of Michigan, traced the sources of the proposed amendment both to the Constitution's Preamble, with its requirement that government promote the general welfare and secure liberty, and to the Declaration. Illinois Representative Ebon C. Ingersoll, who was elected to the Thirty-eighth Congress to fill the vacancy created by the death of legendary abolitionist Owen Lovejoy, voiced the desire to secure slaves "natural" and "inalienable" rights because blacks have a right to "live in a state of freedom." He asserted that they have a right to profit from their labors and to enjoy conjugal happiness without fear of forced separations at the behest of uncompassionate masters.[21]

Moreover, Ingersoll viewed the proposed amendment to apply to the "the seven millions of poor white people who live in the slave States but who have ever been deprived of the blessings of manhood by reason of . . . slavery. Slavery has kept them in ignorance, in poverty and in degradation." Senator Wilson likewise said the Thirteenth Amendment would provide "sacred rights" to whites and blacks.[22]

Representative Thomas T. Davis of New York expounded on civil liberty on January 7, 1865: "Liberty, that civil and religious liberty which was so clearly beautifully defined in the Declaration of Independence. . . . African slavery was regarded as temporary in its character. . . . Our fathers predicted that the time would soon come when the interests of the country would demand that slavery should pass away." Representative John F. Farnsworth of Illinois thought the "old fathers who made the Constitution . . . believed that slavery was at war with the rights of human nature"; on the other hand, Representative William D. Kelly of Pennsylvania thought the "errors" of the founding fathers for compromising with wrongs were being expiated by "blood and agony and death."[23]

Congressional supporters of the proposed amendment did not stop at the exposition of natural rights. Their commitments had a practical component as well. The proposed amendment was generally regarded as a means of granting citizens the right to enjoy their civil rights without arbitrary state or private harassment. Radical Republicans recognized that slavery was privately and publicly perpetuated. They crafted the Thirteenth Amendment to eliminate any incidents associated with both. Many of the amendment's advocates, regardless of whether they held the view that it would alter the fundamental character of the Constitution or explicitly incorporate rights that were already there, believed that the amendment would expand federal control over the administration of government.

There was common agreement that the amendment would empower Congress to pass legislation directed at any incidents of servitude. The conflict between Southern states and the Union brought to power a federalist-minded group of legislators. This turn of events enabled Congress to pass three amendments, beginning with the Thirteenth, which granted the national government a degree of power to protect civil rights that it had never had before. As Representative Frederick E. Woodbridge from Vermont put it, the proposed amendment would assure that at the end of the War "the goddess of Liberty . . . may look north and south, east and west, upon a free nation untarnished by aught inconsistent with freedom."[24]

The national rights that the amendment secured were the practical manifestations of the "great charter of liberty given to them by the American people." Passage of the amendment, Representative M. Russell Thayer argued, was a recognition that each citizen, regardless of his or her social station, had fundamental rights and immunities, which included the rights to enforce contracts, sue, give evidence in court, inherit, and purchase, lease, hold, and convey real property.[25]

To achieve those ends, congressmen sponsored several bills even before passage of the Thirteenth Amendment. Senator Wilson offered a bill that represented the aspiration of those who wanted to secure meaningful liberty. The bill would have nullified any laws that infringed on the civil rights and immunities of persons because of their color, descent, race, or previous enslavement. However, this proposed bill suffered from the same limitations as the Emancipation Proclamation: it extended only to rebel states and was based on presidential war powers. Similarly, Representative John F. Farnsworth sponsored a resolution asserting that the national government must secure the rights and privileges of citizenship to blacks who had served in military conflicts. Well meaning as this formulation was, it excluded many slaves and left untouched the typical dominance associated with wage labor.[26]

The aim of providing civil freedoms to persons of all races, nationalities, and ethnicities appeared time and again during the debates. Senator Harlan had earlier clarified that the incidents of servitude included arbitrary restrictions on parental relations, personal property, receiving legal redress, practicing free speech, and giving trial testimony. Statements about the Thirteenth Amendment's potential impact on civil rights became ever more prominent after the new year. John Kasson of Iowa on January 10, 1865, asserted there were three "fundamental natural rights of human society": the right to conjugal relations, parental rights, and "the right of a man to the personal liberty."[27] The aspirations of the amendment's proponents were truly national in scope. They crossed the line into what had traditionally been state jurisdiction.

Curiously, congressmen who opposed passing the proposed amendment inadvertently lent credence to a nationalist reading of its provisions. Numerous opposition speakers realized that the Radical Republicans conceived that the scope of the proposed amendment would go well beyond outlawing hereditary, physical bondage. The Thirteenth Amendment transformed U.S. legal culture from one where privileges could be based on slave ownership and race to a constitutional republic where the fundamental law substantively secured civil liberties. Outspoken Democrat Robert Mallory exclaimed that he opposed passing the joint resolution because it would make African Americans "American citizens" whose interests would be represented in Congress, and he upbraided Republicans for wanting freedom to lead to racial equality.[28]

Those Democrats who opposed secession while remaining committed to states' rights claims about slavery regarded the only legitimate war aim to be reunification, and they insisted that pursuing the abolition of slavery would only prolong the war. Thus, the amendment's antagonists expected it to grant Congress the power to enact laws enforceable within states, not only on federal property. The congressional debates indicate that progressive congressmen made it their mission not only to destroy Southern battlefield resistance but also slavery and associated forms of discrimination.

Even at the beginning of 1865, passage of the amendment was so uncertain that on January 13, Representative Ashley, who would continue to be a leading proponent of African American civil and political rights well into Reconstruction, postponed the vote by moving for the continued consideration of the joint resolution. Thereafter, the weight of President Lincoln's advocacy for the amendment became increasingly evident in garnering Democratic congressional support. He had successfully pushed for supporting the proposed amendment in the 1864 Republican platform, and, in 1865, personally persuaded some Democratic Congressmen from Union states to vote for the proposal. Ultimately, its passage came two and a half months before John Wilkes Booth assassinated the President.

How critical was Lincoln's contribution to gathering enough votes? Historians LaWanda and John H. Cox argued persuasively that had the Thirty-eighth Congress not passed the amendment, the legislators could not have passed the measure before Southern surrender and, in that case, ratification of the Thirteenth Amendment probably would not have become a condition of readmission.[29]

The day the House passed the joint resolution to send the proposal to the states for ratification was a festive one in Washington, D.C. An "uncontrollable outburst" greeted the Speaker of the House's announcement that the measure received the needed two-thirds majority. Applause and cheers arouse from the House well, and spectators in the galleries joined in the celebration. Lincoln personally received the good news from his friends, who met with him at the White House. In his exuberance, Lincoln unnecessarily signed the joint resolution.[30]

The amendment's potential to improve the country and to set it on the course of liberty presaged great improvements, but first the states needed to ratify it. The Illinois legislature was first to do so, passing a resolution on the first of February, and Rhode Island and Michigan ratified the next day. On February 4, when Massachusetts, Pennsylvania, and West Virginia ratified, Senator Sumner asserted that the votes of the rebel states were not required. He reasoned that since the states that had remained in the Union were able to make laws without rebel state participation in Congress, "the amendment to the Constitution, prohibiting slavery throughout the United States will be valid to all intents and purposes as part of the Constitution whenever ratified by three fourths of the States, *de facto*, exercising the powers and prerogatives of the United States under the Constitution." Lincoln, in his last public address (April 11, 1865), did not outright disagree with Sumner's perspective but thought "such a ratification would be questionable and sure to be persistently questioned." The President therefore favored ratification by three-fourths of all states so that the amendment's authority would be incontrovertible. Lincoln envisioned ratification as part of the process of Southern reconstruction and did not want to alienate states like Louisiana whose legislature had already voted for ratification.[31]

During the summer and autumn of 1865, Andrew Johnson, who took over the presidency after Lincoln's violent death, appointed provisional governors in secessionist states. They promulgated regulations for convening state constitutional conventions. "It was understood that at these conventions the states would abrogate their secessionist ordinances, adopt new constitutions, repudiate their war debts, and ratify the thirteenth amendment." Most of the Southern opposition to ratification focused on Congress's broad-ranging powers. A delegate in the Mississippi constitutional convention explained Southern concerns:

> The second section confers extraordinary power upon Congress. That section gives to Congress broad, and almost, I may say, unlimited power. . . . I fear excessively that there is hidden away in that section, something which may be destructive to the welfare of the South. I am not willing to trust to men who know nothing of slavery the power to frame a code for the freedmen of the State of Mississippi.

The provisional governor of South Carolina found that his state's legislators had the same concern: "They have no objection to adopting the first section of the amendment proposed; but they fear that the second section may be construed to give Congress power of local legislation over the Negroes, and white men, too, after the abolishment of slavery." In fact, Southern premonitions were accurate. Radical Republicans did envision the second section as the source of congressional power against slavocracy. South Carolina's ratification contained a qualification against congressional intervention into the state's political and civil treatment of blacks. The ratifications by Florida, Alabama, Louisiana, and Mississippi contained similar reservations. When, on December 18, 1865, Secretary of State Seward announced that twenty-seven states had ratified the Constitution, that number constituted three-fourths of the whole before secession.[32]

C. *The Immediate Aftermath of Liberation*

1. What Sort of Freedom?

It did not take long for Radical Republicans to discover that passage of the amendment did not automatically put an end to the vast number of injustices associated with involuntary servitude. However, in the immediate aftermath of ratification, plantation working conditions often changed for the better. Persons learning of their freedom typically participated in vivacious celebrations. For them, it was truly independence day. Years later, Charlotte Brown recalled her first free Sunday:

> We was all sittin' roun' restin' an' tryin' to think what freedom meant an' ev'ybody was quiet an' peaceful. All at once ole Sister Carrie who was near 'bout a hundred started in to talkin': 'Tain't no mo' sellin' today,/'Tain't no mo' hirin' today,/'Tain't no pullin' off shirts today,/Its stomp down freedom today./Stomp it down!' An' when she says, 'Stomp it down,' all de slaves commence to shoutin' wid her. . . . Wasn't no mo' peace dat Sunday. Ev'ybody started in to sing an' shout once mo' chile, dat was one glorious time.

Another ex-slave explained the drastic change in labor relations: her former master "never was mean to us after freedom. He was 'fraid the niggers might kill him." Employers often desisted from corporal punishment to avoid antagonizing their laborers. Some black laborers even left employers when threatened with the type of violence that had been commonplace before liberation. Freed people sought to assert their economic independence by hiring out their labor to new employers, entering into sharecropping arrangements, and renting land. While Congressmen Stevens's and George Julian's land distribution plans failed to gain enough support in Congress, after the Civil War tens of thousands of families bought land for depressed prices, seeking independently to earn a living. Institutionalized discrimination nevertheless continued to obstruct freed people's progress. They found little legal redress, even when employers refused to pay field hands promised wages, landowners deceived sharecroppers into running up enormous debts, or marauding gangs stole from black farms.[33]

Freed people sought to make liberation meaningful by exercising their autonomy in ways that previously had been barred to them. Many walked away from plantations to live in less comfortable circumstances in order to enjoy their newfound sense of self-direction. People visited neighbors, sought long-lost family members, set out for the cities, visited previously prohibited places, and assembled in previously forbidden numbers.[34]

One of the most salient changes immediately following the Thirteenth Amendment's ratification was the establishment of an educational system for children and adults. All states in the antebellum South, except Tennessee, prohibited blacks from obtaining literacy instructions. While some owners gave their slaves private lessons in spite of these laws, 90 percent of the South's black adult population was illiterate in 1860. The Freedmen's Bureau and benevolence societies ran schools that became tangible means for emerging from slavery with skills to compete in the job market. Ex-slaves and abolitionists built, taught, and funded schools, recognizing forced ignorance to be a surmountable incident of servitude. Hundreds of thousands of black children attended school in the postbellum South. Presence at schoolhouses was itself sometimes a danger. Roving gangs committed violence against students and educators and set fire to their schoolhouses.[35]

Plantation owners and state authorities recognized that educated blacks were unlikely to remain field hands and, already in 1865, began a concerted campaign to minimize parental autonomy in educational decisions. They were driven by a paternalistic form of racism that regarded blacks as being so degenerate that they were even incapable of raising their own children. Racialist ignorance, born from years of pro-slavery indoctrination, led many to believe blacks had no feeling for family members. One judge, for instance, expressed surprise that freedwomen had "a great antipathy to their children being apprenticed." Freedmen who left their plantations risked leaving their children behind, and the sheriffs pursued those who tried to steal away with their children.

In an attempt to circumvent the Thirteenth Amendment, several states began instituting child apprenticeship laws, binding children to a term of indenture as long as a white judge determined that such service was in the children's best interest. Just as the Fugitive Slave Act of 1850 bribed magistrates by granting them a larger compensation for returning fugitives than if they ruled against the petitioning owners, so too Alabama judges received a one dollar compensation from the masters or mistresses to whom the children were apprenticed. In Mississippi, the apprenticeship law granted former owners preference to exploit the labor of black and mixed orphans or inadequately supported children. Males could be apprenticed until the age of twenty-one and females eighteen, and during the term of indenture masters were permitted to administer corporal punishment. In return, child laborers received room and board and masters were required to teach them to read and write.[36]

Blacks applied to the local provost marshals and Freedmen's Bureau for help against these child abductions, particularly in those cases where children were taken from living parents. Jack Prince asked for help when a woman bound his maternal niece. Sally Hunter requested assistance to obtain the release of her two nieces.[37] Bureau officials finally put an end to the system of indenture in 1867.

Indeed, the pattern around the South was to reinstate a *de facto* slavery, even after the Thirteenth Amendment ended the *de jure* variety. The newly freed persons in the South presented a great demographic problem, which few realized during the congressional debates on the Thirteenth Amendment. Once free, many of them were people without houses, and found themselves in a country with numerous legal barriers and customs against their advancement. In some places conditions improved after the amendment's ratification because blacks were permitted to participate in law suits, own property, and marry, all of which had been forbidden to slaves. But the burdens they faced were far more onerous than their gains.[38] States adopted laws attempting to retain a subservient labor force and a stable social hierarchy, which was favorable to whites.

Southern states enacted a series of obstructionist laws designed to exclude blacks from enjoying the privileges of national citizenship. States like South Carolina and Mississippi passed black codes that affected black lives in much the same way as the pre–Civil War slave codes. The provisions of these statutes suppressed African American aspirations by restricting their freedom of movement, privacy, and labor rights. Lawmakers obfuscated some of these statutes' inequitable aims under the ruse of racially neutral provisions. Even though many of the laws were facially nondiscriminatory, their burdens fell primarily upon the backs of agricultural laborers, most of whom were black. Moreover, some laws were specifically designed to keep farmland in the hands of whites. Since landownership was so important to agrarian Southern society, the bar to black ownership functioned to keep African Americans from holding positions of power. To this end, laws that specifically prohibited blacks from leasing lands outside incorporated cities increased the number of blacks who had no choice but to look for manual agricultural labor, often on their former masters' farms or plantations. Mississippi, for instance, prohibited African Americans from buying or leasing lands outside cities. In Louisiana, the law placed freed people in virtually impossible circumstances by requiring them to obtain a home within twenty days from a certain date, yet forbidding anyone from selling or leasing land to them.[39]

Other laws overtly perpetuated the incidents of servitude. For instance, black codes riddled freed people's lives with "onerous disabilities and burdens and curtailed their rights . . . to such an extent that their freedom was of little value." Black codes included criminal provisions with more stringent penalty provisions for black violators than for white offenders. The Mississippi code denied to civilian blacks equal coverage under the Second Amendment, prohibiting them from owning Bowie knives, firearms, or ammunition.[40]

In the years immediately following ratification, many blacks remained in a state of penal servitude since they could not leave their place of employment without being subject to criminal repercussions. Since the Thirteenth Amendment did not bar involuntary servitude as a form of criminal punishment, another way of refusing freed persons the full benefit of their emancipation was through capricious prosecution and conviction for autonomous acts. Throughout the South, blacks who left plantations to find work were often subject to being whipped.

Georgia passed a statute requiring that any master-servant relationship lasting more than a month must be entered into in writing. Any contractually bound employee leaving his employment before the expiration of the contract forfeited his wages. Such a person could also be imprisoned for four months or fined $500. Likewise in Mississippi, any person leaving an employer before the termination of a labor contract was subject to arrest and forfeiture of up to a year's worth of wages. On the other hand, in Georgia, employers could fire servants for such subjective reasons as "disobedience . . . immorality, and want of respect." This effectually bound employees to a system resembling indentured servitude, giving them virtually no job security in return.[41]

Besides positive legal impediments to black freedom, widespread violence prevented freed people from choosing where to live and for whom to work. White supremacists participated in whippings and lynchings. They denied freed people's humanity, incensed that blacks initiated conversations with whites, refused to call whites "masters," resisted corporal punishment, and protected family members. Citizens wrote congressmen informing them of the brutality perpetrated against blacks, educators, and abolitionists. Laws prohibiting blacks from serving on juries assured that justice would not be colorblind. Many Southern state officials either participated in the mayhem, encouraged it, or did nothing to prevent it. Of the five hundred whites charged with murdering blacks in Texas between 1865 and 1866, all five hundred were acquitted by lilywhite juries.[42]

Many Confederate soldiers returning from the War, still dolled up in their Confederate grays, terrorized blacks, stealing from them and forcing them to sign binding labor contracts. Some former Confederate soldiers joined terrorist organizations such as the Ku Klux Klan and the Black Horse Cavalry. The United States Freedmen's Bureau provided some measure of protection against these injustices, but could not prevent all the criminal assaults. The efforts of persons such as Tennessee governor William G. Brownlow and Arkansas governor Powell Clayton, who were committed to ending repression and stamping out the Klan, were not enough to diffuse the racism that had entrenched itself through generations of indoctrination and practice. Militant support reestablished old social and racial hierarchies that condemned blacks and wage-earning whites to work for inadequate compensation. Throughout the South there were concerted efforts against establishing the civil freedoms assured by the Thirteenth Amendment.[43]

2. Legal Protections

Realizing the need to enact legislation in order to achieve the Thirteenth Amendment's purposes, the Reconstruction Congress began debating substantive civil rights proposals in December 1865, immediately after the states' ratification. Even advocates of legal reform held differing views about the amendment's reach. Radicals argued that it granted Congress authority to end discriminatory practices throughout the North and South, while moderates regarded it as primarily a guarantee of property and labor rights.

Even moderate Republicans like Senator Lyman Trumbull assumed that the Thirteenth Amendment enabled Congress to protect citizens against arbitrary infringements of their basic freedoms. Some of the confusion about the scope of the amendment's coverage resulted from Trumbull's Judiciary Committee's decision to integrate the Northwest Ordinance into the amendment's first section, instead of following Sumner's suggested language that would have assured the protection of equal legal rights. Some committee members later indicated that they chose language designed to end every abuse associated with involuntary servitude, not merely the institution of human chattel. If the amendment meant only to end forced labor, Trumbull asserted during a Senate debate on January 19, 1866, the "promised freedom is a delusion. . . . With the destruction of slavery necessarily follows the destruction of the incidents of slavery." The enforcement clause, he argued, gave Congress the authority to pass laws prohibiting any infringement on civil rights associated with the institution and its "badges." "If in order to prevent slavery Congress deem it necessary to declare null and void all laws which will not permit the colored man to contract, which will not permit him to testify, which will not permit him to buy and sell, and to go where he pleases, it has the power to do so, and not only the power, but it becomes its duty to do so." Later that year, Jacob M. Howard, a Radical Republican senator from Michigan, who was also a member of the 1864 Judicial Committee, gave a similar explanation. The committee anticipated the South's attempt to circumvent the amendment, Howard recalled, and intended the amendment to secure civil rights for blacks and whites. It secured the newly freed with the "ordinary rights of a freeman and nothing else."[44]

While this view was not shared by every Republican, those who were pushing for social reform were able to drive the agenda. Before the amendment's ratification, the federal government had never been in the hands of a group willing to end human rights abuses associated with the system of slavery. Radical Republican leaders invoked the amendment's second section to justify providing freed people with substantive and procedural rights. At various times during the Thirty-ninth Congress, they tried to eliminate employment discrimination, assure freedom of movement, provide a right to education, and prohibit arbitrary arrests. At the beginning of the Reconstruction Congress, Senator Sumner introduced a bill "to enforce the amendment to the constitution by securing the elective franchise to colored citizens" and offered "a joint resolution that prohibited any denial of civil or political rights, on the ground that such denial would violate the Amendment and the constitutional guarantee of the republican form of government." Senator Yates introduced a sweeping bill that assumed that "whereas by virtue of said abolition of slavery all men in all the States and Territories are citizens and entitled to all the rights and privileges of citizens . . . all citizens of the United States, without distinction of race, color, or condition shall be protected in the full and equal enjoyment of all their civil and political rights, including the right to suffrage." Although the Senate did not pass Yates's proposal, the bill exhibited the remarkably broad national mandate that Radicals thought the Thirteenth Amendment granted Congress. Yates's bill included the assumption that, even before the passage of the Fourteenth Amendment, the Thirteenth entitled citizens to all lawful privileges and immunities. The same great expectation is evident from other radical proposals. Less than a week after the amendment passed the House, Senator Henry Wilson introduced a bill (S. 427) prohibiting states, municipalities, corporations, and persons from excluding anyone on account of race from travel on railroads or navigable waters. Companies and individuals violating the proposed bill would have been subject to a $500 fine and up to six months' imprisonment. For Radical Republicans, the Thirteenth Amendment was the foundation on which they hoped to establish nationally recognized civil rights.[45]

Over the next couple of years, four statutes emerged to enforce the Thirteenth Amendment: the Civil Rights Act of 1866, the Slave Kidnaping Act of 1866, the Peonage Act of 1867, and the Judiciary Act of 1867.[46] These laws were radical departures from antebellum legal thought and speak loudest against the revisionist claim that the Thirteenth Amendment meant no more "for the Negro than exemption from slavery."[47] They provided the federal government with the power to prevent human rights abuses committed on the local, state, and national level. This legislative approach committed national government to upholding liberty rights that numerous constitutional provisions, congressional compromises, and Supreme Court decisions had previously abridged.

The Civil Rights Act, officially entitled "An Act to protect all persons in the United States in their civil rights, and furnish the means of their vindication," offers a case study into the practical effects that the amendment's framers intended it to have. Congress passed the Act pursuant to the amendment's second section. Unlike the Freedman's Bureau Act, which was a temporary wartime measure with no application outside the rebel states, the Civil Rights Act's reach was national. Trumbull reported the bill on January 12, 1866. In its initial form, the bill proposed to confer citizenship on all persons, except untaxed Indians who inhabited the states or territories. Further, under the initial proposal, any discrimination against citizens' civil rights and immunities would have been criminal. Language in the initial bill essentially guaranteed equal enjoyment of the privileges and immunities of citizenship but was removed from the bill's final draft. In its enacted form, the Civil Rights Act recognized the civil rights to

> make and enforce contracts, to sue, be parties, and give evidence, to inherit, purchase, lease, sell, hold, and convey real and personal property, and to full and equal benefit of all laws and proceedings for the security of person and property, as is enjoyed by white citizens, and shall be subject to like punishment, pains, and penalties, and to none other, any law, statute, ordinance, regulation, or custom, to the contrary notwithstanding.

The Act granted federal courts jurisdiction to hear cases of any alleged violations. Moreover, anyone who was denied the right to enforce his or her rights under the Act in a state court was permitted to transfer the case to a federal court. State officials who violated the Act under color of law or pursuant to custom were also subject to criminal prosecution. Violators were subject to imprisonment for up to one year and a fine of up to $1,000.[48]

The Act passed over President Johnson's veto. The urging of Secretary of State Seward and Ohio governor Jacob D. Cox, both Republicans who supported Johnson against attacks from those in their own party, made no difference in Johnson's decision to break with congressional reconstruction. In his lengthy message explaining the veto, Johnson said that the rights enumerated in the act were the province of each state and that it was unconstitutional to grant such extensive jurisdiction to the federal courts. Congress overrode Johnson's veto by a vote of 33 Senators for and 15 against, and the House overrode his veto by a vote of 122 for and 41 against.[49]

In its initial stages, the Civil Rights Act had a profound effect on the Southern legal culture. Black litigants transferred cases to federal courts when they found no redress against white defendants in the state court system. For instance, the "District Court in Louisville assumed jurisdiction over hundreds of cases in which whites were accused of murdering, assaulting, robbing, and otherwise maltreating blacks, thereby giving blacks access to impartial justice."[50] Moreover, Southern laws began to criminalize the commission of violence against African Americans. However, after the Freedman's Bureau's presence in the South was scaled back, enforcement became only sporadic.

On the one hand, the Civil Rights Act was a more detailed application of the natural-rights principles Republicans hoped to secure for freed people. Its passage shortly after states ratified the amendment shows how committed Republicans, during the early stages of Reconstruction, were to making freedom a practical reality. On the other, the final draft's exclusion of the explicit guarantee of civil rights and immunities against discrimination was, at best, a miscalculation. If the Republicans had hoped to gradually use section 2 of the Thirteenth Amendment to pass Reconstruction legislation, they would soon learn that President Johnson, using his veto power, would make increasingly more difficult the passage of any measure augmenting the power of national government. Further, with time, even leading antislavery Republicans would become less adamant and more willing to reconcile with the South than protect the rights of the newly freed. This was clear by the time Horace Greeley accepted the Democratic nomination for president in 1872 and even more when President Rutherford B. Hayes entered the Compromise of 1877, agreeing to withdraw federal troops from the South. Further, the Supreme Court soon embraced a narrow reading of the amendment, making district court enforcement almost impossible. The Supreme Court had the most constricting effect on the amendment and the Civil Rights Act.

3

End of Radical Ideals and Judicial Response

A. *Political Abandonment of Reconstruction*

President Andrew Johnson, from the beginning of Reconstruction, thwarted Republican efforts to make real the assurance of freedom. Only four weeks after the joint resolution to amend the Constitution passed through Congress, on May 29, 1865, Johnson issued the Proclamation of Amnesty. It offered amnesty for any rebels willing to swear allegiance to the United States and abide by emancipation policies. Those who were pardoned under this scheme, which required no proof of sincerity, could participate in Reconstruction.

The Democratic Party continued to sway Southern politics. In spite of its nominal support for the Thirteenth Amendment, it remained committed to white supremacy and forced labor, just as before the Civil War. Unreconstructed states passed laws inimical to the amendment. Delaware denied blacks equal access to public conveyances, places of amusement, or hotels. The Democratic legislature in Tennessee quickly repealed Radical laws that had prohibited the segregation of railroads and restricted Ku Klux Klan activities. And the seeming disinterest in the high rate of black illiteracy in states like Florida, Georgia, Louisiana, and Virginia led to a number of congressional proposals for a national education system.[1]

The Republican party, too, began to draw away from the idealism that led to passage of the Thirteenth Amendment. In part, the death of leaders who constituted the core of Radical Reconstruction, men like Salmon P. Chase, Thaddeus Stevens, and Edwin Stanton, reduced interest in passing necessary laws against continued incidents of servitude, such as discrimination in public places. Further, popular discontent with Reconstruction policy contributed to the amendment's disuse. George W. Julian and Benjamin F. Wade, both congressmen who were deeply committed to abolitionism, lost their seats in elections, and Sumner saw a decline of his influence in the Senate.[2]

The new guard of Republican leaders, led by Roscoe Conkling, had ambitions in the politics of bridges, tariffs, and road constructions. Increasingly absent was the commitment to human rights and revulsion for the racist inequality that had driven Stevens, Sumner, Wade, Kelly, and Wilson. Ironically, the moderation of Senators William P. Fessenden and Lyman Trumbull, which was so instrumental to getting the Civil Rights Bills of 1866 and 1875 through Congress, gradually damped the passions for social reform. In time, diehard Radicals were blamed for putting fundamental rights ahead of sectional reconciliation, derisively blamed for "waving the bloody shirt" and exploiting the War for political gain, and some in fact did just that. But those individuals who believed the Thirteenth Amendment was a source of substantive rights, rather than a punishment for rebellion, despaired about the diminishing zeal for passing national laws aimed at eradicating lingering vestiges of servitude. In 1874, Henry Wilson, by then vice president in the Grant administration, wrote William Lloyd Garrison that "anti-slavery veterans" needed to turn back the "counter-Revolution" sweeping away Reconstruction. He warned against men who were "beginning to hint at changing the condition of the Negro." George Julian wrote a despondent entry in his diary after visiting a cemetery monument to abolitionist Joshua R. Giddings: "The abolition element has almost died out in that old stronghold of radicalism, as it has in so many others throughout the country and the few antislavery pioneers who remain seem to feel lonely and lost."[3]

In this political atmosphere, the Supreme Court, beginning in 1873 with the *Slaughterhouse Cases*, also began reconsidering the constitutionality of federal laws prohibiting state and private discrimination. Its holdings put in doubt congressional power to intervene in traditional state-regulated areas such as public accommodations, criminal cases, and education. Thereafter, the increasingly reduced congressional civil rights agenda was linked to the Court's consistent erosion of such legislation. In addition, political events also affected the Court.

In particular, the maelstrom brought on after the 1876 presidential election influenced the judicial trend against a broad application of federal powers. When the votes were counted, Samuel J. Tilden, the Democratic candidate, had 184 electoral college votes, while the Republican, Rutherford B. Hayes, had 165. Twenty votes, which were scattered among four states, remained undecided, and all that was needed to receive the presidency was 185 electoral votes.

A stalemate ensued after much wrangling over the votes of undecided states. Since Congress was unable to decide the issue, it appointed an electoral commission composed of fifteen members. The Republican-dominated Senate received five members, of whom three were Republicans. The Democratic-dominated House received five members, of whom three were Democrats. And five members were chosen from the Supreme Court with a two-to-two split and one, presumably, neutral member. Initially, the neutral member was Justice David Davis, who had been Lincoln's campaign manager in 1860, but then Democrats made a strategic blunder by appointing Davis to the Senate from Illinois. Davis resigned from the Supreme Court and accepted the Senate seat. Consequently, Justice Joseph Bradley, a Republican, became the deciding eighth vote.

The commission then struck a deal that gave the presidency to Hayes in exchange for withdrawing federal troops from the South and effectively putting an end to all Radical attempts to change Southern society and improve black lives. When Hayes saw the precipitous drop in black votes in the 1878 election, he admitted that the "experiment" of entrusting reform to the South "was a failure."[4]

G. Sidney Buchanan, a legal historian, examined the effects of the Compromise of 1877 on judicial decisions, finding that they extended further than the immediate congressional abandonment of Reconstruction legislation. The Supreme Court, too, having sent the key member to the election committee, began determining opinions in line with the Compromise of 1877. Subsequent Court decisions became more averse to federal civil rights jurisdiction, until the Court had rendered the Thirteenth Amendment virtually a hollow guarantee that remained practically unenforceable.[5]

B. Supreme Court Abandonment of Reconstruction

Congress drafted the Thirteenth Amendment broadly enough to end any contemporary or future manifestation of involuntary servitude. Section 2 was the key to promulgating any "appropriate legislation" to that end. At first, the relative ambiguity of the amendment's first section and the lack of specificity about the meaning of "freedom" boded well for congressional use of sweeping powers to enact multivariegated reforms, but, in time, the same ambiguity also provided the judiciary with a basis for reading the amendment as narrowly as those antagonistic congressmen who voted against the joint resolution to pass it onto the states for ratification. The Supreme Court gradually emaciated the amendment's potential to address human rights violations, and only during the 1960s' civil rights movement did the Court recognize its mistake.

1. Early Opinions

A Kentucky federal court's 1866 decision in *United States v. Rhodes* was the first federal decision on the constitutionality of the Civil Rights Act of 1866, which Congress passed pursuant to its Thirteenth Amendment enforcement authority. Supreme Court Justice Noah Swayne heard arguments on the case, while sitting as a designated circuit court justice. Swayne espoused abolitionism even before the Civil War: at one time he and his wife freed slaves they received by marriage. As an attorney, Swayne had even represented fugitive slaves. His political views were closely tied to antislavery sentiments. He had joined the Republican Party in response to the 1850 controversy about the Fugitive Slave Law. And his proclivity to end racial oppression came through in this opinion.

Rhodes offered short-lived hope to the newly freed slaves and their advocates, with Swayne basing his reasoning on "the spirit in which the amendment is to be interpreted." The case arose after the white defendant had allegedly committed burglary against Nancy Talbot, "a citizen of the United States of the African race." The Civil Rights Act granted the federal court jurisdiction to hear the matter because the laws of Kentucky disqualified Talbot from testifying against the white defendants. In effect, the Kentucky law permitted whites to commit crimes against blacks with virtual impunity. In fact, prior to *Rhodes*, the Supreme Court of Kentucky held that the Civil Rights Act intruded on the state's sovereignty and reversed a white man's larceny conviction because it was based on a black witness's testimony. Swayne's opinion on the reach of federal power was much different.[6]

Swayne found that removal to federal courts was appropriate where state law prohibited black defendants from testifying. This was necessary to afford them equal access to redress for civil and criminal cases. The second section of the Thirteenth Amendment, Justice Swayne held, granted Congress the authority to enact legislation enabling blacks to have the same right to testify as any white citizen. He upheld the constitutionality of the Civil Rights Act, securing Talbot's right to legal redress through the federal removal provision. The Civil Rights Act of 1866 gave force to the Thirteenth Amendment; without it, "simple abolition would have been a phantom of delusion."

Swayne's reasoning offered insight into why even today a court must examine the history of American slavery in deciding cases arising from the Thirteenth Amendment. He recited "the state of things which existed before and at the time the amendment was adopted" over a few pages. He began with a narrative on the great civil rights infractions committed against slaves, mentioning prohibitions against teaching slaves, preventing them from assembling, suppressing slave labor unrest, and leaving them defenseless against crimes committed by whites. Further, Swayne seemed to recognize that the root problem was racism and economic exploitation of disenfranchised peoples. In this vein, he understood that the institution of slavery also made free blacks' lives miserable, and that they were saddled with many of the same "badges of bondman's degradation. . . . Their condition, like his, though not so bad, was helpless and hopeless." Federal courts committed to Republican principles had to step in because even after liberation the "worst effects of slavery" resurfaced, as occurred in Kentucky where blacks were at the mercy of whites, not having recourse to the courts against lawbreakers.

State court decisions that were decided shortly after *Rhodes* varied on the extent of Congress's power under the Thirteenth Amendment. Those rulings focused on the effect of the Civil Rights Act of 1866 on state sovereignty. While some courts found that the Act granted people the right to testify regardless of their race or ethnicity, at least one Kentucky court again held that Congress overstepped its constitutional authority by granting blacks the right to testify against whites.[7]

Meanwhile, in an era when Supreme Court justices regularly heard cases in the circuit courts, a duty Congress statutorily imposed in 1789 and ended only in 1891, other antislavery justices, besides Swayne, held that the Civil Rights Act of 1866 was constitutional. In *In re Turner*, Taney's successor, Chief Justice Chase, considered the legality of an indenture contract between a girl, Elizabeth Turner, and her former master, Philemon T. Hambleton. The terms of indenture permitted Hambleton to transfer Turner to another person. The master refused to educate Elizabeth, to which Maryland's indenture statute entitled white apprentices. Chase ordered Turner's release, holding that this labor arrangement violated Turner's civil rights because it failed to provide her with the "full and equal benefit of all laws and proceedings for the security of persons and property as is enjoyed by white citizens," which the Civil Rights Act guaranteed. Furthermore, Hambleton had asserted a "property" interest over Turner that the Thirteenth Amendment had outlawed.[8]

Justice William Strong was even more progressive in his 1873 opinion, which arose from a violation of the Enforcement Act of 1870. Strong found that the Thirteenth Amendment provided a substantive right: "Thus the thirteenth amendment made the right of personal liberty a constitutional right."[9]

Sadly, Strong was also the author of a majority opinion in 1872 that had inimical, long-term consequences. In *Blyew v. United States*, he relied on a legal technicality to deny case removal from a Kentucky court to a federal one. The case was the first blow to the use of the Thirteenth Amendment for ending centuries of racial intolerance. The facts of the case were gruesome, and looking at them with some detail helps one see how important federal relief was in a state that was still wedded to its proslavery past.[10]

The litigated dispute arose between a black family, the Fosters, and two local white men who periodically came to their cabin. Sallie and her husband Jack allowed the two, John Blyew and George Kennard, inside their family home. During the visit, Blyew became angry and hit Richard, the Fosters' sixteen-year-old son, on the head two times with an ax. Blyew and Kennard then began to vent their rage, repeatedly chopping at Jack and Sallie with the weapon. The parents died together in a pool of blood, with Sallie's head on Jack's chest. The perpetrators had also inflicted wounds to other members of the family. Richard was hit several times with the ax, but found safety under his father; his ten-year-old sister, Laura, suffered a head gash, the ax cleaving part of her skull, and the men also cut Amelia, who was only six years old. Neither did Blyew and Kennard spare the children's nonagenarian grandmother: she too suffered a fatal blow. After Richard regained consciousness, even though he was bleeding profusely from his head, he managed to drag himself to a neighbor's house to call for help.

The next morning police arrested Blyew and Kennard at Blyew's mother's home; a fresh foot trail began there and led to the Fosters' house. The two boot prints met the measurements of one of the arrested men and the other prints were linked to the boots of the other. What's more, a bloody ax helped connect the men to the crime, and Richard made a sworn and signed statement about the slaughter before he expired from wounds. Laura also identified Blyew and Kennard, in a crowd, as the murderers.[11]

Kentucky law, in 1868, when the two men were indicted, still forbade black witnesses from testifying against white defendants.[12] The case therefore was heard in federal court, which found both men guilty of the murders. The court sentenced them to death by hanging. The tenth section of the Civil Rights Act of 1866 granted the Supreme Court jurisdiction to hear the final appeal in this case. The United States Solicitor General argued to the Court that the right to testify protected persons and property and was part and parcel of the freedom Congress assured all citizens regardless of race.

After hearing oral arguments, the Supreme Court was convinced by the defendants' procedural argument against federal court jurisdiction and reversed the convictions. The Court decided that only living persons could request removal, making convictions for murder impossible. The Court further found that Congress passed the Civil Rights Act of 1866 to make whites and blacks equal before the law because blacks encountered many obstacles to gaining access to federal courts. The Act was passed at a time when African Americans were often subject to more severe penalties than whites, some states denied blacks the right to a jury trial, and many state courts rendered prejudiced judgments. Nevertheless, in *Blyew* no one had standing to remove the case to federal court since the key victims were dead. Thus, the Court partly undermined the significance of the Civil Rights Act's removal provision, leaving state courts to be the sole arbiters of murder cases, even when those courts barred black testimony.

Justice Swayne continued to maintain his broad reading of the Thirteenth Amendment, and he joined Justice Bradley in the dissent to *Blyew*. They pointed out that by enacting the Civil Rights Act, Congress put former slaves specifically and all blacks generally on an equal legal footing with other U.S. citizens. The majority of the Court misconstrued the Act by using an artificially "narrow" reading, discounting the liberal ideals surrounding its passage. Bradley's dissent asserted that Congress intended to prevent wanton, racist conduct directed at the black community. The legislature attempted to "do away with the incidents and consequences of slavery" and to replace them with "civil liberty and equality." One of the chief aims in abolishing slavery was to assure blacks the "full enjoyment" of their civil rights. Congress enacted the Act, Bradley explained, because merely striking off the "fetters of slavery" would have been an inadequate solution for the years of black repression. The dissent further recognized that the majority opinion legitimized Kentucky's practice of prohibiting blacks from testifying against whites and branding all blacks "with a badge of slavery."

Southern government officials and hoodlums alike used *Blyew* to skirt civil rights legislation. The case significantly diminished the potential for a successful Reconstruction. It branded blacks as easy prey for individuals and groups who continued extolling the Confederacy and sought to reinvigorate its institutions. If the Klan and other violent supremacist groups had been at all leery of being tried in federal courts, *Blyew* relieved them of that worry. The federal government could no longer provide a judicial forum in cases where state laws prohibited blacks from testifying against whites and when the black victims of a crime were unavailable.

Soon, the Court placed substantive limitations on Congress's power, which emasculated the Thirteenth Amendment even more than the procedural strictures set in *Blyew*. The beginning of that trend came in the well-known *Slaughterhouse Cases*, where white butchers sought relief against a Louisiana law that granted a monopoly to a single slaughterhouse company. The butchers brought suit under the Thirteenth and Fourteenth Amendments. The plaintiffs claimed that the state law violated the Thirteenth Amendment because it prohibited them from engaging in a lawful occupation. This argument did not persuade Justice Miller, who held that the Thirteenth Amendment's reach was limited to slavelike relations. He found the amendment inapplicable to cases where individuals sought to assert an interest in pursuing their occupation. The Court thus found the Louisiana law constitutional. Miller's decision limited the national government's power to end the use of economic exploitation in order to deny people work opportunities.[13]

Shortly thereafter, in 1874, Justice Bradley penned a decision on a case he heard as a designated circuit court judge in Louisiana. In his nonbinding dictum to *United States v. Cruikshank*, Bradley again expressed a fairly expansive view of the Thirteenth Amendment. The case involved Ku Klux Klan defendants (members of the "White League") whom a federal jury had convicted under the Civil Rights Enforcement Act of 1870. The defendants had participated in the 1873 Colfax Massacre, where Louisiana whites murdered over one hundred black men for holding a political rally to assert their right to vote. Bradley stated that the second section of the Thirteenth Amendment gave Congress power "not only to legislate for the eradication of slavery, but for the power to give full effect to this bestowment of liberty on . . . millions of people." His dictum seems to have conceded that the amendment was a source of both the negative power to end forced servitude and positive power to extend citizenship rights without regard to people's previous condition of servitude. For him, the grant of freedom was no hollow concept. Congress regarded the demise of slavery to mean that blacks would enjoy "an entire equality before the law with the white citizen." However, Bradley's binding holding in *Cruikshank* was based on the Fourteenth Amendment, which he found protected only "against the acts of the state government itself." Since none of the defendants were members of the state government, the Court overturned their convictions. The Supreme Court affirmed Bradley's decision on Fourteenth Amendment grounds and never reached his Thirteenth Amendment reasoning.[14] Indeed, Bradley himself never returned to that reasoning; instead, he moved away from his earlier convictions.

2. Relinquishment of Thirteenth Amendment Principles

After *Slaughterhouse*, the Supreme Court sharply curtailed the effectiveness of the Thirteenth Amendment. A movement away from abolitionist ideals was already afoot in Congress, and the Supreme Court failed to meet the historical moment with the resolve needed to secure citizens against arbitrary intrusions into their liberties.

The period of significant decline in Thirteenth Amendment jurisprudence began with the *Civil Rights Cases* (1883) in which Justice Bradley drastically qualified his earlier dissent in *Blyew*. His decision further diminished the scope of federal civil rights protections.[15] The case concerned the constitutionality of the Civil Rights Act of 1875, which was enacted, in large part, because of Charles Sumner's heroic efforts. In its original form, Sumner proposed in 1872 to forbid social discrimination in public schools, railroads, steamboats, public conveyances, hotels, restaurants, licensed theaters, juries, and in incorporated church or cemetery associations. Federal courts would have had jurisdiction to hear these cases and to impose fines and imprisonment against violators. However, in the Senate Judiciary Committee, the prohibition against public school discrimination became a sticking point. The bill's opponents argued against abolitionists, claiming that white students would not attend schools with blacks and that integration would harm education. What's more, Southern Republicans claimed President Grant would veto the bill, even though the President kept silent on the issue. Disputes arose between

Southerner and Northern Republicans, leading to an enormous congressional defeat for the party. In the next Congress, Democrats held 168 seats, Republicans 108, and Independents 14.[16]

Even on his deathbed, in March 1874, Sumner did not forget that abolition, *via* the Thirteenth Amendment, meant more than merely setting free millions of people. They had been denied an education by Southern slave codes, and even after emancipation blacks were still excluded from numerous public places. As he lay dying, Sumner was not remiss to remind a visitor, "You must take care of the civil-rights bill, . . . don't let it fail." Sumner died before Congress enacted the Civil Rights Act of 1875.[17]

Sumner's bill also had popular backing. For instance, George Curtis, the editor of *Harper's Weekly*, wrote in favor of its passage. When "hotels and restaurants may turn respectable guests away because they are of the colored race," Curtis unequivocally stated, "and theaters and cars, all doing business by legal licence, may refuse them entrance for the same reason, it is plain that the law fosters the prejudice." However, when "the law enables the colored guest to call the offending host to account . . . the prejudice will begin to wane." Benjamin Butler, who managed the Bill in the House, committed himself to defending "the rights of these men who have given their blood for me and my country."[18]

The Radical Republican influence was by then waning. The Bill passed out of the Senate, without the church provision, only after Vice President Henry Wilson cast the tie-breaking vote. The House then deleted the school and cemetery clauses and passed the Civil Rights Act of 1875. From then until *Brown v. Board of Education* (1954), this country would tolerate a separate and supposedly equal school system. Still, the Civil Rights Act of 1875 prohibited some forms of social discrimination connected to the remaining vestiges of servitude. The Act's first section entitled "all persons within the jurisdiction of the United States" to the "the full and equal enjoyment of the accommodations, advantages, facilities, and privileges of inns, public conveyances on land or water, theaters, and other places of public amusement." Its second sections set out the applicable criminal and civil penalties for violations.[19] The Civil Rights Act of 1875 was grand in its protection of some basic human rights that are essential for living freely, not only for blacks but for the nation as a whole. It was the last civil rights law the Reconstruction Congress passed.

The constitutionality of the Act's first two sections was the subject of litigation in the *Civil Rights Cases*. By 1883, when the case came before the Supreme Court, Reconstruction had come to a grinding halt even though many racialist institutions resembling slavery remained. Litigation involved five joint cases from various parts of the country. The first four cases were reviews of criminal prosecutions. Two of the defendants were charged with denying blacks access to an inn or hotel, a third for prohibiting a black individual from access to the dress circle of a theater in San Francisco, and a fourth for refusing access to a New York opera house. The fifth case was a civil action from Tennessee against a railroad company whose conductor prevented a black woman from riding in the ladies' car. Attorneys for four of the five defendants did not even bother appearing to argue the case before the Court, but they nevertheless received a favorable ruling for their clients. Their success signaled the national consensus to draw away from abolitionist principles.[20]

The government's case was based on two theories. It first claimed that Congress had power to enact the Act in order to prevent intrusions on freedom pursuant to its Thirteenth Amendment power. The second basis of its case was that Congress had power to establish necessary and proper laws for the furtherance of equal protection and due process under the Fourteenth Amendment.

Bradley, who was by then chief justice of the Supreme Court, drafted the majority opinion. All the members of the Court, except Justice John Marshall Harlan, joined the majority. Bradley had steadily moved away from his dissent in *Blyew* toward the narrow construction of both the Thirteenth and Fourteenth Amendments in *Cruikshank*. By 1877, when he headed the electoral commission that gave Hayes the presidential victory, Bradley was a long way from his *Slaughterhouse* dissent. That year he joined the Court in *Hall v. DeCuir*, which found unconstitutional a Louisiana law requiring the desegregation of public conveyance.[21]

The limits on Congress's Fourteenth Amendment power announced in the *Civil Rights Cases* continue to be binding. The *Civil Rights Cases* held that the Fourteenth Amendment only protects citizens against state interference with individual rights but not against individual interference with individual rights. Thus, the Court decided that the Fourteenth Amendment did not authorize Congress to pass the Civil Rights Act of 1875. I will critique the Fourteenth Amendment's state interference requirement in relationship to the Thirteenth Amendment in chapter 6. Suffice it to say here that, in the unreconstructed South, the idea that states themselves would regulate private discriminations was far-fetched. The dissent's view on congressional enforcement power was more realistic and analogous to

Radical Republican ideals of Reconstruction. The fifth section of the amendment, Harlan wrote, enabled Congress to enact "appropriate legislation . . . and such legislation may be of a direct and primary character, operating upon states, their officers and agents, and also upon, at least, such individuals and corporations as exercise public functions and wield power and authority under the state."

Significantly, the *Civil Rights Cases* also provided the Supreme Court with the first opportunity to interpret the Thirteenth Amendment's substance. Bradley conceded that the Thirteenth Amendment did more than simply nullify state laws protecting slavery and release slaves from their masters' control. It also decreed "civil and political freedom throughout the United States." Further, it granted Congress the power to pass all necessary and proper laws abolishing the "badges and incidents of slavery in the United States." However, that part of the decision was dictum because Bradley considered it not germane to the constitutionality of the Civil Rights Act of 1875. In the substantive part of the decision, he distinguished "the social rights of men and races in the community," which he thought the Thirteenth Amendment did not cover, from "fundamental rights which appertain to the essence of citizenship," which he believed were within its province. Even on this point, Bradley was reticent, choosing not to reach the issue of whether the Thirteenth Amendment alone protected those fundamental rights without the later ratification of the Fourteenth Amendment. Bradley concluded that the Civil Rights Act of 1875 was unconstitutional because denying persons admission to public accommodations was not a vestige of slavery nor a fundamental right of citizenship.

Justice Harlan wrote the dissent to the *Civil Rights Cases*. It is worthwhile to pause and recall his political evolution. He developed abolitionist sentiments later in life than did Justice Swayne. During the Civil War, in 1861, at the age of twenty-eight, he became a colonel in the Tenth Kentucky Regiment. Soon after resigning his commission from the Union Army, Harlan became a successful politician, working alternatively as Kentucky's secretary of state, attorney general, and congressman. As attorney general, he argued for a much different position than he would later embrace in his *Civil Rights Cases*'s dissent. The federal government should be limited, he had earlier insisted, and, unless it could show there was an immediate necessity, it possessed no legal justification to remove slaves from Kentucky masters. Most remarkably, in *Bowlin v. Commonwealth* the United States Supreme Court sided with him and his state in favor of a Kentucky law forbidding black testimony against white criminal defendants. Indeed, at first Harlan even opposed the Thirteenth and Fourteenth Amendments because he thought they undermined Kentucky's right to determine its policy on slavery. In a letter, he stressed that his "opposition" was not based "in regard to the future of slavery in Kentucky, or in regard to that institution in its moral, social, or political aspect . . . but on principal." Further in the same letter, Harlan expressed his worry that immediate abolition would result in racial unrest.[22]

Harlan changed his opposition to federal anti-slavery policy upon learning of outrages committed in Kentucky by the KKK and other terrorist organizations such as Rowzee's Band and The Regulators. By the 1870s, Harlan was a Kentucky Republican politician who met with black leaders on a personal level and spoke in favor of civil rights. However, his previous views made him suspect for a time and blocked his immediate confirmation to the Supreme Court. In response to his critics, Harlan made clear in many speeches that he had abandoned his old views.[23]

When he wrote his first great dissent in the *Civil Rights Cases* in 1883, Harlan's support for ending slavery and its concomitant disabilities was no longer in doubt. Years after, his widow, Malvina Harlan, recalled in her memoirs how the Justice would wake in the "middle of the night, in order to jot down" a thought on his dissent "which he feared might elude him in the morning." Harlan realized the momentous significance of the case and sought to fashion a wise and forceful decision. At times during his preparation, he was "in a quagmire of logic, precedent and law." Mrs. Harlan inspired her husband's thoughts by taking out of storage the prized object from his Americana collection, Chief Justice Taney's inkstand. Taney had used it to write his *Dred Scott* decision. Seeing the inkstand, Harlan was stirred to effectuate the opposite result:

The memory of the historic part that Taney's inkstand had played in the Dred Scott decision, in temporarily tightening the shackles of slavery upon the Negro race in the ante-bellum days, seemed that morning to act like magic in clarifying my husband's thoughts in regard to the law . . . intended by Sumner to protect the recently emancipated slaves in the enjoyment of equal "civil rights." His pen fairly flew on that day and, with the running start he then got, he soon finished his dissent.[24]

Harlan found Bradley's majority opinion in the *Civil Rights Cases* "narrow and artificial." He thought it undermined the "substance and

spirit" of the Thirteenth Amendment. The Court had construed "constitutional provisions adopted in the interest of liberty" in such a way as to
"defeat the ends the people desired to accomplish." Harlan approached
the problem from a historical perspective, showing how the amendment
had affected the Court's earlier rulings on the federal duty to recognize
state sovereignty over slavery. In *Prigg v. Pennsylvania*, he recalled, the
Court established that Congress could pass the national Fugitive Slave
Law to protect a master's right to own and recover slaves. Therefore,
Prigg concluded that the national government could use its "implied
power" to aid in the return of fugitive slaves from free states. The second
section of the Thirteenth Amendment, Harlan found, did away with the
use of federal authority to protect against this oppression. Even more im-
portantly, the amendment "expressly granted" Congress the power to
guarantee "universal civil freedom," which trumped the *Prigg* protec-
tionism. The congressional enforcement power made clear the framers'
desire to promulgate national civil rights legislation rather than leaving
civil reform in the hands of the very states that had opposed the abolition
of slavery.

From there, Harlan drew on Chief Justice Taney's finding in *Dred Scott*
that blacks were never citizens of the United States and therefore shared
none of the inherent privileges and benefits of its laws and protections.
The Thirteenth Amendment, Harlan went on, was a direct response to
Dred Scott as it granted national citizenship to every race. Because the
dogma of black inferiority was instrumental to the sustenance of slavery,
the Thirteenth Amendment's guarantee of freedom must have "necessarily involved immunity from, and protection against, all discrimination
against them, because of their race, in respect of such civil rights as be-
long to freemen of other races."

Harlan's dissent showed a keen prescience that the majority's decision
would preclude the national government from putting an end to all impediments to freedom. In contradistinction, Harlan thought Congress
had the power to enact and enforce the Civil Rights Act of 1875. Harlan
then carefully evaluated whether the Thirteenth Amendment guaranteed
the rights of the particular litigants in the *Civil Rights Cases*, finding that
the use of public highways was "so far fundamental as to be deemed the
essence of civil freedom." And in 1875 Congress passed the Act to remove burdens on locomotion "which lay at the very foundation of the institution of slavery." As for the defendants who denied blacks access to
an inn and a hotel, they were engaged in "a *quasi* public employment"

and could not deny service to persons because of their race or color. Likewise, defendants who owned public places of amusement "established and maintained" their business "under direct license of the law." Blacks were part of the public for whom those laws were maintained. Harlan, then, found that the Thirteenth Amendment granted Congress the power to pass laws prohibiting discrimination in places of public accommodation.

> I am of the opinion that such discrimination practiced by corporations and individuals in the exercise of their public or quasi-public functions is a badge of servitude, the imposition of which congress may prevent under its power. By appropriate legislation, to enforce the thirteenth amendment; and consequently, without reference to its enlarged power under the fourteenth amendment, the act of March 1, 1875, is not, in my judgment, repugnant to the constitution.

While Justice Harlan agreed with Justice Bradley that Congress could not regulate social relations, meaning that it could not require blacks and whites to participate in social intercourse, Harlan's dissent proclaimed that no public or private actor could "consistently . . . with the freedom established by the fundamental law" deny any citizen the rights to enjoy public accommodations. Harlan stood alone on the Court in his acute understanding that the vestiges of slavery could only be eliminated by broad-based legal reforms.

In a letter to Harlan, the then retired Justice Swayne highly praised his dissent: "In my judgement, it is one of the great, indeed one of the greatest, opinions of the Court does you infinite honor, is all that could be desired, and will make a profound and lasting impression upon the Country." Former Supreme Court Justice William Strong, similarly, told Harlan that after reading the dissent he too recognized that the majority opinion was "too narrow-sticks to the letter, while you aim to bring out the Spirit of the Constitution."[25]

The Supreme Court's holding in the *Civil Rights Cases*, coupled with a Republican reevaluation of the party's priorities and a presidential policy of appeasing the South following the Compromise of 1877, put a halt to Reconstruction and the systematic attempt to end discrimination. The *Civil Rights Cases* were a missed opportunity to further the racially tolerant vision of the Thirteenth Amendment. The nation had to wait until 1964 to end discrimination in public accommodations.[26] Until then, the country was in the degrading grip of forces opposed to congressional authority in cases of racial discrimination.

A public outcry greeted the *Civil Right Cases*. Black citizens held a mass meeting in Louisville to express their outrage on October 19, 1883, just four days after Bradley issued the opinion. They declared that the Supreme Court could not eliminate their constitutionally guaranteed rights of citizenship. The colored citizens of Birmingham, Alabama, also condemned the decision. They regarded it to be an infringement against their natural human right to enjoy equal accommodations. The *Arkansas Mansion* carried a number of excerpts from various newspapers; this collage or articles showed a lack of a national consensus. On the one hand, various black organizations mobilized meetings throughout the country declaring that the Supreme Court's holding was "foolish and useless." These "indignation meetings" gathered regularly in the months following the holding to express outrage. On the other hand, one editorial claimed that the Court's decision was received "with pleasure by sensible people all over the Union."[27]

In spite of many popular efforts to the contrary, Bradley's decision took firm root in American jurisprudence. The cases that followed on the heals of the *Civil Rights Cases* further curtailed the significance of the Thirteenth Amendment. Supreme Court jurisprudence tended to favor state police powers in the areas of race relations and civil interactions. *Plessy v. Ferguson* overtly discarded the ideals of post–Civil War Reconstruction. As with the *Civil Rights Cases*, eight justices joined with the *Plessy* majority, and only Justice Harlan voiced a dissent.[28]

At center stage was Homer Adolph Plessy, who was born free on March 17, 1862. All his immediate relatives were white, except one of his four great-grandmothers, who was black. Plessy's attorney would later say that his racial mixture was "not discernable." Nevertheless, Plessy was considered black under Louisiana law.[29] He had entered the struggle against enforcement of the state law through the Citizens' Committee to Test the Constitutionality of the Separate Car Law. Plessy entered a railway station and bought a first-class ticket on the East Louisiana Railway. His aim was to challenge the 1890 Louisiana Act 111, section 2 (Louisiana Separate Car Act), which enforced an "equal but separate accommodations for the white and colored races." The train personnel were given the power to enforce the law, and both the railroad employees and passengers were subject to fines for violating it.[30]

Plessy's arrest was probably achieved by prearrangement to create a viable legal case. He sat in a railcar reserved for whites. When the conductor asked for his ticket, Plessy told him that he was one-eighth black and refused to go to the colored car. The conductor then called a detective, who arrested Plessy. The next day, Plessy was released on a $500 bond.[31]

Louis A. Martinet, a prominent black attorney, and Rodolphe Desdunes, one of the founders of the Citizen's Committee, recruited Albion W. Tourgée to represent Plessy at court. Tourgée zealously took up the request and represented Plessy for free. Like many men of his generation, Tourgée fought for the Union during the Civil War and even sustained a spinal injury. After the War, he openly took on African American clients and employees. Of even greater credit to him, though he lived in North Carolina, he boldly criticized the Ku Klux Klan, most memorably in his fictional work, *A Fool's Errand. By One of the Fools*. Tourgée, however, was not licensed in Louisiana, therefore Martinet also retained a local white attorney to represent Plessy.[32]

Criminal district court Judge John H. Ferguson, who presided over *State v. Plessy*, had previously heard another case involving the Louisiana Separate Car Act. The other case involved interstate travelers. That case was brought by Daniel F. Desdunes, also seven-eighths white, who had bought a rail ticket from Louisiana to Alabama. In Desdunes's case, Ferguson determined that the Louisiana law was unconstitutional as applied to travel between states. Therefore, Ferguson seemed like an ideal judge from the Citizen's Committee's perspective.

The Plessy challenge was necessary to end the discriminatory Louisiana intrastate travel restrictions, which Desdunes's victory did not affect. Tourgée determined not to use any interstate commerce argument, which had been critical to the former case. His was a principled attack on the Louisiana law, rather than one based on a legal stratagem. As Tourgée put it, "What we want is not a verdict of not guilty, nor a defect in this law but a decision whether such a law can legally" stand under the Thirteenth Amendment and the Equal Protection Clause of the Fourteenth Amendment.[33]

Plessy did not enter a plea before Judge Ferguson. Instead, his attorneys filed a motion to dismiss the case because the Louisiana law was unconstitutional. At a hearing, Judge Ferguson found the Act constitutional because the state had the power to regulate railroad companies operating exclusively in its borders. On the Thirteenth Amendment issue, Ferguson based his decision on the *Civil Rights Cases*, finding the amendment only applies to slavery and not to the situation of this case. Plessy's attorneys appealed the case to the state supreme court, which upheld the trial court's ruling and subsequently issued a "writ of errors" that brought the case before the U.S. Supreme Court. Thus, the criminal case against Plessy was placed on hold to await the Supreme Court's ruling on constitutional issues.[34]

The *Plessy* decision had consequences on both Thirteenth and Fourteenth Amendment jurisprudence. Indeed, these two aspects of the case intermingle. The Court's finding that the Louisiana law did not violate the Fourteenth Amendment was based on the same complacency with nineteenth-century racism as its holding on the Thirteenth Amendment. The majority's evaluation about the law was guided by the state's "established usages, customs and traditions of the people, and with a view to the promotion of their comfort, and the preservation of the public peace and good order." All of these qualifications of analysis boded well for the advocates of the *status ante-bellum*.

The brief of errors Tourgée and Walker submitted to the Supreme Court set forth their legal arguments. On the Thirteenth Amendment, they claimed that forcefully separating the races perpetuated "observances of a servile character [which were] coincident with the incidents of slavery." Such a regimen perpetuated the badges of servitude by enforcing "the distinction of race and caste among citizens of the United States on both sides." The point was that the Louisiana Separate Car Act maintained the racialist classifications that slavery spawned. Their argument not only pointed out the detrimental effect to the individual traveler, but also to mixed race spouses, whom it forbade from traveling together by rail. Curiously, while Louisiana separated rail travelers, interracial marriage was still legal there. A separate brief pointed out that the travelers suffered not only physical discrimination analogous to slavery but were also forced to submit to "a taunt by the State" related to "that previous condition of their Class."[35]

Justice Henry B. Brown, who penned the *Plessy* opinion, held that the Louisiana Act excluding blacks from white railroad cars did not violate the Thirteenth Amendment. The holding provided judicial legitimization for the Jim Crow system that legally reenforced a system of exclusion reminiscent of slavery. Rather than taking a contextualist approach, reflecting on whether forced segregation was historically tied to involuntary servitude, the Court interpreted "slavery" literally as "control of the labor and services of one man for the benefit of another, and the absence of a legal right to the disposal of his own person, property and services." This definition included only involuntary labor and peonage but none of the myriad legal restrictions on freedom imposed in the postwar South. In fact, to Brown a law "permitting, or even requiring, [racial segregation] in places where they are liable to be brought into contact do not necessarily imply the inferiority of either race to the other."

Justice Brown was remiss in addressing the Southern cultural baggage that continued to haunt black lives. He also devalued black American frustrations, angers, and fears:

> We consider the underlying fallacy of the plaintiff's argument to consist in the assumption that the enforced separation of the two races stamps the colored race with a badge of inferiority. If this be so, it is not by reason of anything found in the act, but solely because the colored race chooses to put that construction upon it.

Further, showing an insensitivity about black living conditions and the sense of abandonment blacks faced from widespread prejudices, Justice Brown speculated that if they were in the majority and whites in the minority, whites would not demand racial integration. His majority opinion took on a typically supremacist approach, extolling whites for their innocence and upbraiding African Americans.

The Court's lack of "understand[ing]" about why the Plaintiff considered "a legal distinction between the white and colored races" to be a badge of servitude was disheartening. *Plessy* discarded the Thirteenth Amendment's potential to herald a renaissance of freedom. That decision made the Union's victory over the Confederacy far less than complete because it allowed the continued spoliation of black civil rights. Segregationist laws, like the Louisiana Separate Car Act, branded blacks with a scarlet letter, inviting state-condoned racial favoritism. Such laws intended both to exclude and to send a message to the African American community. Blacks were tolerated but also subject to arbitrary legal and private barriers against self-expression and civil participation. The *Plessy* decision not only stigmatized black passengers, but also had a residual effect on the nation as a whole, making elaborate avoidance of Thirteenth Amendment principles easier to justify.

Justice Harlan, in his dissent to *Plessy*, once again manifested his commitment to the fundamental rights of U.S. citizens. Disavowing the majority's disregard for the hardships blacks faced, Harlan's dissent drew on "the humanitarianism of the earlier era."[36] The right of persons of various races to share railroad cars was only a subpart of the rights "inhering" in Harlan's notion of "freedom." Harlan drew from Blackstone's *Commentaries*, just as he had in the *Civil Rights Cases*, to explain the significance of "personal liberty." It consists in the general right to "locomotion, of changing situation, or removing one's person to whatever places one's own inclination may direct." The Louisiana law against racial integration in railcars was primarily aimed at restricting "the personal freedom of citizens" to travel on public accommodations.

Justice Harlan realized the majority's opinion would have long-term ramifications; in fact, for years after the holding it affected many facets of Southern culture, including separate public drinking fountains and schools. Indeed, Harlan understood that the majority's opinion would justify much wider state and private restrictions than simply those on rail travel. Harlan reflected on the extensive implications of the majority's holding: "If a state can prescribe, as a rule of civil conduct, that whites and blacks shall not travel as passengers in the same railroad coach, why may it not so regulate the use of the streets of its cities and towns as to compel white citizens to keep on one side of a street, and black citizens to keep on the other?"

The Louisiana Separate Car Act not only limited the free movement of individuals but also hindered black and white interaction. Harlan realized that drawing legal demarcations between the races communicated black subordination and legitimated the ideology of white exclusivity to the privileges of citizenship. Government, he asserted, could not interfere with the personal choice of "a white man and a black man . . . to occupy the same public conveyance on a public highway." Likewise, a railroad corporation using the public way performed a public function. Justice Harlan found disingenuous the notion that separate accommodations for blacks and whites made both races equals before the law. "The thin disguise of 'equal' accommodations for passengers in railroad coaches will not mislead any one, nor, atone for the wrong this day done." Separation of the races, to the contrary, was a continuing mark of slavery that denied blacks the full enjoyment of "civil freedom and equality before the law established by the constitution."

Plessy created a two-tiered system of civil rights based on racial characteristics. On this point, Harlan restated his view that although the Reconstruction Amendments eradicated the holding in *Dred Scott*, some states continued to erect racial barriers that prevented blacks from exercising civil liberties. Since state regulations damaged relations between the races, Harlan concluded that the national government had an interest in preventing "race hate to be planted under the sanction of law." As constitutional scholar T. Alexander Aleinikoff pointed out, Harlan's dissent in *Plessy* regarded citizens' liberty to be the fundamental unit that government must protect.

If the health of a society can be measured by the extent to which it respects the fundamental rights of all its citizens and augments social welfare, the prognosis for the United States after *Plessy* was of a malignant disregard for oppressed and weak minorities. Justice Harlan predicted, quite accurately, that *Plessy* would "prove to be quite as pernicious as the decision made by the tribunal in the *Dred Scott* case." Generational acceptance of purported black inferiority, coupled with legally countenanced inequality, legitimized discrimination in public places, and even violence.

It would take decades for the country to recover from the Supreme Court's constriction of the human rights protections that Radical Republicans had fought to include in the Constitution. In 1903, a federal district court judge, sitting in Arkansas, sought to reverse the trend. The case of *United States v. Morris* dealt with indicted persons who prevented African Americans from leasing and cultivating lands. The Court found that the defendants had violated black citizens' Thirteenth Amendment rights by preventing them from exercising their "inalienable" and "fundamental rights, inherent in every free citizen." Both the amendment and the Declaration of Independence, the court held, secured those "fundamental rights."[37]

The Supreme Court, however, soon snuffed this brief flicker of hope. *Hodges v. United States* arose in 1903, when a mob of white men used deadly weapons, threats, and intimidation to violently drive eight African American citizens from their lumber mill jobs. The mob thereby prevented the employees from fulfilling their labor contracts. A federal grand jury in Arkansas indicted the defendants under § 5508 of the United States Code, which criminalized two or more people from conspiring "to injure, oppress, threaten, or intimidate any citizen in the free exercise or enjoyment of any right or privilege secured to him by the Constitution or laws of the United States, or because of his having so exercised the same." Another pertinent national law gave all persons within the jurisdiction of the United States a coequal right to enforce contracts.[38]

The Court held that Congress overstepped its Thirteenth Amendment power by enacting these laws. It viewed the Thirteenth Amendment's prohibition against slavery in its "natural sense," meaning that it relied on a Webster Dictionary definition of the term rather than considering the debates and social circumstances surrounding the amendment's ratification. Under the Court's interpretation, states retained the power to prevent mob obstructions of liberty, and the Thirteenth Amendment granted Congress no power to do so. The Court further constricted Congress's ability to prevent coercive infringements on liberty, holding that the conduct covered by the charging legislation included many acts that were not exclusively related to slavery. Construing organized racist aggression as no different than any other crime, the Court held that "no mere personal assault or trespass or appropriation operates to reduce the individual to a condition of slavery." Essentially, the Court found the Thirteenth Amendment did not reach the use of force to intimidate laborers from performing their obligations under employment contracts. In the final analysis, *Hodges* construed the Thirteenth Amendment to reach only a small set of cases involving forced labor.

The majority's assault on congressional section 2 power did not convince Justice Harlan. Indeed, his dissent, which Justice Day joined, gave the clearest distinction he had ever formulated between the Thirteenth and Fourteenth Amendments. The Thirteenth established certain freedoms, he wrote, that the Fourteenth protected against inconsistent state actions. His dissent also laid out some of the essential rights protected under the Thirteenth Amendment, exhibiting a clear divergence from the majority. His views will be essential in helping us understand, in Part II, why the Thirteenth Amendment continues to be the source of substantive autonomy rights. Liberty, Harlan wrote, adopting the language of an earlier case,

> means not only the right of the citizen to be free from the mere physical restraint of his person, as by incarceration, but the term is deemed to embrace the right of the citizen to be free in the enjoyment of all his faculties; to be free to use them in all lawful ways; to live and work when he will; to earn his livelihood by any lawful calling; to pursue any liveli-

hood or avocation, and for that purpose to enter into all contracts which may be proper, necessary, and essential to his carrying out to a successful conclusion the purposes above mentioned.

The amendment entitled all free persons to these rights.

The dissent's perspective on the Thirteenth Amendment embraced ideas that were similar to those Radical Republicans had explicated during congressional debates on the amendment. Harlan and Day recognized that the amendment's guarantee of liberty, the very liberty the Preamble to the Constitution ensured, prohibited racists from preventing law-abiding persons from pursuing jobs of their choosing. We may infer, then, that to the dissent the right to personal freedom meant being able to choose an employer without violent interference.

But the *Hodges* majority abandoned blacks to the whims of Southern state legislators who already used Jim Crow laws to stigmatize blacks. They could no longer turn to federal prosecutors for help, even in cases overtly linked to the harms of involuntary servitude.[39] The majority's recognition that the Thirteenth Amendment "reaches every race and every individual" was an empty concession since the Court's holding precluded Congress from wiping out remaining incidents of servitude. Indeed, *Hodges*'s statement on the amendment's racially neutral applicability was a snide way of asserting that the emancipation "of the colored race" was "not an attempt to commit that race to the care of the nation." Supreme Court jurisprudence made Thirteenth Amendment challenges to human rights violations virtually impossible.

The last of the series of cases the Court decided prior to the 1960s civil rights reforms dealt with a restrictive covenant between thirty white people, prohibiting the covenanted parties from selling or leasing parcels of land to any black person. In 1922, a contractee agreed to sell one of the lots to a person of the black race. In response, one of the other contractees filed suit requesting a court to enter an injunction against the sale. In *Corrigan v. Buckley* the Court held unanimously that it could not reach the merits of the case. It decided that neither the Thirteenth Amendment nor any existing federal statutes granted it jurisdiction to hear a case involving private covenants on the sale of real estate. *Corrigan* relied on *Hodges*'s narrow construction of the Thirteenth Amendment, finding that it only applied to "a condition of enforced compulsory service of one to another" but that it did "not in other matters protect the individual rights of persons of the negro race." By 1926, when the

Court ruled on *Corrigan*, Justice Harlan was no longer on the bench, and we can only speculate about whether he would have filed a dissent. But without him, the Court was unanimous in its decision.[40]

The holding in *Hodges* had dealt a fatal blow to civil rights litigation that relied on the Thirteenth Amendment. The Supreme Court dealt its first punches in the *Slaughterhouse Cases* and *Civil Rights Cases*, and the impact of those cases continued to wax through the years. The Thirteenth Amendment remained a viable source of constitutional rights only in peonage cases. Labor activists attempted in the 1930s to rely on the Thirteenth Amendment as the primary source of their right to collectively organize and bargain with management. But these efforts were soon abandoned. Instead of the Thirteenth Amendment's human rights approach, organized labor and civil rights organizations increasingly relied on the Commerce Clause.[41]

Until 1968, when the Supreme Court decided *Jones v. Alfred H. Mayer*, the underlying ideals of the Thirteenth Amendment, freedom with dignity and the right to self-governance, were buried in the avalanche of Supreme Court equivocations. Since the Supreme Court cut off the federal avenue of redress, hundreds of thousands of people suffered from legally sanctioned racism that eroded their freedom, through both tyrannical state legislation and private discrimination.

C. A Ray of Hope: Jones v. Alfred H. Mayer

After a long dormancy, the Thirteenth Amendment emerged from the cocoon to which the late nineteenth and early twentieth-century Supreme Court had relegated it. *Jones v. Alfred H. Mayer* interpreted the amendment as a broad protection of civil liberties. The case gave civil rights advocates new opportunities to further the broad aims of abolition. The Supreme Court, with Chief Justice Earl Warren still at the helm, rendered its decision during a period of great civil rights reform.

Jones offers a viable means for using the Thirteenth Amendment as a vehicle for improvement.[42] It remains a critical case defining Congress's power to pass laws that protect liberties and prohibit discrimination. Although little used, *Jones* is, in some ways, as revolutionary for Thirteenth Amendment reform as *Brown v. Board of Education* was to the application of the Equal Protection Clause of the Fourteenth Amendment.

Justice Stewart, writing for the majority in *Jones*, overturned the narrow construction of the amendment that the Supreme Court had adopted in *Hodges v. United States* and *Plessy v. Ferguson*. Those decisions had incapacitated the amendment in any circumstances except those involving forced labor. The seven to two majority in *Jones* turned to the principles which Justice Harlan expanded in his earlier dissents. Beginning with his dissent in the *Civil Rights Cases*, Harlan had pointed out that racialist barriers are inimical to freedom, even when private actors carry them out. And *Jones* accepted his premise.

The *Jones* holding, therefore, signaled the Court's renewed commitment to put an end to practices that left blacks in little better circumstances than their enslaved ancestors. The Court ceased following Radical ideals even before the legislative branch abandoned Reconstruction. *Jones* heralded a return to the basic principle that any incident or badge of servitude, whether imposed by a private or state actor, violates individual freedom and the federal government can prohibit it. Its holding presaged a new era of civil rights litigation.[43]

Mr. and Mrs. Jones wanted to purchase a new house from the Alfred H. Mayer Corporation, a private real estate developer. The company refused their offer to buy because Mr. Jones was black. The broad issue in the case was whether the Thirteenth Amendment granted Congress the power to prohibit Alfred H. Mayer's private racial discrimination.[44]

The Court held the Joneses could in fact bring a private cause of action to enjoin the company from discriminating pursuant to 42 U.S.C. § 1982. That statute had its roots in the Civil Rights Act of 1866, which Congress had passed based on its section 2, Thirteenth Amendment power. It provided that "all citizens of the United States shall have the same right, in every State and Territory, as is enjoyed by white citizens thereof to inherit, purchase, lease, sell, hold, and convey real and personal property." The company violated the Act by not entering into a real estate contract with the Joneses for racist reasons.

Justice Stewart's opinion relied on the principles of Radical Republicans, who had not expected the amendment to become a "paper guarantee." The Court evaluated the legislative debates surrounding passage of the Civil Rights Act of 1866. It determined that many of the congressmen who enacted the statute had two years earlier passed the proposed Thirteenth Amendment. Consequently, the Act represented the type of protection the framers intended the amendment to provide. Following the reasoning of the first Justice Harlan's dissents, Justice Stewart found that the second section to the Thirteenth Amendment empowered Congress to pass legislation specifically designed to promote personal autonomy and to eliminate the "badges and incidents" of servitude. Stewart recognized that the framers anticipated that the liberation of slaves would not eliminate prevailing discriminatory attitudes toward blacks. They affixed the second section to the amendment as a legislative tool for battling local prejudices and giving practical effect to abolitionist ideals. The amendment was not meant to merely set people free and then abandon them to the whims of militias and unscrupulous governmental entities.[45] The second section granted Congress the power to effectuate the cause of freedom through all laws "necessary and proper" for ending involuntary servitude.

The *Jones* Court arrived at that conclusion by evaluating the legislative intent, plain meaning, and judicial history of the Civil Rights Act of 1866. It found that Congress had wanted to end the type of discriminatory practices that Alfred H. Mayer committed. Maintaining a segregated society, even by privately excluding them "from white communities," deprived blacks of constitutional liberty and functioned as a "substitute for the slave system."

John Marshall Harlan the younger, grandson of the earlier John Marshall Harlan, drafted the dissent to *Jones*. The younger man's dissent, however, was very much different from the dissents his grandfather wrote on the Thirteenth Amendment. Harlan's central premise in *Jones* denied that the amendment applied to private actions. As an alternative to relying on the Civil Rights Act of 1866, he preferred that housing discrimination be litigated under the recently passed Federal Fair Housing Act. Circuit courts in later years would find that even Harlan's suggested approach did not eliminate the need to consider whether housing discrimination is a vestige of servitude. In fact, several circuits have found the Federal Fair Housing Act to be constitutional under the Thirteenth Amendment. For instance, the Eighth Circuit in 1974 found that "[l]ike the 1866 Civil Rights Act, the Fair Housing [Act] is an exercise of congressional power under the thirteenth amendment to eliminate the badges and incidents of slavery." And in 1972, the Fourth Circuit found the Fair Housing Act "is a valid exercise of congressional power under the Thirteenth Amendment to eliminate badges and incidents of slavery." Thus, Harlan's nascent distinction between the two amounted to a nonstarter.[46]

As the *Jones* majority had done in its opinion, Harlan reviewed the legislative history of the Civil Rights Act of 1866, concentrating particularly on the congressional debates. His principal contention was that the Act meant to prohibit state-sponsored, not private, limitations against the enjoyment of the enumerated rights, including the right to obtain housing. The Act, in his eyes, aimed to counteract the Black Codes that Southern legislators developed to elude the Abolitionist Amendment's prohibition against slavery and its incidents. The rights secured under the Act were ones that provided free persons with equal legal status but not redress against purely private discrimination, according to Harlan.

His conclusion seems analogous to, although certainly not as inimical as, the holding in *Plessy*, which allowed segregation to continue as long as the segregated accommodations were equal. Likewise, Harlan believed the Act left intact private restrictions on where a person wished to live. This would have allowed persons to enter into racist real estate covenants with legal impunity. In this, Harlan seemed to ignore how many postbellum private intrigues hurt blacks in ways that were about as harmful as the black codes. For instance, plantation owners in the postbellum South often agreed to keep blacks from purchasing and renting land. These agreements, along with the laws against African American mobility, aimed at keeping the newly freed from departing from their old plantations and assuring their old masters that they could keep exploiting those who had been their slaves. This was one of the practices Congress wanted to end with the Civil Rights Act of 1866, and it was one that Harlan overlooked in his dissent to *Jones*.

Harlan also responded to the majority's holding that section 1 of the Act had "far broader" application than to the black codes and laws from the Old South. The majority wrote that the Reconstruction Congress wanted to address the codes and "the mistreatment of Negroes by private individuals and unofficial groups, mistreatment unrelated to any hostile state legislation." Justice Stewart found historical support for this principle from the congressional debates prior to passage of the Civil Rights Act of 1866. In response, Harlan noted that at the time of the Act's passage, racial discrimination was common in the North also, in public accommodations and education, yet those practices received no criticism during the debates.

While Harlan made a poignant point about a shortcoming of the Radical Republican agenda, he did not convincingly respond to the majority. Justice Stewart, for instance, pointed out that the 1866 act was reenacted in 1870, after the states had ratified both the Thirteenth and Fourteenth Amendments. Thus, by then *de jury* both Southern and Northern states were to have eliminated the vestiges of servitude and the laws that perpetuated them, including the black codes. Then, "congressional concern had clearly shifted from hostile statutes to the activities of groups like the Ku Klux Klan operating wholly outside the law." Based on these historical antecedents to the passage and reenactment of the Civil Rights Act, the majority found no basis for exempting "private discrimination the operations of the . . . Act."

The logical implication of *Jones* is that Congress has the power to legislate against any state and private infringements that arbitrarily prevent individuals' rights to live freely. Thus, the freedom that the Declaration of Independence extolled from the beginning of the American project became an enforceable right, and the source of that substantive right is the Thirteenth Amendment. In the Supreme Court's words: "Surely Congress has the power under the Thirteenth Amendment rationally to determine what are the badges and the incidents of slavery, and the authority to translate that determination into effective legislation." The rationality standard is a low one that Congress can meet by examining the historical landmarks of slavery, evaluating what existing practices perpetuate it, and promulgating laws to end them.

Congress, then, has the power to end any existing coercive and arbitrary injustices analogous to involuntary servitude. *Jones* elevated the Thirteenth Amendment to a high constitutional pedestal, among the pantheon of human rights protections designed to make a society where people can achieve their potentials. Persons can now bring law suits for injunctions under existing federal statutes that are rationally tailored to prohibit arbitrary interference with their right to live self-guided lives. As for the federal government, it can sue for criminal penalties.

Jones recognized that the United States is responsible for protecting its citizens against arbitrary infringement of fundamental rights. National civil rights laws, therefore, can directly confront civil rights violations and need not operate behind a veil of Congress's commercial powers (chapter 6). Moreover, *Jones* required courts to analyze human rights violations in a way significantly different from the state action analysis under the Fourteenth Amendment. Beyond this, the decision raises intriguing questions about whether even absent congressional action, persons can bring suit both against states and individuals for violating the Thirteenth Amendment's first section. For, the second section authorizes Congress to pass federal laws rationally tailored to end the badges and incidents of servitude, while the first section is a self-executing, that is a judicially enforceable, prohibition against any remaining incidents of involuntary servitude, and the institution's injustices far exceeded forced labor. Admittedly, such a reading of the first section is my attempt to extend Thirteenth Amendment doctrine beyond current Supreme Court holdings.

In the Supreme Court cases that followed *Jones*, the Court continued holding that Congress could prohibit private racial discrimination. The Court in *Runyon v. McCrary* addressed the narrow issue of whether 42 U.S.C. § 1981, which was originally enacted as section 1 of the Civil Rights Act of 1866, prohibited private schools from refusing to enroll students based on their race. Its holding had broad social ramifications on the integration of private schools. The relevant part of § 1981 provided that "all persons within the jurisdiction of the United States shall have the same right in every State . . . to make and enforce contracts . . . as is enjoyed by white citizens." Justice Stewart based his decision on the law's prohibition against contract discrimination. The school violated the law because it refused to enter into a contract with the parents of potential students who happened to be black. The Court found that the free association and privacy rights of parents who wanted to keep the school segregated did not trump the rights of parents whose children the school refused to enroll on racial grounds. Parental desire to send their children to a private, segregated school also did not override the federal government's reasonable prohibition against the school's discriminatory contracting practices.[47]

The Court could have sent an even stronger message about the nation's commitment to freedom had it used a more historical, rather than contractual, analysis. The Court's holding could have been based on the right to parental autonomy, which had been denied both through slave codes and by individual slave masters. Schools that refuse to enroll students because of their race violate more than the parents' contractual right. Such schools also interfere with parents' Thirteenth Amendment autonomy right to educate their children.

The Court's 1973 decision in *Tillman v. Wheaton-Haven Recreation Assn.* provided even stronger ammunition in the civil rights arsenal. Justice Blackmun wrote the majority. The litigation involved a private swimming club that discriminated against blacks in its membership and guest policies. Three African Americans, to whom the association denied access, sought damages and an injunction against the practice pursuant to 42 U.S.C. §§ 1981's and 1982's prohibitions against racist leasing and rental practices. Blackmun, for the majority, reasoned that since the association's membership was tied to a narrow geographic location, persons who lived and purchased property valuated their real estate partly on the expectation that they could join the recreation center. The holding was thus again rooted in contract law rather than a fundamental right to enjoy public accommodations. The Court limited itself to examining the discrimination on the basis of the existing statutes instead of the Thirteenth Amendment's underlying principles.[48]

In a 1975 case, *Johnson v. Railway Express Agency*, Justice Blackmun further extended the applicability of § 1981, finding that it allowed recovery for the discriminatory conduct of a private employer. The case provides a rich distinction between employment discrimination claims under § 1981 and Title VII, which is the traditional avenue for relief for employment discrimination. The Court's holding makes clear why plaintiffs often fair better in employment discrimination claims filed under § 1981 instead of Title VII. For instance, Title VII's relatively short statute of limitations is not applicable to § 1981 claims. Instead, § 1981 claims, à la *Johnson*, apply the pertinent personal injury statute of limitations from the plaintiff's state. In *Johnson*, the Court applied Tennessee's one-year limitation period, which was significantly longer than Title VII's 180-day requirement to file the employment claim with the Equal Employment Opportunity Commission (EEOC), or 300 days to file with a state Equal Employment Opportunity investigator. Other courts commonly apply two- or three-year state personal injury statutes of limitations to § 1981 cases.

Further advantages to the Thirteenth Amendment–based employment discrimination claims are that § 1981 does not exempt employers who are improper parties under Title VII and § 1981 does not require the exhaustion of administrative remedies. On the other hand, Title VII also has advantages. It provides certain remedies, such as the recovery of attorneys' fees, which § 1981 does not. All in all, *Johnson* offers a meaningful alternative to persons seeking creative litigation strategies to obtain equitable and pecuniary relief for employment discrimination.[49]

In a 1989 case, the Supreme Court ruled that § 1981 only applies to racial discrimination perpetrated during the contract-formation process, but not to the postformation discrimination.[50] Congress superseded the Court's ruling by passing the Civil Rights Act of 1991, codified as 42

U.S.C. § 1981(b). The section provides that "the term 'make and enforce contracts' includes the making, performance, modification and termination of contracts, and the enjoyment of all benefits, privileges, terms, and conditions of the contractual relationship." Furthermore, the amended version of § 1981 explicitly covers private and state violators: "The rights protected by this section are protected against impairment by non-governmental discrimination and impairment under color of State law."[51]

This overview of case law since 1968 shows just how broadly the Thirteenth Amendment reaches even when its potency rests only on a civil rights statute enacted in 1866. Congress can go much farther and pass new statutes pursuant to its section 2 authority, particularly in light of the sensitivity against discrimination that has burgeoned since the 1960s. Certainly discrimination in real estate transactions and private schools is not literally slavery or involuntary servitude; rather, the Court used its interpretive method to find that Congress could determine that these were rationally related to the incidents and badges of servitude. The Court's analyses in *Jones*, *Runyon*, and *Johnson* indicate that Congress can reasonably pass laws in order to end social and economic injustices that abridge fundamental liberties.

Even so many years after ratification, questions remain about the Thirteenth Amendment's reach. The Supreme Court has never determined whether a private party can bring a cause of action under the first section of the Thirteenth Amendment. The Court's current stance on this issue is ambiguous. Generally, lower court decisions proscribe independent judicial use of section 1 to determine which discriminations are rationally related to the incidents and badges of servitude.[52] However, there is a faint glimmer of hope in Supreme Court dicta that suggests a more progressive position.

Palmer v. Thompson, decided in 1971, addressed the section 1 issue but left it unresolved. In 1962 Jackson, Mississippi, closed four segregated swimming pools and surrendered the lease of a fifth segregated pool. Whites had exclusively used four pools, and only blacks used a fifth one. The City Council's decree was based on its finding that continuing to operate the swimming pools would be too costly and that closing the facilities was necessary for preserving public order. The Court, Justice Black writing for the majority, refused to second-guess the legislators' motives. The Court determined that the stated legislative purposes were beyond the scope of judicial review and affirmed the District Court's denial of injunctive relief.[53]

The petitioners had argued that "the city's closing of the pools to keep the two races from swimming together violates the Thirteenth Amendment." Justice Black determined that absent a federal law requiring the Court to open swimming pools, the Court could not "legislate new laws to control the operation of swimming pools throughout the length and breadth of this Nation." The Court implicitly recognized Congress's second section authority to pass a law prohibiting governmental entities from purposefully refusing to desegregate. However, the Court refused to use its section 1 power to determine whether the City Council's actions were discriminatory. Court dictum, nevertheless, came close to recognizing that section 1 by itself authorized the Court to find a discriminatory law unconstitutional: "Should citizens of Jackson or any other city be able to establish in court that public, tax-supported swimming pools are being denied to one group because of color and supplied to another, they will be entitled to relief." This statement leaves open the question of whether litigants could obtain an injunction, absent statutory authority, if they petition to desegregate open swimming pools rather than praying to reopen closed ones. The dictum is particularly intriguing because it comes at the very end of the opinion, almost inviting a citizen law suit to rely on section 1 to petition for an injunction. However, the likelihood that the Court would issue such an injunction is small, given the absence of decisive precedent on the matter.[54]

One of *Palmer's* greatest weaknesses lies in the Court's failure to analyze the extent to which the category "badges and incidents of servitude" extends to social discriminations, such as swimming pool segregation. Nowhere in the decision did the Court conduct anything resembling an analysis of whether racism and its coercive practices developed through forced, public racial segregation. If the Court concluded that segregation in public places stamped blacks with a badge of inferiority that limited their autonomy rights and helped maintain a divisive society, granting an injunction would not have amounted to making new laws. Rather, the Court would have acknowledged that slavery extended beyond the plantation system and that it continues to plague the United States. Such a finding would not have required the Court to micromanage "thousands of towns and cities." Instead, it would have granted victims standing to file claims pursuant to section 1. Litigation, then, would have focused on ripe issues.

The Court's decided avoidance of a timely issue was question-begging. The Court in *Palmer* could have relied on Justice Harlan's dissent in

Hodges, where he asserted that section 1 did much more than free slaves: "By its own force, that Amendment destroyed slavery and all its incidents and badges, and established freedom."

Ten years after *Palmer*, the Court again considered whether the first section of the Thirteenth Amendment went any farther than simply abolishing slavery. In *City of Memphis v. Greene*, black citizens objected to the closing of a street running between a predominantly black area and a white residential community, claiming that the closing constituted a badge of servitude because it affected black citizens' ability to enjoy their property. The Court held that the city's motives were to protect children's safety and preserve residential quietude, not to discriminate. So, the street closing imposed a "routine burden of citizenship" and, therefore, was not a badge of servitude.

The Court in *Greene* did, however, emphasize the Thirteenth Amendment's self-executing first section. The decision further indicates that, under the right circumstances, the Court might allow a claim directly under section 1, even absent congressional action. Memphis had based its argument on *Palmer*, claiming that absent direct congressional enabling legislation the Court could not hold for the plaintiffs. The Court rejected Memphis's argument and stated that "[p]ursuant to the authority created by section 2 of the Thirteenth Amendment, Congress has enacted legislation to abolish both the conditions of involuntary servitude and the 'badges and incidents of slavery.'" This exercise of authority the Court went on "is not inconsistent with the view that the Amendment has self-executing force." In the final analysis, however, *Greene* did not determine whether section 1 of the amendment allows citizens to file civil actions absent existing federal law governing the matter because the Court did not specify whether the amendment's self-executing force extended beyond the unshackling of slaves.[55] The dictum in *Greene* indicates that, given a relevant legal controversy, the judiciary could decide whether a particular cause of action amounts to involuntary servitude.

The Supreme Court has not subsequently returned to clarify this important point, and on it hang two issues: whether a private claim is available under section 1 absent an ancillary statute, and, if such a cause of action is available, whether it may be filed against public or private actors.

D. *Summing Up*

Thirteenth Amendment jurisprudence has emerged from the narrow Supreme Court holding in the *Civil Rights Cases*. This decision precluded any petitions to courts seeking to end discriminatory practices on public accommodations. Had the Court come to the opposite conclusion, a civil rights movement could have bourgeoned immediately after the Civil War and the Thirteenth Amendment could have helped end many stigmatizing practices, such as racial segregation, which continued into the 1960s. By the 1896 *Plessy* decision, the Supreme Court virtually nullified the amendment's effectiveness, having become complicit in legitimizing separate-but-equal practices. Finally, with the 1906 *Hodges* decision, the Supreme Court undermined Congress's ability to prevent the perpetuation of any badges and incidents of servitude, except those directly associated with peonage and chattel slavery. Only in 1968, with the ruling in *Jones v. Alfred H. Mayer*, did the Court recognize its earlier mistakes.

Even today, the Thirteenth Amendment remains a sparsely used and little-defined part of the Constitution. *Jones v. Alfred H. Mayer* returned the Thirteenth Amendment to its place among other cornerstones of federal civil rights. However, both in *Jones* and in the Thirteenth Amendment cases that followed it, the Court presented its holdings within the rubrics of contract claims, pursuant to §§ 1981 and 1982. These Reconstruction-era laws continue to serve as the primary congressional means of providing redress for anyone who still suffers from oppressions analogous to involuntary servitude. Sections 1981 and 1982 were passed over a century ago, when the country was far less sensitive to racism than it is today, and are in great need of supplementation. New legislation should be rooted in Reconstruction, the civil rights movement of the 1950s and 1960s, modern sensibilities, and principled analysis. Statutes derived from the Civil Rights Act of 1866 are limiting because they are phrased in terms of economic interests in freedom. Congress might find that discrimination on public accommodations is rationally linked to involuntary servitude even if the victim's economic interest is not affected. So, the full wisdom of the Thirteenth Amendment's humanistic principles is yet to be tapped.

New laws and a deeper jurisprudence, based on a contextual reading of the Thirteenth Amendment, should be developed to end those social injustices that place racist and ethnocentrist impediments in the way of freedom. For this, legislators and judges must look to the meaning of freedom and involuntary servitude through historical and theoretical analysis. This approach will reveal the injustices the amendment seeks to eradicate and the social welfare it aims to achieve. The first Justice Harlan's dissent, in the *Civil Rights Cases*, drew attention to the constraints on the victim's liberty imposed through social discrimination on public transportation. Now, almost 140 years after the abolition of slavery and ratification of the Thirteenth Amendment, Congress should return to passing laws pursuant to its section 2 power. Congress has virtually plenary federal power under that section to protect freedom against arbitrary infringements. The Supreme Court, in its turn, should use the amendment to better refine its jurisprudence on civil liberties. This would be consequential for deciding cases involving the rights to travel freely, raise a family, and make professional choices.

4

Summing Up and Looking Ahead

While the language of the Thirteenth Amendment was am-
biguous enough to give rise to segregationist decisions like *Plessy v. Ferguson*, its potential to change U.S. society lay in its breadth of application
to abolish all contemporary and future vestiges of servitude. Understand-
ings of the amendment's grant of authority diverged in part because during the congressional debates its advocates tended to focus only on slavery and general principles of republican government. They spent little
time on the issue of what civil protections freed people would have after
liberation. Radical Republicans, who were the driving force behind the
Thirteenth Amendment, determined that to get enough votes for
ratification, they had to adopt conservative language for the amendment,
derived from a readily recognizable source, Thomas Jefferson's Northwest Ordinance. The vagueness inherently built into the amendment provided ample means for differing interpretations; some of these favored
providing blacks with the full range of citizenship rights while others only
wanted to emancipate people who would *de facto* still be bound to forced
labor. This political strategy was effective in passing the amendment
through Congress and states ratifying conventions, but in the long run it
left a "legal snarl."[1]

Reflecting on the debates with a critical eye, however, is not meant to
be a condemnation of the framers' motives. Radicals persistently evinced
their commitment to protecting all citizens' fundamental liberties. Initially, the executive and the judiciary stood in the way of Radical Reconstruction. In 1866, Congressman Isaac Arnold, a veteran Radical Republican, laid out the military and political steps that led up to the Thirteenth
Amendment:

First, The army was prohibited from returning to rebel masters, fugitive
slaves: *Second,* The employment of fugitive slaves as laborers in the

army was sanctioned: *Third*, The passage of a law confiscating and con-
ferring freedom upon slaves used for insurrectionary purposes: *Fourth*,
The abolition of slavery at the National Capital: *Fifth*, The prohibition
of slavery in all the territories: *Sixth*, A law giving freedom to all who
should serve as soldiers in the army or in the navy: *Seventh*, A law emancipating the slaves of rebels: *Eighth*, And most important of all, the great
Proclamation of Emancipation; emancipating the slaves in the rebellious
States: *Ninth*, A law emancipation of the families of all those who
should serve in the army or navy of the United States: *Tenth*, The repeal
of the fugitive slave code: *Eleventh*, The Constitutional amendment
abolishing and prohibiting slavery throughout the Republic.

Eventually two more Reconstruction amendments followed, but the congressional framers initially considered the Thirteenth Amendment as the
bedrock of Reconstruction.[2]

Laws, such as the Civil Rights Act of 1866 and the Freedmen's Bureau Acts, which passed soon after the ratification of the amendment,
began giving content to the liberties the framers expected to protect.
These laws were rooted in an ideal of liberty that grants all citizens the
same rights to make meaningful decisions about their lives and to obtain
judicial redress for coercive infringements to their autonomy. The
statutes' provisions made federal authorities responsible for preventing
public and private injustices in the areas of property transaction, contract enforcement, and litigation. Radical Republicans envisioned a
sweeping reconstruction that would cover discrimination committed in
the North and South. In the minds of progressive humanists, this was
only to be the start of abolition, encompassing all institutions associated
with slavery and heralding in constitutionally guaranteed freedom, the
likes of which had never existed in the United States. Those hopes were
never realized: they were swept away by popular prejudices, in both re-
gions of the country.[3]

War jarred the nation enough to develop a popular consensus for abolishing slavery. Without the violent conflict, universal freedom could not
have gained enough support to pass the joint resolution through Congress, and without the pressure wrought from defeat, the South would
not have ratified the amendment. Following the Civil War, the old racially
intolerant complacence reemerged throughout the country, particularly in
the South. The Compromise of 1877 was a final stake in the heart of civil
rights progress.[4]

Yet the amendment, with its latent potential for civil rights activism, remains imprinted in the Constitution, even though politicians have, for the time, virtually ceased using it. In spite of its dormancy, the amendment's enforcement clause is still a powerful legal provision for passing civil rights legislation. The first section was a self-executing declaration that freed slaves and can, with the aid of some litigating sophistication, be extended to other personal liberty issues. Courts have found the amendment's long-term substance in the next clause, which empowered Congress to pass positive laws to protect all citizens' fundamental right to live unobtrusive, autonomous lives. The second section grants an enormous power to the federal legislature, providing it with the authority to end generations of disabilities and to instantiate the Preamble's principles. Without that power, the aspirations of Reconstruction would have rung hollow. Time has come to renew their vision of a nation devoted to protecting individual autonomy against arbitrary coercion.[5]

While the amendment's preeminent goal was the abolition of slavery, it further aimed to protect fundamental liberties. The United States, which had since the earliest days of the republic been committed to an often contradictory version of the natural-rights theory,[6] came to grips with its implications: each person has the same essential rights, and African Americans' degraded state was not an innate condition but one which was socially and legally imposed. The eradication of slavery, therefore, should have a social and legal component for achieving equal liberty.

Judges can determine whether laws or actions resemble badges or incidents of servitude by evaluating how much they interfere with important liberties, such as the rights to make parental decisions, to travel, to enter into employment and real estate contracts, and any other freedoms that are intrinsic to living a fulfilling life in a constitutional republic. This scheme values individual autonomy, but it is not oblivious to the fact that individuals live in a national community where adjudicators must balance conflicting rights. The analysis should not stop at the disabilities existing contemporaneously with the passage of the amendment and the federal laws that followed on its bootstraps. The broader question is whether there continue to be indicia of servitude that interfere with the lives, liberties, and well-being of persons within the United States or areas subject to its jurisdiction. Federal statutes should offer avenues of judicial redress for the victims of such exploitation. But congressional inaction should not render the Thirteenth Amendment impotent. The judiciary, too, has a role to play in protecting liberties against infringements, and common law will be critical to opening new avenues of redress.[7]

The Thirteenth Amendment assures persons of all races striving to attain a better life that they will not be subject to the indiscriminate use of private or official power. It seeks not only to eradicate forced labor but also any remaining "spectacle of slavery" that lingers, "unwilling to die." Current exclusionary practices and denigrations against outgroups, including official state uses of Confederate symbols, bias crimes, and labor peonage must be eliminated to comply with the constitutional assurance of personal autonomy.[8]

The Abolition Amendment empowers legislators to pass any laws necessary to assure citizens of their rights to self-determination, accomplishment of reasonable aspirations, and freedom from harassment tending to arbitrarily diminish citizens' range of available alternatives. It grants the judiciary the jurisdiction to end private and governmental abuses. Of course, these are only beginning musings that need to be elaborated. Clearly not all discriminating conduct falls within the framework of the Thirteenth Amendment. For instance, it is overreaching (indeed even an absurdity) to think that a private remedy can extend to preferences about whom to marry; indeed, the ability to make that choice is exactly the sort of freedom the amendment protects. It could not grant a remedy to someone who is upset because the object of his adoration will not marry him on account of his race. The Thirteenth Amendment, however, does allow Congress to pass laws prohibiting parties from interfering with the right to choose a marriage partner.

If I am correct, then the Thirteenth Amendment is not only a prohibition against slavery but also a grant of negative and positive freedom. The amendment is a negative grant of freedom in that it prohibits arbitrary infringements against autonomy. Historical analysis is necessary to determine the extent to which such infringements are analogous to involuntary servitude. And it is a positive grant of freedom insofar as it obligates the federal government to protect citizens' opportunities to enjoy their lives.

"Freedom" is an organic concept that takes both history and principle into account. The past is educative, but social change comes not only from its instruction but also from a forward-looking approach that is founded on constitutional principles. While we must not forget that the roots of the Thirteenth Amendment are planted in the abolition movement, we should also gaze prospectively to improve our understanding of the features necessary to a free and fair society.[9]

PART II

5

Theoretical Foundation

In the symphony of United States values, freedom has always been paramount. Liberty has a conspicuous place in the country's statements of national purpose: the Declaration of Independence and the Preamble to the Constitution. Those manifestos were so powerful that their ideals influenced a generation of abolitionists. The makers of the Constitution, as Justice Brandeis explained in a dissenting opinion, set out "to secure conditions favorable to the pursuit of happiness. . . . They conferred, as against the Government, the right to be let alone."[1]

The Thirteenth Amendment disentangled the principle of freedom from its previous favoritism for property-owning white males and made universal the liberty to live an uncoerced, self-directed life. Adopted in the immediate aftermath of the Civil War, the amendment was both designed to abolish slavery and protect people's right to act independent of arbitrary coercion.

A. Abolition and Natural Rights

Radical Republicans established the Thirteenth Amendment on the natural rights principles that had guided the abolitionist movement from its founding in 1833. As Unitarian leader William Ellery Channing explained in 1835, the abolitionist argument rested on the Declaration of Independence's assertion of "the indestructible rights of every human being." Each person was "born to be free," and the desire for wealth, especially in human capital, could never trump individual rights. Slavery was inimical because it stripped "man of the fundamental right to inquire into, consult, and seek his own happiness." Similarly in 1857, the National Anti-Slavery Convention expressed its devotion for "[t]he only self-evident truths of the Declaration of Independence . . . and the Golden Rule of the Gospel—nothing more, nothing less."[2]

During the Civil War, many Republicans adopted radical abolitionist principles about the federal government's obligation to eradicate slavery. The Thirteenth Amendment's grant of power to Congress over matters resembling the incidents of servitude signaled a break from moderate antislavery leanings. Moderates wanted states gradually and separately to end slavery. Even Lincoln, who also thought slavery was "a total violation" of the Declaration of Independence, initially held to a gradualist, state-by-state approach. His views changed only during the War when he realized that Southern states would not be appeased into abandoning their expansionist ambitions.[3]

The Declaration takes for granted that the possession of natural rights is "self-evident."[4] Implicitly, this means people are intuitively empathetic and can recognize that others are endowed with the same rights. An advocate of the Thirteenth Amendment detailed a similar view during the House debate on the proposed amendment: "What vested rights so high or so sacred as a man's right to himself, to his wife and children, to his liberty, and to the fruits of his own industry? Did not our fathers declare that those rights were inalienable? And if a man cannot himself alienate those rights, how can another man alienate them without being himself a robber of the vested rights of his brother-man?"[5] Slavery was an anomaly in a country formed in opposition to British violation of American civil liberties. Within this national context, the Thirteenth Amendment brought the Constitution, which originally protected the institution of slavery, into harmony with the Declaration of Independence. Charles Black has pointed out that Thirteenth Amendment principles had been dormant in the Declaration of Independence. Abolitionists changed legal culture to accord with ideals that had existed since 1776.

Radical Republicans used the amendment process, under Article V, to alter the Constitution's initially inimical provisions. The Continental Congress compromised the ideals of liberty to special interests who regarded the right to property, particularly in the chattel of people, to be more important for achieving a national federation than the right to freedom. In spite of Charles Sumner's contention that it was absurd to argue that the Constitution contradicted the Declaration, the Three-Fifths Clause and the Fugitive Slave Clause hung like an asphyxiating cloud above the United States. With its passage, the Thirteenth Amendment immediately provided an enforceable right for the protection of those civil liberties that until the amendment's ratification had been valued but not implemented. The amendment allows Congress to secure liberty, life, and the pursuit of happiness through positive laws.[6]

Behind its enforceable provisions lies a national commitment to secure personal liberties that are integral to civil welfare. Progressive advocates of the first Reconstruction amendment made an earnest effort to remove impediments standing in the way of civil rights. They regarded the Thirteenth Amendment as a means of restoring the natural rights long denied to both blacks and wage earners. According to Radical Republicans, former slaves were not only freed from bondage; they also gained the right to make fundamental choices about their jobs and families. Congressman M. Russell Thayer of Pennsylvania expressed the same point in general, rhetorical terms: "What kind of freedom is that which is given by the amendment of the Constitution, and if it is confined simply to the exemption of the freedom from sale and barter? Do you give freedom to a man when you allow him to be deprived of those great natural rights to which every man is entitled by nature?"[7]

The Thirty-ninth Congress opened in 1865 with a statement by Schuyler Colfax, the incoming Speaker of the House of Representatives. Given shortly after Congress passed the proposed Thirteenth Amendment and before the introduction of the proposed Fourteenth Amendment, the statement was indicative of how Congress planned to use the Thirteenth Amendment for Reconstruction. "[I]t is yours," Colfax told the House, "to mature and enact legislation which, . . . shall establish [state governments] anew on such a basis of enduring justice as will guarantee all necessary safeguards to the people, and afford, what our Magna Charta, the Declaration of Independence, proclaims is the chief object of government—protection of all men in their inalienable rights."[8]

Representative E. C. Ingersoll of Illinois asserted, in more practical terms, that former slaves had a right to profit from their labors and to enjoy conjugal happiness without fear of forced separations at the behest of uncompassionate masters. He also voiced the desire to see blacks "live in a state of freedom."[9] Republicans like Representative Ignatius Donnelly of Minnesota recognized that "slavery is not confined to any precise condition. . . . Slavery consists in a deprivation of natural rights. A man may be a slave for a term of years as fully as though he were held for life; he may be a slave when deprived of a portion of the wages of his labor as fully as if deprived of all." Senator John Sherman of Ohio regarded the amendment's second section to be the grant of congressional power to actively secure freed people their liberty rights "to sue and be sued . . . [and] to testify in a court of justice."[10] When they found that President Andrew Johnson opposed virtually all of their Reconstruction proposals, Radicals passed the Fourteenth Amendment to add specificity to the Thirteenth Amendment's general grant of freedom.

B. *Thirteenth Amendment and Universal Liberty*

The Thirteenth Amendment granted Congress the power to enliven the moral principles contained in the Declaration of Independence and the Preamble to the Constitution. The amendment's framers recognized that they were creating a monumental change in the entire structure of U.S. civil society. And their ideas are invaluable for understanding the amendment's meaning; however, we are not constrained to precisely follow them but only to include them in analyzing solutions to contemporary vestiges of servitude. Historic analysis helps to define constitutional limits but needs normative supplementation to achieve progressive aims. In this regard, the Thirteenth Amendment was both a new beginning for the nation and a constructive means for enforcing its foundational principles of liberty and general well-being.[11]

The amendment drastically altered the Constitution. Its first section eliminated, or more euphemistically amended, all the federalist provisions of the 1787 Constitution that protected slavery, and the amendment's second section provided the U.S. Congress with the power to protect individual rights and thereby better the nation.[12] The Thirteenth Amendment is the legal causeway from slavery to freedom. Accordingly, the Thirteenth Amendment secured two fundamental principles, which both emanated from the Preamble. The first principle protects the right to unobtrusive autonomy in carrying out deliberative decisions. The second principle limits autonomy whenever it arbitrarily interferes with other citizens' sense of purpose. The guarantee of freedom protects individual choices as long as they do not infringe on the coequal liberty rights of others. This approach balances autonomy with welfare in order to achieve a liberating sense of mutual purpose for civil society.

The Thirteenth Amendment, thus, not only ended slavery but also created a substantive assurance of freedom. It prohibits all the vestiges of involuntary slavery, whether imposed by public or private actors, and it grants Congress the right to enact laws, making "universal liberty" a matter of national concern, not merely of state prerogative. The Thirteenth Amendment not only secures delineated civil freedoms, such as those specifically enumerated by the Bill of Rights, but also secures freedom from all forms of arbitrary domination. In this regard, legislative initiatives must balance individual liberties against the national interests of a diverse but equally free people. The enforcement clause of the Thirteenth Amendment provides lawmakers with the power to craft laws that are tied to the Declaration of Independence's ideal of a free and equal citizenry. The framers of the Thirteenth Amendment refined that ideal to include persons of all races.[13]

The Thirteenth Amendment's liberty guarantee is expansive enough for each generation to abolish continued coercive practices, not just those incidents of forced domination the Thirty-eighth Congress recognized when it debated the proposed Thirteenth Amendment. Indeed, the range of liberty rights the Thirteenth Amendment secures is just as broad as those the Due Process Clause guarantees. Accordingly, Justice Harlan's description of a broad-concept freedom in the context of the Due Process Clause bears striking resemblance to the description of freedom his grandfather expounded in the dissents to *Civil Rights Cases*, *Plessy*, and *Hodges*. Our nation, Harlan wrote in dissent to *Poe v. Ullman*, balances

> respect for the liberty of the individual . . . and the demands of organized society. If the supplying of content to this Constitutional concept has of necessity been a rational process, it certainly has not been one where judges have felt free to roam where unguided speculation might take them. The balance of which I speak is the balance struck by this country, having regard to what history teaches are the traditions from which it developed as well as the traditions from which it broke. That tradition is a living thing. . . . [T]he imperative character of Constitutional provisions . . . must be discerned from a particular provision's larger context. . . . "[L]iberty" is not a series of isolated points pricked out in terms of the taking of property; the freedom of speech, press, and religion; the right to keep and bear arms; the freedom from unreasonable searches and seizures; and so on. It is a rational continuum which, broadly speaking, includes a freedom from all substantial arbitrary impositions and purposeless restraints.[14]

The constitutional right to freedom, then, is linked to this country's struggle to break with racial enslavement and to its moral growth through the Reconstruction amendments.

At this point, it is important to note that the Supreme Court has extended the Thirteenth Amendment's applicability to coercive acts committed against the members of any race, not only against blacks. Historically, Radical Republicans passed civil rights legislation, such as the Civil Rights Act of 1866 and the Ku Klux Klan Act of 1871, to protect their black and white allies. The risk to missionaries, teachers, and politicians who came to the South after the Civil War was almost as great as the danger blacks faced from mob violence.[15] Over the years common law has guided the determination of whom these statutes are meant to protect. The Court in the *Slaughterhouse Cases* found the amendment applies to "Mexican peonage and the Chinese coolie labor system." Since race is a fluid term, the Supreme Court later held that contemporary racial classifications should not constrict the amendment's applicability. In *Shaare Tefila Congregation v. Cobb*, a case arising from the private desecration of a synagogue, the Court found that when the 1866 Congress passed the Civil Rights Act of 1866, Jews and Arabs were among the groups classified as distinct races. Therefore, the Court held that the Civil Rights Act prevents property discrimination reminiscent of servitude from being committed against Jews and Arabs.[16]

The Thirteenth Amendment, indeed, prohibits all repressive conduct rationally related to the impediments of freedom, not simply racist labor practices.[17] The amendment's protections apply to anyone who is subject to arbitrary restraints against the enjoyment of freedom. Congress must only find that those restraints resemble the badges and incidents of involuntary servitude. Laws passed pursuant to the Thirteenth Amendment should protect free and equal persons' conceptions of and quest for qualitatively good lives. Masters had suppressed slaves' life aspirations, prohibiting them from entering into marital contracts, from choosing professions, and from making a host of other important life decisions. Slavery devalued the commitment of our pluralistic society to respect the individual and collective right to live free of arbitrary intrusion on freedom. Consequently, laws that are passed under section 2 against any badges of involuntary servitude must make it easier for people to express their individuality and prevent arbitrarily domineering private and state actions.[18]

The Thirteenth Amendment shifts the balance of authority for protecting civil rights away from states and in favor of the national government. A federal polity that is composed of independent citizens must protect individual opportunities to pursue self-defined goals and establish reciprocal rights for fair dealing. The Thirteenth Amendment requires that one of the federal government's primary functions be to protect the common good; that is, laws must aim to improve people's lives, as much as feasible, and to help them flourish as individuals with unique interests.

This account presupposes that the coequal freedom of self-determination and self-realization is conducive to the overall good of U.S. society. Laws that require citizens to deal fairly with others are the best means of reducing the number of conflicts and, thereby, of increasing social tranquility. So, a policy designed to promote liberty as a means of achieving the common good has an antidiscriminatory principle built into it: one cannot arbitrarily restrict another's liberty through the badges or incidents of servitude and credulously insist that such an act benefits everyone.

Stated generally, civil freedom is a condition where the members of a polity may not be arbitrarily restricted from pursuing their plans. Neither are individuals allowed to deliberately, recklessly, or negligently interfere with the liberty rights of others; so, civil liberty is not an absolute right, but limited by the coequal rights of others. Further, within an organized society, freedom involves the opportunity, available to all citizens and residents, to contribute to society and the right to experience fulfilling lives that are restricted only by impartial and necessary laws. Indeed, freedom, in this sense, implies the individual pursuit of reasonable choices to affirm the meaning of one's life and to help achieve social betterment. Accordingly, the Thirteenth Amendment negatively prohibits arbitrary domination and positively allows pluralistic self-determination.

This differs from Isaiah Berlin's influential dichotomy of liberty. In his seminal essay "Two Concepts of Liberty," Berlin divided freedom into two categories he thought to be distinct. The negative sense of freedom, according to him, refers to the absence of external interference or obstruction on people's choices. It addresses the question, "What is the area within which the subject—a person or group of persons—is or should be left to do or be what he is able to do or be, without interference by other persons?" On the other hand, the positive sense of freedom relates to self-mastery. It answers the question: "What, or who, is the source of control or interference that can determine someone to do, or be, this rather than that?"[19]

Berlin's mistake was in thinking that these two perspectives of freedom are separable. In fact, they work in concert. Freedom from slavery under the Thirteenth Amendment has a necessary corollary of freedom to choose a self-assertive life; otherwise, there would seem to be no reason for desiring liberty over involuntary servitude. The yearning to be free from brutal coercion, or even the domination of a benevolent master, is also linked to the urge to follow one's perspective of a good life. Individuals *qua* humans have the right to pursue their aims because people are innately self-directed. Slavery undermined people's ability to express their individuality. Accordingly, freedom is a unified concept that harmonizes the negative and positive views and adds a third condition for a free life: it must be one that rational people, being apprised of the full set of possible alternatives, would find to be worth pursuing.

Freeing slaves or ending any of the badges of servitude is only an initial step for protecting the human rights necessary to make life meaningful for free persons. A society that promotes the common good, which is the national government's obligation under the Preamble, allows each of its members to develop his or her talents. This constitutional framework judges the United States' ability to free itself of remaining vestiges of bondage by the extent to which civil rights laws increase people's ability to choose their unique paths in life. The Thirteenth Amendment requires the legislature to pass laws conducive to welfare and recognizes the value of individual lives to social improvement. The federal concern for individual freedom derives from the changed balance of power that the amendment effectuated. As Eric Foner has pointed out, to newly freed slaves the end of bondage meant the freedom to make essential determinations about how to live and the ability to pursue choices that would improve their lives. Foner's views are commensurate with the Thirteenth Amendment whose full range of meaning requires "eradicating a multitude of historic wrongs—segregation, disenfranchisement, exclusion from public facilities, confinement to low-wage menial jobs, harassment by the police, and the ever present threat of extralegal violence."[20]

The Thirteenth Amendment provides Congress with the power to end any private or state-sponsored domination that prevents individuals from participating in civil society as rational, autonomous agents. The amendment requires Congress to provide the legal protections necessary for people to pursue their personal and public aspirations. Laws passed under section 2 should outlaw practices reminiscent of slavery because they impede persons from living self-directed lives and undermine their ability to contribute to civil society. The amendment's first section, which guarantees freedom from arbitrary constraints on personal choices, harmonizes with both the positive protections under its second section and the more abstract guarantees in the Declaration and Preamble to the Constitution.

The Supreme Court recognized this unified concept of freedom in the landmark *Jones v. Alfred H. Mayer* case, holding that the Thirteenth Amendment vested "Congress with power to pass all laws necessary and proper for abolishing all badges and incidents of slavery in the United States." The Court found that the Civil Rights Act of 1866 protected the Joneses' right to enter into a binding contract for the real estate they sought to purchase from the Alfred H. Mayer Company. That opinion works on two levels. From the negative perspective of liberty, *Jones* prevents discrimination in the making of contracts, and from the positive, it recognizes the right to choose where to reside.

Although each person possesses the fundamental right of freedom, the right to live freely in a constitutional republic is not without its limitations. For instance, people living in an organized society may not exercise their liberty to intentionally cause more than a trivial amount of harm to others. The amendment is not a right for license but rather for independence of choice. It does not sanction indiscriminate behavior that disregards the rights of others. Instead, it provides national assurance of legal redress against arbitrary constraints on independent and unobtrusive choices.[21] This is not a prescription for libertarianism; to the contrary, the Thirteenth Amendment prevents the use of liberty to interfere with other people's quest for a good life. This constraint on the amendment's significance derives from slavers' abuse of freedom. After all, masters had abused their freedom of choice to possess and sell slaves. The amendment ended this atomistic and domineering perspective of autonomy because it denied the application of the Declaration and Preamble to a host of persons for whom the drive for a good life was just as fundamental as it was for their tormentors. The amendment was meant to counteract that abuse of power by enabling Congress to prohibit any abridgments on people's rights to be self-directed and self-motivated. I draw this conclusion not only from the theoretical construct of liberty but from the denigrating nature of the master servant relationship.

Laws based on the Thirteenth Amendment should safeguard the right of citizens to live meaningful lives that are unobstructed by acts of arbitrary domination. In creating meaningful civil rights legislation, pursuant to the amendment, legislators should reflect on the nation's history in order to evaluate whether the United States has cleansed itself of all vestiges of involuntary servitude. With those vestiges that remain, expiation must come from enacting and then enforcing laws rationally designed to end the oppressions.

Federal laws against such practices should be drafted to best benefit the entire populace, rather than a particular interest group.[22] The nation rises or falls as a whole. Even if an ingroup temporarily dominates others, as whites dominated blacks in the antebellum South, human rights violations create destructive frictions that often culminate in the violent destruction of the domineering order, as was the case with the Civil War. The Thirteenth Amendment made available to all the full enjoyment of a free society. The United States is a whole composed of individuals. Where prejudices and dominance relationships leave no choice to exercise personal autonomy, overall welfare is likely to suffer.

Social progress is freedom's primary boon because it integrates and benefits from the unique ingenuities and capabilities of all its members. Where persons are not arbitrarily prevented from choosing their respective aspirations, society augments input into how best to decrease social blights and increase boons. Legislative preservation of the right to seek and achieve personal objectives has a collective benefit. For instance, where professions are open to all, cures for diseases are more likely to be found because more input is available both because educational opportunities are not restricted by discriminatory limitations and because employment opportunities are not stifled by arbitrary subordination. There is also more widespread opportunity for economic mobility where all can exercise an entrepreneurial spirit. Thus, the Thirteenth Amendment's ban on the incidents of servitude affects society as well as individuals.

It does not take for granted that each person will act with reciprocal concern and respect for fellow citizens. Instead, the Thirteenth Amendment grants Congress the power to enact laws against arbitrary domination. By securing personal safety and stability, the amendment protects the nation's citizenry against whimsical coercion. Judicial review serves to check congressional power from being hijacked for autocratic purposes.

An evolving understanding of how best to protect fundamental rights and improve social harmony should inform congressional and judicial interpretation of the Thirteenth Amendment. Such an aim comports with the Preamble's assertion that the national government's purpose is to secure the blessing of liberty and to promote the general welfare. Civil rights laws should be passed and judged pursuant to this dual purpose of national government.

Congress has thus far done little to fulfill its role under the Thirteenth Amendment, and only a handful of cases interpret it. With only a smattering of meaningful laws passed to effectuate the amendment, its potency remains minimal but its potential is great. In spite of more than a century of virtual neglect, the amendment has a deep-reaching effect on the constitutional significance of liberty.

6

Thirteenth Amendment and Constitutional Rights

A. Thirteenth and Fourteenth Amendment Freedoms

Both the Thirteenth and Fourteenth Amendments protect pluralistic freedom; nonetheless, each has a unique role in the constitutional scheme. While this book is not the appropriate place for a detailed analysis of the Fourteenth Amendment, some examination about its relative place with respect to the Thirteenth Amendment is in order. To begin, I regard the Thirteenth Amendment to be a more specific and unequivocal guarantee of civil liberties than the Fourteenth Amendment. This part will demonstrate that the Thirteenth Amendment remains the principle constitutional source requiring the federal government to protect individual liberties against arbitrary private and public infringements that resemble the incidents of involuntary servitude. Moreover, the Thirteenth Amendment is a positive injunction requiring Congress to pass laws to that end, while the Fourteenth Amendment is "responsive" to "unconstitutional behavior."[1] I believe the Thirteenth Amendment takes a mixed liberty approach to liberty: its first section guarantees freedom *from* arbitrary domination. The second section authorizes Congress *to* enact federal laws protecting people's coequal liberties to establish meaning *for* their lives.

The Thirteenth Amendment is an even more unambiguous federal mandate than the Fourteenth Amendment. The prohibition against involuntary servitude is absolute, thus any incidents or badges of it are ineluctably proscribed. The Thirteenth Amendment vests Congress with the power to protect the unobtrusive exercise of freedom against arbitrary infringement. In at least some cases, such as those involving specific instances of slavery, not even a compelling state interest can justify a state or private infringement of autonomy.

In contrast, the state may infringe on the personal liberties the Fourteenth Amendment otherwise secures where there is an overriding public interest. The Supreme Court, in *City of Cleburne v. Cleburne Living Center*, carved out this Fourteenth Amendment exception to the usual prohibition against the use of race, alienage, and national origin classifications. Such laws "are subjected to strict scrutiny" analysis and will only be found constitutional if they "serve a compelling state interest." The Court later clarified that governmental restraints on fundamental freedoms must be "specifically and narrowly framed to accomplish" the compelling purpose. Such a restrictive law cannot be "merely rationally related, to the accomplishment of a permissible state policy."[2] Fourteenth Amendment jurisprudence allows government to infringe even on fundamental liberty interests for compelling public reasons.[3]

The Court's most recent decisions on the Fourteenth Amendment adopt a "responsive" rather than a proactive reading of congressional section 5 powers. In *City of Boerne v. Flores*,[4] the Court invalidated the Religious Freedom Restoration Act in part because it found the statute "so out of proportion to a supposed remedial or preventative object that it *cannot be understood as responsive to*, or designed to prevent, unconstitutional behavior." The case limited Congress's section 5 powers to passing congruent laws for remedying state violations of Fourteenth Amendment guarantees: "The Fourteenth Amendment's history confirms the remedial, rather than substantive, nature of the Enforcement Clause." The Court's rationale was based on statements made during congressional debates over the proposed Fourteenth Amendment to the effect that "[t]he proposed Amendment gave Congress too much legislative power at the expense of the existing constitutional structure." In a recent article, Ruth Colker maintained that the Court misleadingly resorted to the record of the debates that preceded passage of the proposed Fourteenth Amendment. The Court relied on the statements of four congressmen to bolster the *Boerne* rationale without ever mentioning that only one of them voted for the proposed amendment.[5] Relying on the understanding of the ratification opponents is a dubious method of judicial interpretation.

The Court maintained the remedial interpretation of Congress's section 5 power in *Kimel v. Florida Board of Regents*, finding that Congress overstepped its enforcement authority when it extended the applicability of the Age Discrimination in Employment Act (ADEA) to states and local governments. The Court in *Kimel* held that Congress's decision to apply the ADEA to states was "out of proportion to its supposed remedial or preventive objectives." Other recent cases dealing with section 5 have applied the responsive "proportionality and congruency" test to the Patent Remedy Act, the Violence against Women Act (VAWA), the Americans with Disabilities Act of 1990, and the Family and Medical Leave Act.

In addition to authorizing laws that responsively remedy specific past discrimination, the Thirteenth Amendment also grants Congress the power to pass laws that are substantive guarantees. Pursuant to the Thirteenth Amendment, the standard for passing "effective legislation" is that it be "rationally" related to "the badges and the incidents of servitude."[6] The Thirteenth Amendment, thus, envisions the passage of positive legislation that furthers people's ability to enjoy their lives. It provides a substantive right to freedom that Congress must maintain and cannot override. Under the Thirteenth Amendment, the federal legislature may, and indeed should, pass laws that are conducive for autonomy to thrive. The amendment enables Congress to substantiate the promises of freedom in the Preamble and Declaration of Independence.

Congress may use its section 2 power to pass laws that protect the nonintrusive use of personal freedom and punish its abridgment. Moreover, Congress may pass civil legislation, more sensitive to human rights concerns than §§ 1981 and 1982, allowing for private compensation. Such legislation must be compatible with the twin ideals of the Preamble: they must both guard personal autonomy and secure general welfare. Congress's enforcement power under the Thirteenth Amendment not only aims to prevent interference with fundamental rights, which is the extent of Congress's authority under the Fourteenth Amendment, but also enables the federal government to instantiate ideals of the Declaration of Independence and the Preamble.[7]

The Thirteenth Amendment's lack of a state action requirement is another reason for sometimes preferring the Thirteenth to the Fourteenth Amendment. The Supreme Court created this dichotomy as early as 1883, in the *Civil Rights Cases*, and never strayed from it. As we saw earlier, that case invalidated the Civil Rights Act of 1875. The Court found that the Fourteenth Amendment enforcement power is limited to state actions:

> It does not authorize congress to create a code of municipal law for the regulation of private rights; but to provide modes of redress against the operation of state laws, and the action of state officers, executive or judi-

cial, when these are subversive of the fundamental rights specified in the amendment. Positive rights and privileges are undoubtedly secured by the fourteenth amendment; but they are secured by way of prohibition against state laws and state proceedings affecting those rights and privileges, and by power given to congress to legislate for the purpose of carrying such prohibition into effect: and such legislation must necessarily be predicated upon such supposed state laws or state proceedings, and be directed to the correction of their operation and effect.

The *Civil Rights Cases* accorded with post–Reconstruction political decisions, such as the Compromise of 1877, which favored Northern and Southern reconciliation at the expense of meaningful improvements for blacks.[8]

Boerne took the state action requirement for granted and further straight-jacketed Congress by finding that section 5 allows it "to enforce" but not "to determine what constitutes a constitutional violation." The Supreme Court also embraced the state action requirement in *United States v. Morrison*, a case that found the VAWA unconstitutional. The majority explained that it would not deviate from "the time-honored principle that the Fourteenth Amendment, [which] by its very terms, prohibits only state action." *Morrison* asserted that it was based on the doctrine of *stare decisis* and the "insight attributable to the Members of the Court at that time," since they had "intimate knowledge and familiarity with the events surrounding the adoption of the Fourteenth Amendment." The Court's historical analysis again failed to account for the events immediately preceding the *Civil Rights Cases*. Chief Justice Bradley wrote the decision shortly after he cast the deciding vote on the electoral commission that gave Rutherford B. Hayes the presidency and secured the Compromise of 1877. Bradley and the other members of the electoral commission abandoned blacks to the injustices of segregation.

The Rehnquist majority drew on precedent covered with the cobwebs of a racist era instead of advancing progressive arguments born from the abolitionist movement. The Court, in *Morrison* also quoted from another 1883 case, *United States v. Harris*, for the principle that section 5 refers to "[s]tate action exclusively, and not to any action of private individuals." *Harris* struck section 2 of the Ku Klux Klan Act, which had made it criminal for two or more people to conspire to deprive anyone from enjoying the equal protection of the law or the privileges and immunities of national citizenship. The Court's continued reliance on these two decisions, both of which moved the country in the direction of *Plessy v. Ferguson* (1896), indicates the difficulty of using a Fourteenth Amendment strategy to end injustices such as violence against women or hate crimes generally.[9]

Ever since it decided the *Slaughterhouse Cases*, *Civil Rights Cases*, and *Harris*, the Court has severely handicapped national power in the area of the Fourteenth Amendment. On the other hand, beginning with *Jones*, the Court expanded federal authority to prevent interference with civil liberties.

The schema I propose authorizes Congress to pass laws preserving the right to freely pursue goals that do not arbitrarily interfere with the others' legitimate interests. This schema provides both a positive grant of power, insofar as it recognizes that the Thirteenth Amendment provides Congress the power to expand opportunities, and a negative grant of freedom, because it prohibits the government and individuals from intrusively abusing others' autonomy. Such a perspective makes more evident Congress's authority to rationally decide that a law, such as the VAWA, is necessary for protecting women's freedom of movement against misogynistic intrusions into their lives. A law against other hate crimes would likewise use federal power to punish and prevent the types of interference with liberty that the Reconstruction Congress sought to end.

Thus, the Thirteenth Amendment provides a substantive alternative for passing civil rights laws. This interpretation of the amendment is based on Supreme Court precedents. The Supreme Court has consistently found that the Thirteenth Amendment does not contain any equivalent to the Fourteenth Amendment's state action requirement.[10] Congress has great latitude, pursuant to its Thirteenth Amendment section 2 power, to end any remaining vestiges of servitude and their concomitant forms of subordination. The judiciary, I argued in chapter 3.C, should use section 1 even absent congressional action. The practices to which both sections of the Thirteenth Amendment apply need not be overtly tied to forced labor; they may be masked in institutional discrimination and private behavior that arbitrarily deny victims the opportunity to live meaningful lives.

Finally, the two amendments complemented each other in how they altered voting eligibility. The Thirteenth Amendment voided the Three-Fifths Clause, thereby extending the vote to the newly freed. The second and third sections of the Fourteenth Amendment provided conditions for representation and franchise. The second section of the Fourteenth

Amendment counted all persons in a state, except untaxed Native Americans, in apportioning the number of Representatives. Further, it contained a provision, which has never been enforced, reducing the congressional delegation of those states that disenfranchised any male inhabitants of that state. Section 3 of the Fourteenth Amendment prohibited former political officeholders who participated in the rebellion from ever again holding federal or state elective offices. The bar was not, however, absolute as it allowed two-thirds of Congress to pardon the offenders.[11]

The Fourteenth Amendment made the Thirteenth no less significant. The Fourteenth Amendment added greatly to constitutional protections of freedom. It provided specific protections as well as added provisions which, had they been enforced from the time of the Fourteenth Amendment's ratification, would have covered civil liberties. However, this amendment in no way minimized the importance of the Thirteenth Amendment, which continues to be a guarantee of substantive liberties. In fact, numerous landmark Supreme Court cases fit even better under the Thirteenth Amendment's rubrics than they do under the Fourteenth Amendment's.

B. Source for Substantive Freedom

The Supreme Court has done little to examine what civil liberties Congress may protect pursuant to the Thirteenth Amendment. Instead, the Court has used various constitutional provisions to establish its decisions concerning privacy and liberty rights. For example, the Court has repeatedly held that liberty rights are imbedded in the Due Process Clause of the Fourteenth Amendment, which gives the Court little guidance about which liberties it protects. Typically, the Court simply asserts that a human decision, such as choosing whether to travel, is a historically fundamental liberty that is immune from state infringement absent a compelling state interest. This kind of unspecific historical reasoning exposes holdings to the originalist detraction that courts are engaging in judicial lawmaking.[12] Critics of opinions like *Roe v. Wade* have called the Court's reflective method "unprincipled," "illegitimate," and lacking "connection with any value of the Constitution."[13] A Thirteenth Amendment approach sidesteps these criticisms because, instead of an intuitive assertion, it requires a finding that an abridgment of liberty is significantly connected to the incidents or badges of servitude.

The legality of protecting liberties through the Thirteenth Amendment is difficult to gainsay because interpreting the amendment begins with the historical injustice it ended. My approach is analogous to the Supreme Court's two-tiered analytic method in substantive due process cases:

> First, we have regularly observed that the Due Process Clause specially protects those fundamental rights and liberties which are, objectively, "deeply rooted in this Nation's history and tradition," and "implicit in the concept of ordered liberty." . . . Second, we have required in substantive-due-process cases a "careful description" of the asserted fundamental liberty interest. Our Nation's history, legal traditions, and practices thus provide the crucial "guideposts for responsible decisionmaking." . . . This approach tends to rein in the subjective elements that are necessarily present in due process judicial review.[14]

Similarly, a court adjudicating matters under the Thirteenth Amendment must compare contemporary harms to past practices. Once the plaintiff establishes a *prima facie* case, the burden shifts to the defendant to prove that the limitation is no more restrictive than is necessary to protect the public's ability to live freely in a constitutional republic. A court is likely to find that only civic duty, such as a military draft during a just war, jury duty, or public highway work, is an adequate reason for demanding subservience.

The Thirteenth Amendment's declaration of liberty is the source of many unenumerated freedoms.[15] Every generation must develop an understanding of fundamental freedoms by critically examining the nation's past, its core documents, and its moral standing as a constitutional republic. This mode of collective self-reflection aims at empathic decision making that avoids past injustices. Freedom is a progressive civic condition that best expands through an affective comprehension of moral obligations and social limitations. I take it as a given that persons are relational animals who innately empathize and therefore can understand fellow citizens' desire to achieve goals without coercion or arbitrary domination. Constitutional development should never come at the cost of human autonomy and social welfare; otherwise, it would interfere with the reasonable goals of individuals' living in a community of equals. Nevertheless, some limits on freedom are necessary in organized societies where people often have conflicting goals. Normative principles are critical to constructing laws for a pluralistic society. To avoid religious or philosophical absolutism, the Thirteenth Amendment requires a historical basis for asserting that an interest falls under the amendment's purview. Protecting essential freedoms through the amendment's enforcement power means that Congress can pass rational laws punishing acts of exploitation and conducing to the common good.

Before explaining the amendment's reach, a word of caution is in order. Cases should not be decided solely on a judge's proclivity for one philosophy of liberty or another. This lesson was learned during the Gilded Age in which contractual liberty came to stand for a brand of liberty that allowed powerful individuals and groups to take advantage of persons in weaker bargaining positions. Freedom of this ilk disproportionately favored wealth, class, or other characteristics in common with a dominant group. This self-centered philosophy had a strong support during the Civil War and was augmented by the popularity of Herbert Spencer's brand of Social Darwinism. In his *Synthetic Philosophy*, Spencer opposed aid to the poor because "[t]he whole effort of nature is to get rid of such, to clear the world of them, and to make room for better." In the United States, this meant that persons on the bottom end of the socioeconomic scale, who were disproportionately blacks, Native Americans, Chicanos, Chinese, and women of various ethnicities, were left unprotected against suave robber barons. The labor movement was also undermined by cases like *In re Jacobs* (1885), the first major decision invalidating legislation designed to protect workers. Courts, too, limited the freedom of labor unions to organize against companies, granting more than eight hundred injunctions against strikes between 1880 and 1931.[16] The lesson from the domination such supposed freedom actually created is that liberty is not the unlimited right to exploit others in a weaker social station. Moreover, humans are not mere monads unconnected to a social realm. Neither are they indistinguishable blots who are only valuable as parts of a Rousseauistic community. Rather, freedom is an individual interest that enables people to make their lives more significant, both to themselves and to others. Persons living in the United States who are free to exercise their creative powers add to the total national output.

Law protects this dual purpose. Legislation against acts of domination, whether they are perpetrated during employment or in any other setting, is essential in a country devoted to civil liberties. Laurence H. Tribe, a leading constitutional scholar, correctly wrote that based on existing case law, "Congress possesses an almost unlimited power to protect individual rights under the Thirteenth. Seemingly, Congress is free within the broad limits of reason, to recognize whatever rights it wishes, define the infringement of those rights as a form of domination or subordination and thus an aspect of slavery, and proscribe such infringement as a violation of the Thirteenth Amendment."[17] Likewise, the Supreme Court should adjudicate cases implicating personal liberties through the lens of the Thirteenth Amendment. In order to provide consistency and predictability to citizens and litigants, both the legislature and judiciary should use a normative historical analysis.

The Thirteenth Amendment approach can sharpen judicial decisions about the extent to which persons may enjoy fundamental rights, particularly when the exercise of those rights conflicts with other members of a pluralistic community. The basis of such an analysis need not be *ad hoc*; instead, it should be based on the recognition that slavery and involuntary servitude were inimical to fundamental, human liberties. The woefully incomplete post–Civil War American project involves ending racist practices. Twentieth-century Court decisions on constitutionally protected liberty and privacy rights reflect this trend. Those rights are not, however, absolute. To the contrary, the Thirteenth Amendment bars certain uses of freedom, particularly those used for domination or exploitation. After all, in 1857, the Court favored Dred Scott's master's interest to freely travel throughout the states with his slave property to Dred Scott's interest to freedom from slavery.

Liberty rights are well established in United States jurisprudence. The Supreme Court has often invoked the Due Process and Equal Protection Clauses in privacy rights cases; however, the Court has not always provided even this degree of specificity.[18] Its frequent resort to tradition provides little explanation for the protection of fundamental rights. The Thirteenth Amendment is a more explicit guarantee of freedom than other constitutional provisions on which the Court has relied. For instance, *Roe v. Wade*, upholding a woman's right to choose an abortion, relied on the Fourteenth Amendment's liberty provision but also endorsed the District Court's view that the source of that right is the Ninth Amendment.[19] While the Court in *Roe* provided an expansive historical analysis to justify its conclusion,[20] its reliance on tradition was a two-edged sword since the dissent also resorted to tradition to derive the opposite point of view on the right to abortion.[21]

Without a specific nexus on which a court must ground references to tradition, privacy-rights cases rely on the predispositions of judges, and when racists like Chief Justice Taney sit on the Supreme Court, decisions like *Dred Scott* are the product. In order to prevent the hijacking of tradition analysis into the shadier parts of U.S. history, the Thirteenth Amendment requires a very clear judicial analysis: Is the act an incident or a badge of servitude? Or, in the case of legislation, did Congress rationally determine that the statute was a necessary and proper means to end an incident of servitude? The rather obvious shortcoming of this method is that the antagonist of a particular law or judgment can argue that it is unrelated to involuntary servitude. Such criticism does little, however, to limit the virtually plenary power that the Supreme Court found section 2 of the Thirteenth Amendment grants to Congress. Moreover, in spite of the amendment's specific focus, it allows for a broad reading.

Familial liberties are principal examples of how Thirteenth Amendment analysis works outside the context of contract and property-rights cases, where the amendment has most commonly been applied. Indeed, the first use of the term "incidents of servitude," which Senator James Harlan of Iowa coined during the 1864 Senate debate on the amendment, was within the context of slavery's detriments to marriage: "[T]he prohibition of the conjugal relation is a necessary incident of servitude." If Harlan was correct, then the federal guarantee to marry the partner of one's choice is linked to the rights of free people. Traditionally, however, the Court has located the right "to marry, establish a home and bring up children" in the Due Process Clause.[22]

Choice of a marriage partner is fundamental because it reflects so many aspects of an individual's character traits. Family-rights issues provide further insight into why the Thirteenth Amendment is as relevant to protecting civil liberties as the Due Process Clause. Both involve a continuum of interests that are not subject to any "substantial arbitrary impositions and purposeless restraints."[23] Denying adults the right to family autonomy signifies a lack of respect for the individuals' decisions, passions, hopes, and sense of self. Moreover, in this country arbitrary deprivation of family freedoms is linked to slavery.

In both the antebellum and postbellum South, slaves were degraded to a social rung below their masters and other whites. Intermarriage was forbidden to them. A typical argument against abolition was that it would lead to miscegenation. A back-country farmer's attitude was typical: "[H]ow'd you like to hev a nigger steppin' up to your darter? Of course you wouldn't; and that's the reason I wouldn't like to hev 'em free; but I tell you, I don't think it's right to hev 'em slaves so; that's the fac—taant right to keep 'em as they is."[24]

The Supreme Court held that laws against intermarriage violate the Due Process and Equal Protection Clauses in the 1967 case of *Loving v. Virginia*. The Court found, in large part based on the Due Process Clause, that a Virginia statute that prohibited racial intermarriage was unconstitutional. The Court recognized the right to marry "as one of the vital personal rights essential to the orderly pursuit of happiness by free men."[25] The decision, which is one of the most pregnant the Supreme Court ever issued, could have been even more thoroughly grounded through an understanding about the history of U.S. oppression. Prohibitions against intermarriage are related to slavery and subservience. Any arbitrary burdens placed on marriage formation implicate the Thirteenth Amendment.[26]

The abolition of slavery further rejected the racist stereotype that made black families subject to personal and legislative whims. Any contemporary burdens on familial living arrangements that resemble the hardships faced by slave families are unconstitutional. Black families in the antebellum South faced great obstacles in maintaining stable family relationships. Many masters considered slave marriages only temporary and subject to forced termination. Since all Southern states forbade blacks from entering into formal marriage contracts, masters had an absolute right to sell one or both spouses. When slaves married persons on other plantations or free blacks, they were limited in how often they could visit their spouses. Spouses who lived on different plantations were even more likely to be sold apart than those with a common owner, and even when they remained on nearby plantations, their new masters sometimes prevented them from contacting each other.[27]

The dominant stereotype that claimed that blacks were indifferent about their families proved groundless. During and after the Civil War, many freed persons wandered far off plantations in search of loved ones. Ben Dodson, a sixty-five-year-old plantation preacher, cried out in joy when he was reunited with his wife after years of estrangement resulting from their master's decision to sell them separately: "Glory! glory! hallelujah! Dis is my Betty, shuah," he said, glancing again at her face to reassure himself. "I foun' you at las'. I's hunted an' hunted till I track you up here. I's boun' to hunt till I fin' you if you's alive." After emancipation, parents were reunited with children, often not recognizing each other but for a scar or some other unusual feature. Sometimes they discovered that their newly found loved ones had been brutalized during the years of slavery that separated them. One woman located her eighteen-year old-daughter, who had been sold from her, to have been cut "[f]rom her head to her feet . . . just as . . . her face."[28]

The variety of chores on big plantations also often resulted in family separation, especially among extended family members. If one family member worked in the plantation house, he could not live with those members of his family who worked in the fields. The most devastating form of family disruption came from sales, which had even less regard for relationships between cousins, nephews and uncles, or grandparents and their grandchildren than they did for parental and spousal ties.[29]

The Thirteenth Amendment prohibits such disruptions to family structure. The amendment complements due process jurisprudence and expands the scope of prohibited conduct. In *Moore v. City of East Cleveland*, the Supreme Court found the Due Process Clause grants extended families the right to live together. The Court recognized that "the institution of family is deeply rooted in this Nation's history and tradition." Familial bonds are matters of personal choice that are protected.[30] The Court's holding properly targets governmental entities that interfere with familial choice. The Thirteenth Amendment yields added protection of this fundamental right. Pursuant to section 2 of the Thirteenth Amendment, Congress can prohibit private and state interference with family living arrangements.[31]

In another relevant context, the Court in *Griswold v. Connecticut* further guaranteed the protection of family rights. Marriage, the Court observed, "promotes a way of life . . . a harmony of living . . . bilateral loyalty." The Court based its decision on "several constitutional guarantees" of liberties that contain "penumbras, formed by emanations from those guarantees that help give them life and substance." In particular, the Court found a right to marital liberty in the Due Process Clause. The Connecticut anti-contraception law was an affront to the marital relationship because it enabled the state to interfere with the intimate rights of spouses.[32]

Justice Douglas's majority opinion in *Griswold* has been the subject of a variety of criticisms that would not apply to a Thirteenth Amendment approach. One critic of the decision was Justice Black, who wrote in a dissenting opinion that the majority based its decision on the ambiguities of procedural due process. Black rejected the decision because he could "find in the Constitution no language which either specifically or implicitly grants to all individuals a constitutional 'right to privacy.'" Similarly, Robert H. Bork later criticized *Griswold* for failing "every test of neutrality. . . . *Griswold* . . . is an unprincipled decision, both in the way in which it derives a new constitutional right and the way it defines that right, or rather fails to define it."[33]

Griswold's critics, however, fail to realize that finding a substantive guarantee to family privacy does not rely on novel legal reasoning. Substantive guarantees like the First Amendment's guarantee of religious liberty and the Fifth Amendment Just Compensation Clause's guarantee of property rights, are strewn about the Bill of Rights.[34] The Thirteenth Amendment's substantive guarantee of marital freedom is another reason critics are mistaken. The liberty to choose a spouse is grounded in its historic setting and the organic nature of constitutional interpretation. The Thirteenth Amendment facilitates Felix Frankfurter's vision of the Constitution as a "stream of history" which the Supreme Court directs within "a living framework" for growth.[35] Likewise, the amendment is compatible with Justice Ginsburg's view that "[a] prime part of the history of our Constitution . . . is the story of the extension of constitutional rights and protections to people once ignored and excluded."[36]

The Thirteenth Amendment could have further bolstered Justice Goldberg's concurrence to *Griswold*, which convincingly asserts that the Ninth Amendment's sweeping protection of unenumerated rights. The amendment unequivocally condemns any laws and practices intrusive of marital autonomy because such restrictions resemble the coercion of involuntary servitude. The Thirteenth Amendment's first section provides the judiciary with the power to hear cases against individuals, officials, or governmental entities who use arbitrary characteristics, such as race, to intrude on conjugal rights.

The Thirteenth Amendment is relevant in other family autonomy contexts as well. Its applicability is clear, for example, in the area of parental autonomy over children's education. Theodore Weld, in 1839, exclaimed that enslaved parents had "as little control over [their children] as have domestic animals over the disposal of their young."[37] Parents were particularly restrained from educating their children. Many states forbade slaves from receiving any form of education, even though some blacks learned clandestinely, many of them with the help of sympathetic or self-interested whites. Parents were altogether excluded from the decision of whether to educate their children. Such a practice prohibited parents from helping offspring achieve their potential for private and public accomplishments.

As we saw earlier, the Supreme Court in *Runyon v. McCrary* recognized the Thirteenth Amendment's applicability to parental decisions over their children's education. The plaintiffs were parents who wanted to contract for education with a private school. The Court held that the Civil Rights Act of 1866 prohibited the school from refusing to enroll the children on racial grounds. The Court concluded that parents have the liberty right to enter contractual agreements with the school of their choosing.[38] The Court could have refined its reasoning with a discussion of the disadvantages that slaves faced and of the act's liberating aim. Rather than basing its decision on a contractual right, the Court should have defined the universal human right to educate one's children. After all, parents' rights go well beyond the right to contract for their children's education and include a privacy interest in improving their children's lives.

Indeed, a whole series of parental autonomy cases regarding educational issues fit in with the Thirteenth Amendment's criteria so well as to make it plausible that courts could find unconstitutional arbitrary restrictions on parental autonomy, even absent congressional action. This would require the Court to recognize that section 1 grants the judiciary deliberative powers, which, in turn, could have significant ramifications on litigants' ability to sue under the amendment, especially in those circumstances where Congress has failed to address educational discrimination.

Other parental autonomy cases do rely on broad historical reasoning that the Thirteenth Amendment can buttress. In *Meyer v. Nebraska*, the Court struck down a state law that forbade teaching students a language other than English before they finished the eighth grade. The Court relied on the liberty protection of the Due Process Clause and decided the law violated the parents' right to decide how to educate their children. The decision is somewhat ambiguous because the majority did not attempt "to define with exactness the liberty thus guaranteed." The Court provided a more useful criterion in *Wisconsin v. Yoder*, where it invalidated a state law requiring children to attend school until the age of sixteen. The Court held that the law violated Amish parents' rights to exercise parental control and religious authority. The Court stated that "[t]he history and culture of Western civilization reflects a strong tradition of parental concern for the nurture and upbringing of their children." Using similar reasoning in *Santosky v. Kramer*, the Court noted "[t]he fundamental liberty interest of natural parents in the care, custody, and management of their child." And it reiterated the "historical recognition that freedom of personal choice in matters of family life is a fundamental liberty interest protected by the Fourteenth Amendment."[39]

The Court clothed these cases in the historical recognition that the government must not interfere with parental decisions absent a compelling state interest. Thirteenth Amendment analysis could better link that aspect of American legal history to specific constitutional landmarks. Such an analysis would reflect on the institutional denial of parental autonomy in the antebellum United States and critically consider whether barring parents from particular educational or custody decisions resembles the conditions of involuntary servitude. The liberation from slavery extended to all parents the freedom to make critical decisions about their children's education. The Thirteenth Amendment approach, then, may be even better grounded in U.S. history than the one based on the Fourteenth Amendment. The Thirteenth Amendment sifts through specifics rather than generalities and has the further advantage of providing a cause of action against private and public schools.

I am not advocating abandoning the generalities of the Fourteenth Amendment. The point, rather, is that many parental autonomy cases that are analyzed under the Fourteenth Amendment could be made less vulnerable to criticism by bringing the Thirteenth Amendment's self-executing first section into the judgment or, preferably, by enacting federal family protections pursuant to the Thirteenth Amendment.[40]

Although greater methodological certainty makes the Thirteenth Amendment an attractive alternative for civil rights strategists, it is not the best alternative for all cases related to family life and reproduction. Some cases do not fall under the amendment's ambit, even though at first they seem to fit it. For example, in *Skinner v. Oklahoma*, the Court appropriately resorted to the Equal Protection Clause of the Fourteenth Amendment to find an Oklahoma law requiring "habitual criminals" to undergo sterilization violated their fundamental right to procreate. "We are dealing here" the majority wrote, "with legislation which involves one of the basic civil rights of man. Marriage and procreation are fundamental to the very existence and survival of the race." The decision remains open to critics like Bork, who criticized the Court for failing to adequately ground the right to procreate and thereby enabled judges to exploit "substantive equal protection" in order to "embed their notions of public policy in the Constitution."[41] Bork's criticism would be entirely inapplicable to a Thirteenth Amendment prohibition against the arbitrary infringement of liberty rights. His textualist argument, which rests on the premise that there is no constitutional guarantee to procreate, comes undone at the infusion of Thirteenth Amendment analysis. Masters interfered with many aspects of their slaves' procreation. They castrated slaves with relative equanimity since it was generally considered a medical procedure that masters could perform on chattel. Further, some states permitted castration as part of the punishment for black rape of white women.[42] Thus, impediments to procreation interfere with a free life.

In spite of this seeming fit, the problem of using the Thirteenth Amendment in cases like *Skinner* or *Turner v. Safley*, which found that prisoners retain the right to marry under the Fourteenth Amendment, is that they both dealt with prisoners' rights. Even where limiting marriage and procreation rights has some resemblance to the incidents of servitude, the first section of the Thirteenth Amendment does not seem to protect persons who have been duly convicted of crimes. This is a disturbing conclusion for human rights activism, making the Fourteenth Amendment the best means for convicted criminals to proclaim their limited right to exercise fundamental freedoms. Further, it presents a dilemma that can only be rectified by amending the Thirteenth Amendment's exception for the use of involuntary servitude "as a punishment for crime whereof the party shall have been duly convicted."

It is worth taking a step outside cases dealing with family privacy rights to see whether the historically based approach to involuntary servitude that I have been advocating applies to another area of law. The effects of slavery were experienced well outside family relations, so the Thirteenth Amendment, too, must apply to other liberty rights. In this regard, right-to-travel cases further indicate that the Thirteenth Amendment is a substantive guarantee of freedom.

Justice Douglas found the right to travel abroad and within the United States was "a part of our heritage" that the Due Process Clause of the Fifth Amendment protects. In *Kent v. Dulles*, he explained the subtle nature of that right: "Travel abroad, like travel within the country, may be necessary for a livelihood. It may be as close to the heart of the individual as the choice of what he eats, or wears, or reads. Freedom of movement is basic in our scheme of values."[43] However, Douglas did not provide a reason for finding that right in the Bill of Rights. Indeed, slaves' inability to freely travel without their masters' permission indicates that the Fifth Amendment did not adequately protect that right.

Slaves were restricted from relocating. Even those slaves who worked for their masters outside the homestead or plantation only traveled at the masters' sufferance.[44] After liberation, many blacks wandered in the country and settled in cities away from their plantations. The newly freed people desired freedom from manacles and the ability to live and work where they wished. Often they were financially strapped, but preferred freedom to the security of their old homes.

This was the situation Sidney Andrews found during his travels in 1866, while reporting on the defeated South. Throughout Georgia he found many freed people who were living in destitution after leaving their former homes. "Who shall have the heart to blame them?" Andrews asked rhetorically. "For they were in search of nothing less noble and glorious than freedom. They were in rags and wretchedness, but the unquenchable longing of the soul for liberty was being satisfied." Andrews asked one elderly woman why she had left a mistress who "would have given you a good home as long as you live." To the freewoman the response seemed obvious, "What fur? 'Joy my freedom.'" In another place he found eleven people living in a hut with rags for bedding. To Andrews's inquiry about whether he had a kind master, an elderly inhabitant responded, "I's had a berry good master, mass'r, but ye see I's wanted to be free man."

Another narrative tells of an elderly slave, named Si, who left a plantation one night with his wife. In the morning, the master came across Si bending down in a nearby forest by his deceased wife, who had died of exposure. "'Uncle Si, why on earth did you so cruelly bring Aunt Cindy here for, through all of such hardship, thereby causing her death?' Lifting up his eyes and looking his master full in the face, he answered, 'I couldn't help it, marster; but then, you see, she died free.'"[45]

After the ratification of the Thirteenth Amendment in 1865, states could no longer arbitrarily deny citizenship or access into their borders. Senator Trumbull explained during an 1866 congressional debate that the Thirteenth Amendment's enforcement power allowed Congress to pass laws that would, in effect, prevent racist isolationism in both the North and South. "It is idle to say that a man is free who cannot go and come at pleasure, who cannot buy and sell, who cannot enforce his rights. These are rights which the first section of the constitutional amendment meant to secure to all; and to prevent the very cavil which the Senator from Delaware suggests today, that Congress would not have the power to secure them, the second section of the amendment was added."[46] Even after the Thirteenth Amendment's ratification, states clandestinely ended the amendment's grant of freedom and placed legal barriers limiting freed people's movement.

In 1865 and 1866, all former Confederate states except Tennessee and Arkansas passed sweeping vagrancy laws. These made any poor man who did not have a labor contract subject to discretionary arrest. Vagrancy laws disproportionately targeted unemployed blacks and were designed to keep them from leaving their former masters' plantations. Some Southern cities enacted similar ordinances designed to thwart black movement. The mayor of Mobile, Alabama warned vagrants that if they did not find employment or leave that city, they would be arrested and forced to work on public streets. Other towns had similar punishments to prevent blacks from staying in urban areas. Nashville, Tennessee and New Orleans, Louisiana sent black "vagrants" to workhouses, San Antonio and Montgomery required that they work on the streets to pay for the expense of keeping them in jails. In a move reminiscent of the antebellum system of passes, without which slaves could not leave their masters' property, some cities arrested any blacks who stayed out on the streets after curfew without their employer's permission. This scheme was meant as much to inhibit blacks from intrastate and interstate travel as it was to perpetuate a system of involuntary servitude.[47] The substantive guarantee of freedom was meant to end these sorts of practices; yet, even today, cities like Chicago continue enforcing loitering and begging ordinances that inhibit movement. The Supreme Court has never considered whether modern-day loitering laws are vestiges of involuntary servitude.[48]

The Court has recognized that the right to travel is "firmly established and repeatedly recognized." Similar to the family privacy cases, the Court has found support for protecting the right to travel in a variety of constitutional provisions, including the Privileges and Immunities Clause, the Due Process Clause, the Equal Protection Clause, and the Commerce Clause.

Shapiro v. Thompson involved a state welfare eligibility provision that imposed a one-year residency requirement. The Court ruled that absent a compelling interest, state interference with the fundamental right to travel violated the Equal Protection Clause. In another case, *Saenz v. Roe*, dealing with the availability of welfare benefits to persons who recently moved to a new state, the Court ruled that prohibitions on the right to travel violated the constitutionally guaranteed privileges and immunities of newly arrived citizens. The majority in *United States v. Guest* found that the constitutional right to travel "and necessarily to use the highways and other instrumentalities of interstate commerce in doing so, occupies a position fundamental to the concept of our Federal Union." The majority linked the right to travel to the Commerce Clause because it regarded "the constitutional right of interstate travel [as] a right secured against interference from any source whatever, whether governmental or private . . . that is quite independent of the Fourteenth Amendment." The Court's preference of the Commerce Clause as the source of the right to travel again artificially linked a fundamental right to an economic power rather than to a human interest existing independently of governmental powers.[49]

Of course, it is accurate that limits on travel can both be detrimental to commerce and violate citizens' privileges and immunities, but, to date, the Supreme Court has inadequately examined the connection between slavery and restraints on movement. A Thirteenth Amendment approach adds a needed reflection on whether impediments to free movement resemble the burdens of involuntary servitude. This approach recognizes that some extreme burdens on the right to move about freely can resemble the constraints of enslavement.

In *Griffin v. Breckenridge*, the Court nearly acknowledged the connection between the Thirteenth Amendment and right to travel but failed to make the logical connection between them. The case dealt with a racially motivated assault perpetrated on a public highway. In his opinion, Justice Stewart referred to a variety of right-to-travel cases, including *Shapiro*, and found that "[o]ur cases have firmly established that the right of interstate travel is constitutionally protected, does not necessarily rest on the Fourteenth Amendment, and is assertable against private as well as governmental interference." Furthermore, Stewart determined that Congress had the power to create a cause of action against private, racially motivated conspiracies under § 1985(3), the Ku Klux Klan Act. In later years, the Court explained that "the conspiracy at issue [in *Griffin*] was actionable because it was aimed at depriving the plaintiffs of rights protected by the Thirteenth Amendment and the right to travel guaranteed by the Federal Constitution."[50] The clear indication in *Griffin* is that the right to travel and the Thirteenth Amendment granted Congress the authority to pass the Ku Klux Klan Act, thereby providing redress against individual conspiracies that interfere with movement—even absent a state action, negative effect on commerce, or interference with the privileges and immunities of citizenship. The case is unclear, however, about why the right to travel should be separated from core Thirteenth Amendment interests. This dichotomy is particularly obscure because Congress passed the Ku Klux Klan Act, in part, pursuant to the Thirteenth Amendment. The amendment, therefore, was a logical place for the Court to find congressional power to prohibit conspirators from interfering with citizens' right to travel.

The Court has located the right to travel in so many constitutional provisions because, like family autonomy, it is a fundamental interest. The right to live free of arbitrary impediments that prevent enjoyment of such interests sometimes implicates the Thirteenth Amendment. Securing "the blessings of liberty" is a national aspiration to which the Preamble to the Constitution commits the federal government. The amendment made that national aspiration enforceable against state and private infringements. The amendment enhances, clarifies, and enforces contemporary civil rights decisions.

C. Commerce Clause and Thirteenth Amendment

The next issue to analyze is whether the Thirteenth Amendment alternative can bolster civil rights cases that have relied on the Commerce Clause for their authority. This analysis requires a preliminary explanation of the case law and then a critical comparison to Thirteenth Amendment authority.

By the 1960s, civil rights lawyers began resorting to the Commerce Clause in litigation. Part of their aim was to adopt creative strategies to get around the eighty-year-old state action restrictions in *United States v. Harris* (1882) and the *Civil Rights Cases* (1883). These two cases placed a roadblock in front of litigants seeking to assert their human rights by invoking the Fourteenth Amendment. By the 1990s, use of the Commerce Clause was well established in civil rights litigation; however, conservative members of the Court have now reversed the trend in a series of cases. The Rehnquist court reduced Congress's effectiveness to enact legislation pursuant to its Commerce Clause power in *United States v. Morrison*, where the Court struck down a national law prohibiting gender-motivated violence, and *United States v. Lopez*, where it found unconstitutional a federal statute against the possession of firearms near a school.

Enter the Thirteenth Amendment, which offers an alternative to recapture, and indeed build upon, civil rights gains.

Congress passed numerous 1960s civil rights statutes pursuant to its Commerce Clause authority. The successes of presidents John F. Kennedy and Lyndon B. Johnson in spurring a civil rights agenda culminated in the Civil Rights Act of 1964. That statute continues today to provide remedies against a variety of discriminations, including those perpetrated in public accommodations, employment, and housing. The Supreme Court, under the leadership of Chief Justice Earl Warren, avoided the need to alter the post–Reconstruction jurisprudence on Congress's power under the Fourteenth Amendment by turning to the Commerce Clause to justify congressional enactments against private discrimination.

In a 1964 watershed case, *Heart of Atlanta Motel*, the Supreme Court determined that Congress could use its power to regulate interstate commerce to prevent a private motel from discriminating on the basis of race, color, religion, or national origin. The motel refused to rent rooms to African Americans while advertising nationally and serving clientele from interstate highways. The Court held that the motel's segregation caused blacks to be "subject of discrimination in transient accommodations," forcing them to travel greater distances to find another motel or to impose on friends willing to put them up for the night.[51] Oddly, it was the motel that raised the Thirteenth Amendment claim, arguing that requiring it to provide accommodations to unwanted customers would subject the business to involuntary servitude. The Court rejected the motel's reasoning and held that the Thirteenth Amendment granted Congress authority to pass rationally designed antidiscrimination laws for bettering the general welfare. Nevertheless, the Court refused to reverse the *Civil Rights Cases*'s Fourteenth Amendment bar against federal laws prohibiting public accommodation discrimination.[52]

That same year, the Court found in *Katzenbach v. McClung* that the Civil Rights Act of 1964 constitutionally prohibited a family-owned restaurant from discriminating against potential patrons. In the District Court, the plaintiff had relied on a Thirteenth Amendment argument. The trial court had found the amendment irrelevant to the issue because it neither permitted nor denied Congress power to pass laws against discrimination. The trial court had also found that there was no "close and substantial relation" between the restaurant and interstate commerce. The Supreme Court did not follow the "close and substantial relation" test.

Instead, it determined that Congress had a "rational basis" for adopting the Act's regulatory scheme based on evidence that segregated restaurants hindered business, inhibited travel, and therefore detrimentally affected interstate commerce. However, the Court refused to reach the Thirteenth Amendment issue.[53]

For decades, *Heart of Atlanta Motel* and *McClung* stood for the deferential principle that Congress could pass any laws rationally connected to interstate commerce. Two recent decisions have significantly beveled down the weight of those opinions and have, inadvertently, made more clear the increased relevancy of the Thirteenth Amendment.

Chief Justice Rehnquist reduced congressional Commerce Clause power in *United States v. Lopez*. The case dealt with the Gun-Free School Zones Act of 1990, which provided criminal penalties for persons who knowingly possessed firearms in a school zone. Rehnquist, writing for the majority, found the Act unconstitutional. In the course of his decision, the Chief Justice weakened Congress's Commerce Clause power by foregoing the rational basis inquiry and, instead, examining whether the law has a "substantial effect" on interstate commerce. The Court found no congressional showing that guns carried in a school zone had a "substantial effect" on interstate commerce. Rehnquist's language also indicated that the Commerce Clause would henceforth only apply to cases involving "economic enterprise."[54]

Five years later, the Court, in *United States v. Morrison*, relied on *Lopez* to find unconstitutional the Violence against Women Act, a federal statute that provided a private remedy for gender-motivated violence. The Chief Justice again wrote for the majority, further embedding into jurisprudence his views on the centrality of economics to congressional powers over interstate commerce. Congress had provided abundant information about the interstate effects of gender violence. Nevertheless, the Court did not find sufficient evidence to prove that violence against women substantially affected interstate commerce. In *Morrison*, Rehnquist asserted that Congress could not enact law "based solely on that conduct's aggregate effect on interstate commerce." And the aggregation doctrine, he held, was inapplicable in cases of gender-motivated violence that are "not directed at the instrumentalities, channels, or goods involved in interstate commerce."[55] On the other hand, both of the dissents in the case, written by Justices Souter and Breyer, wanted to restore the rational basis test.

The recent developments in Commerce Clause cases illustrate the chief problem with relying on that part of the Constitution to support Congress's power to end arbitrary intolerance. This strategy relies too heavily on an economic, rather than humanitarian, basis. The use of Commerce Clause powers leaves open economic counterarguments that an intolerant act is not substantially connected to interstate commerce.

Although the Court found that violence against women is not an economically directed activity, that finding is irrelevant in deciding whether the Thirteenth Amendment grants Congress the power to prevent violence against women. The Thirteenth Amendment perspective allows congressmen to review the connection of gender-motivated violence to slavery. Such violence was regularly perpetrated against slaves on plantations, and women, as Andrew Koppelman has pointed out, were particularly vulnerable to sexual brutality by masters and others who exploited their strengths and positions of power.[56]

Federal laws relying on the Thirteenth Amendment need only be rationally related to the vestiges of slavocracy. The Court has never overturned the *Jones* rational basis test. Had Congress relied on it, the Court might have deferred to Congress provided a legislative finding that gender-motivated violence is rationally related to the incidents of servitude and that the VAWA was a necessary and proper means of dealing with such acts. The only question left for the Court would be whether the statutory means chosen by Congress were "reasonably adapted to the end permitted by the Constitution."[57]

The Commerce Clause does little, if anything, to examine the legacy of slavery or to look at its remaining manifestations, making it susceptible to a purely economic interpretation like the one the Rehnquist majority has adopted. Instead, the Commerce Clause bodes back to what we may call Lockean social religion, which elevates property above the Preamble's guarantee to safeguard citizens' life and liberty for the general welfare. After all, Congress has had the power to regulate all manner of commerce between states at least since 1824, pursuant to *Gibbons v. Ogden*, when slavery flourished in the United States. In fact, one author has argued that the Commerce Clause was an important part of the founders' compromise with slavocracy at the Constitutional Convention. Even though the clause granted Congress the power to regulate the slave trade between states, the national government tolerated the practice, preferring national consensus to human rights reforms.[58]

By its very terms, the Thirteenth Amendment is not given to a neutral reading on the subject of private or state-sponsored discrimination; on the other hand, the Commerce Clause nowhere specifies that it empowers Congress to end human rights abuses. Further, the Thirteenth Amendment extends to interstate and intrastate activities, regardless of whether they have any effect on commerce. The amendment thereby recognizes that involuntary servitude is not merely an economic harm, but one that affects society in a more profound way. It detracts from people's ability to participate in national commerce, limits their right to move about freely, and impedes a broad variety of other autonomous actions. Denying a group to use grocery stores, theaters, and other public places of accommodation infringes on more than national economic interests, it violates the right of persons to decide where to shop, eat, and play. Concerted acts of discrimination, particularly those committed in public places, foreclose opportunities to interact, relax, and unwind. Discriminatory practices in public places bode back to Jim Crow laws and black codes that kept blacks in a virtual state of slavery, even after abolition. So too with discriminatory employment practices, which cause people much more misfortune in their lives than just economic ones. The Rehnquist opinions in *Lopez* and *Morrison* have not reduced the availability of the Thirteenth Amendment to deal with these and other injustices.

The Thirteenth Amendment's special role in employment discrimination cases is illustrative of its continued vitality. The link between employment discrimination and slavery is obvious, as slavery directly restricted blacks from choosing professions. Nationally, even in nonslave states, discriminatory practices barred blacks from competitive jobs. Therefore, Congress can rationally determine that exclusion of a group from equal participation in the workplace is related to forced subservience and an impediment to commerce. Based on this finding, Congress can pass legislation prohibiting employment discrimination currently not covered under federal laws. For instance, Title VII of the Civil Rights Act of 1964, which Congress passed on the basis of its Commerce Clause powers, is more restrictive than the Thirteenth Amendment. Title VII permits the federal government to regulate employers with at least fifteen employees. A law passed on the basis of the Thirteenth Amendment need not be so restrictive. Indeed, even absent new legislation, the Supreme Court has already indicated that § 1981, a Reconstruction-era statute based on Congress's Thirteenth Amendment authority, provides a private remedy to persons working for employers with fewer than fifteen people. Remedies under Title VII and § 1981 are separate, distinct, and independent. The Court stated in a 1994 dictum that "even in the employment context, § 1981's coverage is broader than Title VII's, for Title VII applies only to employers with 15 or more employees, whereas § 1981 has no such limitation."[59]

At times, the Thirteenth Amendment strategy is preferable to the Commerce Clause alternative because of the amendment's unique communicative value. Tying discrimination to the economy is not enough to alter racist views that have, in some circles, been culturally condoned since the country's founding. A legal framework designed to protect liberty and improve the general welfare conveys a powerful message about this country's underlying commitments. Legal norms can influence a people's desires and interests. They create entitlements society must honor. Laws protecting human rights on the basis of the Thirteenth Amendment effectively communicate a federal commitment to the protection of the general welfare against domineering conduct. Such legal remedies "express recognition of injury and reaffirmation of the underlying normative principles for how the relevant [social] relationships are to be constituted."[60]

The Thirteenth Amendment is a more obvious source for civil rights protections than the Commerce Clause. The former protects individual autonomy against state and private interference, and recent Supreme Court decisions indicate the latter principally concerns regulation of interstate economic transactions. The amendment was ratified to increase the federal government's ability to prevent human rights violations, and the Commerce Clause was included to provide a central authority for regulating commercial interactions across state borders. There is no doubt after *McClung* and *Heart of Atlanta Motel* that the Commerce Clause is also relevant to ending racist practices—even *Lopez* and *Morrison* did not overrule them—however, given the Court's trend away from its earlier deference to congressional Commerce Clause authority, the centrality of the Thirteenth Amendment has become manifest.

7

Contemporary Settings

The Thirteenth Amendment remains at center stage in the struggle against practices tending to restrict autonomy. Its uses extend beyond uprooting only those institutions that existed in the antebellum South. They encompass any barriers reminiscent of involuntary servitude that tend to limit people from participating in and contributing to civic society. These barriers might be erected by states or individuals and might not all be linked to physical coercion.

The use of Confederate symbols on official state logos is one of the remaining badges of slavery. While states no longer formally condone involuntary servitude, some continue to promote the mentality of the Old South by lionizing it on state symbols. Another national problem calling for congressional action is the perpetration of hate crimes. Contemporary peonage in labor settings is a third vestige of slavery. This chapter explores these issues not as an exhaustive analysis of the amendment's applications, but as a starting point for utilizing it to further civil rights reforms.

A. *Confederate Symbols*

1. National Symbolism

States that officially adopt Confederate icons exhibit a nostalgia about the Old South. In evaluating these symbols' expressive role, it is significant to consider how they may affect people's lives. Objects, like flags, that harken back to a racist past reflect at least a tolerance for its ideology.[1] In this section, I take issue with governmental veneration of Confederate symbolism but do not oppose historical displays about the Confederacy, regardless of whether they are located in public museums or on other state property. Nor is my criticism directed at individuals who use those symbols.

Symbols play a role in constructing a worldview. They categorize objects into "accepted types, . . . current patterns . . . [and] standard versions." Social psychologist Howard J. Ehrlich has pointed out that "the codability of a category can be determined by measuring the amount of information about an object that is required to assign it to a category. . . . It can be seen that the greater the codability of a social object, the less information is needed to assign it to a social category." This is especially true when governmental or political entities display identifying symbols.[2]

A symbol's public meaning depends on the context in which it is used. Symbols can connect even disparate elements of people's experiences, filling them with cultural content and internal coping mechanisms. National flags are not merely signals representing information, they also symbolize ideas with value contents. The implication is that images such as burning crosses and Confederate flags have some static definitions related to their historical backgrounds. They are derived from and perpetuate the badges and symbols of servitude, discrimination, oppression, and persecution. Motivating persons through age-old images requires finding symbols that are readily identifiable by their cultural contents. Misethnic symbols borrowed from previous social movements harken back to their fundamental ideals.[3]

Organizations and states choose particular banners because of their signification and power to move others to action. Groups seeking to express a particular message can choose emblems that bring to mind the ideology of bygone eras. The purposeful reintroduction of previously used colors or shapes on a flag or official state seal is filled with meanings that contain past-pointing references. While present circumstances and motivations add to a symbol's meaning, and therefore modify its significance to later situations, its history cannot be eviscerated. Propagandists can use those symbols to carry a traditional message into modern situations. The interpretation of history is often the subject of dispute because historical memory "is always already a selective tradition . . . a present view of a past that best serves the purpose of . . . justifying the status quo." By embracing symbols whose roots are well known, the leaders of governments and political movements are more likely to attract followers. Neophytes can later be convinced of novel ideas, but it is easier to attract their attention with images of a romanticized past. Reuse of traditional symbols can be manipulated to fresh circumstances in order to gain more adherents than the propaganda would have otherwise reached. Tradition gives new movements an air of solemnity and gravity, even when the ideas they express are banal. Such incorporation of past into present is most effective when its discontinuity can be obfuscated and any applicable past practice can be integrated into present-day circumstances.[4]

Officially adopted symbols tend to reinforce political orientations and social outlooks. Symbolism can then enliven preconceptions about the status of political and social actors. Stereotypes are particularly influential when they are displayed under governmental auspices. A banner can be instrumental for marshaling various peoples with otherwise differing interests. Take, for instance, the numerous festivities surrounding the display of flags at a time of war. Rather than concentrate on controversial issues that might cause disunion (like decreased civil liberties required to strengthen state security or the reduction in social spending to increase the military budget), the government rallies citizens behind the national flag. The symbol has differing meanings for each person, but seemingly it forms a common bond among a nation, much of which is ready for action against a real or perceived enemy. The expressive content of a flag is pregnant with meaning about a country's national aspirations, be they communist, democratic, or something else.[5]

An effective symbol, then, changes perspectives, thereby influencing personal attitudes. Persons are thus mobilized, whether it be constructively or destructively, by socially legitimized symbolization. Movements associated with familiar rallying symbols have an added power because they elicit strong feelings through mental images of culturally or regionally significant events. Flags and national icons are not only ornamental, but also evoke strong emotions for national allegiance and political parties, and even among social groups.

The socially constructed meanings behind rallying symbols make it easier for popular leaders to manipulate their followers. Political symbols are not strictly decorative, but are instead designed to lead adherents to commit time and effort for the advancement of various causes. Therefore, governmental incorporation of Confederate symbols can promote the socialization of prejudice. It can also encourage the uninhibited expression of racism through unfair hiring practices and hate crimes. Even though the use of symbols connoting white supremacy does not always lead to overt discrimination—nor is everyone who displays Confederate symbols necessarily prejudiced—displaying exclusionary symbols on state property nevertheless violates the Thirteenth Amendment. Those displays brand blacks as outsiders of the dominant narrative, whose enslavement was defendable on states'-rights grounds. These symbols breed attitudes that might lie dormant during times of political and social tranquility. Yet the danger of racism is that during times of unrest, it offers readily available scapegoats, images, and banners for venting unrelated frustrations.[6]

Symbols can have a practical function; they are not merely aesthetic images. They can be used for strategic social effects, such as the dissemination of political messages. The significance of a governmental symbol is connected to the state and its ethos. One of the Confederacy's key beliefs, as its constitution readily asserted, was the interminable white men's right to own black slaves. The battle flag of the Confederacy, then, carries an exclusionary message that stigmatizes blacks as outsiders of the political community. Official utilization of symbols extolling repressive regimes legitimizes the dogma of hate groups.

Prejudice more readily spreads through a nation when government incorporates symbols that represent racist convictions. The association between police power and bigotry intimidates a large segment of the population and inhibits their free access to social boons, such as freedom to decide where to live, thus infringing on their Thirteenth Amendment autonomy right. Racist symbols, placed conspicuously in public places, can bolster persons resolved to act on prejudiced ideology. Hate groups that have incorporated the same Confederate symbols into logos, such as the KKK and Aryan Nation, are keenly aware that they are joined by some state governments in lauding the Confederate cause and its heroes.[7]

2. Peculiarities of Confederate Symbols

The Confederate states' rallying symbol, the Confederate battle flag, carries the message of the Confederate Constitution, the tenor of which was anti-American. The Thirteenth Amendment grants Congress the power to prohibit states from incorporating it into their official symbols.

In the United States, the Confederate battle flag represents a regime that was devoted to an incongruous brand of freedom. Its demagogy spurred a mass following that disregarded millions of people's right to be self-directed. The highest echelons of society had convinced themselves that the Declaration of Independence granted fundamental rights only to whites and not blacks.[8]

The Confederate Constitution, unlike the U.S. Constitution, explicitly protected black slavery. The Confederate Constitution prohibited the enactment of any law "denying or impairing the right of property in Negro slaves." The Confederate Constitution assured its citizens privileges and immunities, including the right to transport their slaves to other Confederate states without fear that those slaves would be liberated there. Escaped slaves had to be returned to slave owners upon demand. Any new states entering the Confederacy would be granted the right to practice "the institution of Negro slavery."[9]

Unlike the United States, the Confederacy never passed any amendments to abolish slavery. In fact, the language of the Confederate Constitution leaves in doubt whether any rectifying amendment was even permissible. And even if the Confederacy legally could have abolished slavery, it never did. The Confederacy's support for slavery is static: since it no longer exists, there is no way to alter its Constitution's repressive clauses. Whether states in the Confederacy would have ever changed the proslavery provisions is speculative. Therefore, Confederate symbols continue to be interconnected to the repressive institution for which they fought.[10]

The Confederate battle flag and the hero worship of Confederate leaders, through official displays of John Calhoun and Jefferson Davis statues, are also signals indicating support for the racist plantation lifestyle these men supported. The Confederate vice president, Alexander Stephens, explained that the "cornerstone" of his government rested "upon the great truth that the Negro is not equal to the white man; that slavery, subordination to the superior race, is his natural and normal condition." Confederate symbols embrace a message that is very different than the one expressed in national symbols like the Lincoln Memorial, which is a beacon of freedom.[11]

Portraying the leading supporters of slavocracy as liberators besmirches the memory of the thousands of blacks who died during the Middle Passage and contributed to the growth of this country by the uncompensated sweat of their brows. The United States would do better to remove symbols of the Old South from its halls. I do not mean that images of slave owners like James Madison, James Monroe, George Washington, and Thomas Jefferson should be carted away from government property. These men realized and wrote about slavery as an evil, even as they hypocritically owned slaves during their lifetimes. In the end, their ideas, as they came down in documents like the Declaration of Independence and private correspondences, had a sustaining influence on American freedom that their practices did not. However, a statue glorifying an unflinching nullificationist like John Calhoun, who never abandoned the view "that it is a great and dangerous error to suppose that all people are equally entitled to liberty," should find no place in the U.S. Capitol's Great Rotunda, where it is now prominently displayed. This has much the same exclusionary effect as Germany's erecting a statue to Adolf Hitler or Heinrich Himmler would have on Jews, especially those living in Germany. These men were not the heroes of all their subjects. Surely, monuments to these men are not inspirational to the groups they perse-cuted.[12]

The cost of nostalgia about Confederate heroes, who fought to main-tain an inequitable culture, is black alienation. The message to victims is that the government does not consider the Confederacy wholly abom-inable; in fact, it regards it as having redeemable qualities. This is some-what like saying that even though the Nazi attempted genocide of Jews was abhorrent, the swastika can be benignly affixed to official symbols because the Nazis also had some redeeming qualities; after all, they brought Germany out of a recession. The victims of misethnicity cannot view these displays as benign, but only as signs of continued socialized su-premacism. They are stamped with the badge of servitude that violates the Thirteenth Amendment, regardless of whether or not most blacks are thereby affected.[13]

Enacting state legislation to pay for monuments to the apologists of the South's peculiar institution sends an exclusionary social message to black Americans, particularly those living in the communities that adopt confederate symbols. State flags that either incorporate Confederate sym-bols into their flag designs or those states that honor the Confederacy by flying its flag on state grounds create a polity that stigmatizes blacks and countenances discriminatory attitudes toward them. Active state promo-tion of such a message violates the Thirteenth Amendment because it cre-ates a divisive political environment, which is detrimental to civic respect for human rights. Those symbols refer to a heritage in which the white race benefited from a racial hierarchy that undermined the liberty for which the American Revolution was fought. The only freedom they rep-resent is the "freedom of the white Southern plantation owners to bask in economic prosperity at expense of the liberty and freedom of African Americans."[14]

The Confederate flag is a nostalgic symbol for the days when legal in-stitutions reflected an unquestioning commitment to black subordina-tion. Some statements by the framers of the Thirteenth Amendment indicate their belief that its ratification would require Confederate states to tear down St. Andrew's Cross and replace it with Old Glory. In 1864, Mr. Kellogg of New York looked forward to the day when the Union flag would be raised above the rebellious states "and the promise of freedom then be fulfilled." Senator Henry Wilson prophesied that "when the war drums throb no longer and the battle-flags are furled, our absent sons, with the laurels of victory on their brows, will come back to gladden our households. . . . Then the star of the United America . . . will reappear . . . to illume the pathway . . . of struggling humanity." Another congressman contended that the Confederates were "defenders of slavery in arms," and those who defected to the Union lines were coming "to rally around the old flag." New York Representative Elijah Ward, on January 9, 1865, spoke about the ratification of the proposed amendment in terms of winning "back the seceded States under the glorious flag of that Union." Immediately following the Civil War, loyalty to confederate symbols was so great that it was not unheard of for an angry mob to murder a person raising the Stars and Bars.[15]

3. Revival of Confederate Symbolism

The revival of interest in Confederate symbolism during the 1950s occurred contemporaneously with a vocal defense for segregationism. As part of the move opposing civil rights legislation, some Southern leaders, including Governor Fielding Wright of Mississippi, organized the States' Rights Democratic Party, better known as the Dixiecrats. The Dixiecrats purposefully associated the Confederate flag with aggressive white supremacism. They proudly displayed St. Andrew's Cross as a statement of their defiance against laws requiring public school desegregation. The flag was meant as much to intimidate blacks and to galvanize hate groups as it was to voice opposition to social policy.[16]

Several states continue conspicuously to promenade Confederate symbols on their properties. For instance, the Confederate battle flag covers one-third the surface of the Mississippi flag. Mississippi first adopted this design during an era when it enacted laws purposefully drafted to limit black political autonomy. Mississippi emphasizes the public lesson value of its flag, requiring that it be displayed on public buildings, including schools. The history behind the flag's design must be taught in public schools. Lifelong indoctrination is transmitted to students whose curriculum includes studying the pledge of allegiance to the state flag. The pledge instructs them to take "pride in her history and achievements," which, based on the image that it proudly displays, must include the infamous history of slavery. The educational value of the Confederate design promulgates a message that is favorable to the continued racial stratification that the framers to the Thirteenth Amendment had hoped to uproot.[17]

In 2001, Mississippi voters by a 65 percent popular majority reaffirmed their commitment to their secessionist heritage by voting to retain the Confederate symbol on their flag. In 1998 and 2000, the Mississippi Supreme Court found it constitutional for the state to display the Confederate battle flag in public. The court found that having the battle flag on a portion of the state flag does not violate the United States Constitution. In its decisions on this subject, the state supreme court never reflected on whether the Confederate battle flag's exclusionary message violates the Thirteenth Amendment.[18]

The widespread commitment to a symbol full of racist meaning indicates a disregard for the impediments continued racism imposes on blacks who, like other citizens, seek to live meaningful, unfettered lives. The Mississippi flag is a continued badge of servitude that has a detrimental effect on state and national life because it sends a message of disrespect for some of the state's population. It places a wedge between Mississippi whites and blacks by recalling a social vision that was favorable only to whites.

Until recently, two-thirds of Georgia's state flag was covered with St. Andrew's Cross. Unlike Mississippi, Georgian law has no qualms in asserting that part of its state flag design was derived from markings on the "flag of the Confederate States." Georgia evinces the same public commitment as Mississippi to the symbolism of its flag by requiring its exhibition in public and private schools. Georgia statutorily proclaims that no one can prevent the "patriotic" display of the Confederate "flag, standard, color, shield, ensign, or other insignia." The state legislature makes clear its veneration of the Confederacy: "The flags of the Georgia troops who served in the army of the Confederate States, and which have been returned to the state by the United States government, shall be preserved for all time in the capitol as priceless mementos of the cause they represented and of the heroism and patriotism of the men who bore them." The racist implications of this pronouncement are associated with human rights abuses that Confederate states perpetrated prior to the ratification of the abolition amendment and the supremacist practices Confederate states maintained following its ratification.[19]

Georgia adopted its state flag in 1956 as a protest against federal decisions, such as *Brown v. Board of Education,* which forced the South to desegregate. Governor Marvin Griffin, in 1956, expressed his state's activist opposition to civil rights, exclaiming that "there will be no mixing of the races in public schools," and announcing that "the rest of the nation is looking to Georgia for the lead in segregation." In a Court of Appeals case, *Coleman v. Miller,* evaluating the constitutionality of covering part of the Georgian flag with St. Andrew's Cross, the Eleventh Circuit recognized that the symbol was adopted as an expression of white supremacism. The appellant argued that displaying the Georgian flag with its Confederate symbolism violated the Equal Protection Clause of the Fourteenth Amendment. At trial, he testified that the flag placed him in imminent threat of harm and that his friend pled guilty on a parking ticket violation after feeling intimidated by a Confederate flag in the courtroom. This dearth of factual evidence in *Coleman* was insufficient for the court to hold that Georgia's flag had a disproportionate impact on blacks as a group.[20]

Coleman would have been better off arguing that his Thirteenth Amendment rights were violated, rather than posturing from the Equal Protection standpoint. The first section of the Thirteenth Amendment is amenable to a private cause of action arising from the state saddling persons with a badge of servitude and intimidating them from fully enjoying life in Georgia's civil society. From an Equal Protection standpoint, the *Coleman* court relied on that unnecessarily narrow construction of the Fourteenth Amendment adopted by the *Civil Rights Cases.* The *Coleman* court should have considered whether equal protection violations resulted from private injuries, in order to accurately evaluate whether the appellant's claims of private harm were actionable. Moreover, the discriminatory assertions surrounding the adoption of the Georgian state flag, which the court reviewed in its opinion, made clear that retaining a racial hierarchy favorable to whites, and thereby negatively impacting blacks as a group, was the intent of Georgia's legislators in 1956.[21]

After much public pressure, Georgia finally changed the design of its flag. The new state flag still retains the Confederate design, which is now depicted by a small emblem—one among five banners previously flown in Georgia. The retention of the Confederate flag indicates a continued reverence for the Confederacy. The prevalence of this attitude toward the Old South became evident when several months after changing the face of Georgia's flag, the state's legislators passed a resolution encouraging people to fly Confederate flags during Confederate History and Heritage Month.[22]

The continued retention of St. Andrew's Cross on the Georgian flag, no matter how small, is analogous to modern Germany keeping a swastika in the design of its flag. After all, that symbol represents part of Germany's history, just as the Confederate battle flag refers to Georgia's past. While the brutalities that the Confederacy committed and those of the Nazis were in many ways different, both were responsible for enslaving people. Flaunting symbols that inflame racist impulses should have no place in a democracy. Otherwise, the advances in civil liberties become attenuated, weakened by a social psyche that lauds a government whose central tenets included a devotion to stigma and degradation.

South Carolina likewise tried to defuse boycotts against its state by removing the Confederate flag from the State Dome, where it flew between 1962 and 2000. The South Carolina legislature voted to move that flag to the site of a monument for the state's Civil War dead, located on the front lawn of the state capitol grounds. Arkansas' flag has a star on its face expressly dedicated to the Confederacy. For its flag, Tennessee chose the colors of the Confederate states. Texas, too, expresses pride in its slaveholding heritage. Its official state seal, adopted in 1991, reflects Texas's nostalgia for all the flags that have flown above it, including those of Confederate states and the Republic of Texas. Florida and Alabama have flags that incorporate symbols on their flags "reminiscent" of St. Andrew's Cross. Alabama flew the Confederate flag above the state capitol until April 1993, when Governor Jim Folsom ordered that it be taken down. The flag had originally been raised by Alabama governor George Wallace during his "Segregation Forever" campaign.[23]

Confederate symbols have been linked with white supremacism, both before and after ratification of the Thirteenth Amendment. When governments sanction those symbols by placing them in visible public places, they give their referent, the Confederacy, an air of official respectability. By maintaining and paying for the upkeep of Confederate symbols, states reinvigorate the hurdles that still face blacks living in the United States. It also sends a mixed message to children who hear of racial equality and at the same time experience a public iconography dedicated to the Confederacy.

Even the federal government uses symbols that positively portray the defenders of slavery. I was surprised during a 2001 visit to Washington, D.C., while on my first tour of the White House, to find a large-sized painting of President John Tyler hanging in the Blue Room. The painting has been there since 1972. What so amazed me was that this same John Tyler had been elected to the Provisional Congress of the Confederacy, and in 1861 he was elected to the Confederate House of Representatives. He, in fact, was the only former president of the United States to be elected to a Confederate political office. And yet, an image honoring this devotee to the institution of slavery hangs in one of the most prominent places in the United States, there to be viewed and praised by common U.S. citizens and foreign dignitaries alike. That painting, coupled with John Calhoun's impressive statue in the U.S. Capitol rotunda and the many statues of Jefferson Davis around the country evidence a continued callousness about the plight of blacks, throwing governmental support behind the vestiges of slavocracy.[24]

Confederate symbols are associated with an intolerant society, much the same way as are the swastika and hammer and sickle. The inclusion of any of these on modern-day flags is troublesome. While displays about the Confederacy can teach historical lessons, when Confederate symbols are incorporated into government emblems they indicate a persistent social failure to come to terms with the South's violent defense of slavery.

Confederate symbols are divisive to a multiethnic society. Once a label has been attached to an outgroup, it becomes more difficult for persons raised with derogatory preconception to disassociate the stereotype from real individuals. State symbols refer not only to persons who fought bravely for a cause, but also to the ideology behind the cause. Official symbols are standards behind which disparate groups can find consensus. Prior to committing racist injustices on a grand scale, an exclusionary mentality must be in place, conceptually placing some groups outside the pale of full citizenship and regarding them to be unworthy of full legal protections. Confederate flags may reaffirm heroism, but we must ask, heroism for what? The answer is: for the very injustices that the Thirteenth Amendment sought to eradicate.

4. Federal Authority

The elimination of Confederate symbols on state property through federal legislation falls within the ambit of the Thirteenth Amendment because such symbols are the badges of servitude. The First Amendment is not a barrier against legislation prohibiting state use of racist symbols. Protection of political expression in a constitutional republic is meant to guard the speech of individuals who make controversial statements, especially those questioning governmental policies. The right to free speech is not a license for state-sponsored hate speech. In the words of James Madison: "If we advert to the nature of Republican Government, we shall find that the censorial power is in the people over the Government, and not in the Government over the people." The First Amendment does not protect the intentional, governmental promotion of racist speech. Symbolism harkening back to destructive social movements relegates minorities to the place of outsiders. It limits minorities' autonomy, diminishing their ability to participate in politics and governance.[25]

Government speech extends to important public functions such as formulating policies and disseminating information about legislation. However, a state cannot hide behind a First Amendment veil to abridge individuals' constitutional rights. The civil rights gained through the Reconstruction amendments, beginning with the affirmation of freedom in the Thirteenth Amendment, trump government speech. There is a more compelling interest in protecting civil rights than in countenancing state displays of racist symbols. States exist not to perpetuate a hollow bureaucracy proud of its ignominious past, but to assure individual rights and to increase the benefits of the social community. The incorporation of Confederate imagery into state symbolism is a Thirteenth Amendment problem, not one raising First Amendment issues.[26]

States have far more resources than any private persons to express official messages. The states' ability to be heard in the marketplace of ideas is overwhelming compared to the audibility of other voices. States have no authority to use tax revenues for undermining their citizens' liberties. Confederate symbols in places of power send a message that fuses racist rhetoric with governmental legitimizing messages.

If Congress were to enact legislation, pursuant to the second section of the Thirteenth Amendment, prohibiting glorifying displays of Confederate symbols on state and federal property, private parties could seek legal redress for damages and injunctive relief in federal courts. Taken at its word, the Supreme Court in *Jones v. Alfred H. Mayer* regarded Congress's power to protect civil rights, pursuant to the Thirteenth Amendment, to be even more sweeping than its power to regulate interstate commerce. Accordingly, Congress has an interest in prohibiting state uses of Confederate symbols because they play a role in retaining the regressive social stratification that was essential to preserving slavery. Removing those symbols from public places would likely lessen racial tensions and make people more secure in this constitutional republic. If a federal cause of action were created, federal courts could issue injunctions forbidding states from displaying markers of social and political bigotry. Whether a particular object is a badge of servitude would be a question of fact for the trier of fact to decide. If a state symbol were found to further racial discrimination, the government would have to show a compelling state interest for maintaining it, and it is infeasible that any such interest could be formulated.[27]

Litigation of these cases may be costly because they will probably require the use of expert testimony. This is a lesson from *Coleman v. Miller* and *NAACP v. Hunt*, where the Court of Appeals held that personal testimony about how Confederate symbols harmed individuals was insufficient to prove those symbols were unconstitutional.[28] Therefore, besides testimony from private parties, plaintiffs to future litigation will probably have to prove the symbols' social and psychological effects on blacks in particular and on U.S. democracy as a whole. Proving a case may also require testimony from a historian who is aware of the legislative debates surrounding the Thirteenth Amendment and of the Confederacy's legacy.

B. Hate Crimes

Bias crime laws enhance the penalties for wrongdoing motivated by prejudices against a salient group. Such laws predominantly function on the state level. Their provisions and applications differ from state to state as to whom they protect, the behavior they prevent, and the punishments they exact. This situation makes human rights protections dependent on the geography of where an offense was committed. Activists for a national bias crime law argue that current laws are insufficient, but have found jurisdictional objections difficult to gainsay.[29] Detractors of a federal bias crime law argue that neither the Commerce Clause nor the Fourteenth Amendment justify a federal law against bias crimes. They believe that in this, as in almost all other criminal cases, states should be responsible for the policing.[30]

The Thirteenth Amendment's enforcement clause, however, certainly permits Congress to pass laws for policing the incidents of servitude within states. Civil rights scholar Andrew Taslitz has pointed out that "[s]lavery was a massive racial hate crime, sustained by, and consisting of, the many individual hate crimes that were committed against slaves every day."[31] Congress can pass a criminal statute that punishes bias crimes because they infringe on personal freedoms and diminish social welfare.

Several proposed hate crime laws have recently failed to gain congressional passage. The most notable was the Hate Crimes Prevention Act, which would have amended Title 18, section 245, of the United States Code. Among its other provisions, the HCPA would have removed the current jurisdictional requirement that the victim be engaged in a federally protected activity, something that has, over the years, allowed many bias crimes to elude federal authorities.[32] The HCPA would have partly relied on the Commerce Clause to show Congress could pass the law because such crimes affect interstate commerce. Congressional findings of authority were also based on the Thirteenth Amendment because "eliminating racially motivated violence is an important means of eliminating, to the extent possible, the badges, incidents, and relics of slavery and involuntary servitude." Hate-motivated violence, Congress found, "disrupts the tranquillity and safety of communities and is deeply divisive" and is "a relic of slavery."[33] The most recently proposed alteration to the federal bias crimes law, known as the Local Law Enforcement Enhancement Act of 2003, also explicitly recognizes the relevance of the Thirteenth Amendment to protected vulnerable groups from bias crimes. The sponsors of the bill found that "eliminating racially motivated violence is an important means of eliminating, to the extent possible, the badges, incidents, and relics of slavery and involuntary servitude." Yet the LLEEA, like the HCPA, places too much reliance on the Commerce Clause, basing Congress's enforcement power on situations in which the defendant crosses state or national borders or affects interstate or foreign commerce. Even if Congress passes this bill, its commerce limitations will unnecessarily bootstrap federal agents from enforcing the law against criminal cases occurring within states, which Congress's Thirteenth Amendment authority allows it to reach.[34]

The Thirteenth Amendment has been made ever more pertinent to this area of law because, as we saw in the previous chapter, the Supreme

Court recently lessened Congress's Commerce Clause power in *Lopez* and *Morrison*. A new bias crime statute should prevent bias-motivated crimes tending to perpetuate the incidents of servitude through arbitrary attacks that diminish personal choice. Increased security will allow people to move more freely about the country and assert their preferences on where to live and educate children.

Vigorous legislative action is required to prevent bias crimes. Such a law should meet all the rigors of any other criminal legislation (it must require proof beyond a reasonable doubt both in the hearing and sentencing phases, federal prosecution, speedy trial, etc.) and grant federal district courts jurisdiction to try cases. Of course, this would somewhat increase the federal docket, but that is part of the cost of maintaining a free society that is beholden to humanistic principles. I will work out the details of that law elsewhere; here I am interested simply in its legitimacy. The aggravated harm associated with biased motivation and the increased detriment to group relations requires a more severe punishment than would be imposed for the parallel crime alone.

The Federal Bureau of Investigations, which has the statutory responsibility of reporting hate crime incidents, found that bias crimes against Arabs increased in 2001. This was probably linked to misplaced anger against all Arabs following the September 11, 2001, Islamicist terrorist attack on the World Trade Center. Crimes against blacks continued to be the most common bias offenses, and an alarming number of bias crimes were committed against homosexuals and Jews. While the U.S. Supreme Court has never considered whether sexual orientation falls under the Thirteenth Amendment, it has found that the other three groups are protected under laws enacted pursuant to it. Ultimately, any bias crime legislation passed under the amendment must cover all groups who have endured past civil impediments analogous to involuntary servitude. Thus, homosexuals, who continue to have opportunities closed to them through violence motivated by hatred, may fall under this broader definition.[35]

In 2002, there were 9,222 victims of bias crimes. Approximately 50 percent of bias crime victims were targeted because of their race. Of the single-bias race crimes, 67.2 percent were motivated by anti-black sentiments and 19.9 percent were motivated by anti-white sentiments. The victims' religion figured in 18 percent of all bias crimes. About 65.3 percent of religion-motivated bias crimes were committed from anti-Jewish bias, about 10.5 percent from anti-Islamic bias, and about 8 percent from anti-Christian bias. In addition, the victims' sexual orientation figured in 16.4 percent of total single-bias hate crimes, with most of these crimes being committed from an anti-male homosexual motivation.

Groups who have endured lasting discriminations are more likely to be widely stereotyped. Attacks based on stereotypes are unlike ordinary crimes, which tend to be random or arise from personal conflicts. Bias crimes isolate victims because they commonly reflect the intolerant sentiments of many people rather than only the culpability of an individual committing a particular act. Since the perpetrators of prejudice-motivated crimes perpetuate historical wrongs, their injuries spread more broadly and thereby cause more enduring suffering than isolated crimes.[36]

Bias crimes not only hurt a victim directly, they also infringe on the victims' right to travel. Vulnerable groups are forced to be extra cautious about making plans because of the added risks they face. To reduce threats to themselves and their families, many people move from neighborhoods, change jobs, or avoid public places. Bias crimes are distinct from others because of their effects on individuals, the targeted community, and on the overall social stability. Victims are doubly traumatized. They experience stress both because of the underlying crime, which is peculiar to themselves, and for being a part of a historically disempowered group, whose right to enjoy life and achieve their dreams have been coercively stifled.

Persons define themselves, to some greater or lesser extent, by their membership in those groups. Thus, crimes motived by outgroup characteristics hurt persons both materially and existentially. For fear of being victimized, outgroup members sometimes even try to efface their identities, for instance by denying their African ancestry or Jewishness, in order to avoid being associated with the denigrated group. The targeted community understands that the violent conduct is meant to intimidate them and to prevent them from accomplishing their aspirations, whether that means not pursuing professions that have historically been closed to them or choosing not to purchase property in racially or ethnically exclusionary communities. And, on a social level, bias crimes add to intergroup tensions, reducing the degree of trust and cooperation among various groups and thereby diminishing the exchange of creative ideas for improving essential governmental functions, such as the provision of health care and public housing.[37]

Perpetrators intend not only to harm the individuals they attack but also to terrorize a vulnerable community. For example, persons who burn crosses on the lawns of black churches or paint swastikas on synagogues intend to achieve more than the mere act of vandalism. They intend to drive groups of people from their places of worship and neighborhoods. This form of vandalism adopts the imagery that hate groups used to maintain *de facto* slavery in the postbellum South and that Nazis adopted to rally support for the Holocaust. Augmented penalties are warranted for the commission of bias crimes because they harken back to a period of violent domination.

Critics of bias crime legislation often argue that the motive element of the crime, which I think would be an important component of a bias crime law, would violate the defendants' First Amendment rights because they would be punished for their beliefs. Steven G. Gey, for example, states that making motive an important element in bias crime legislation "would permit the government to punish antisocial beliefs and expression without establishing the existence of a threatened harm independent of the one already punished by the original criminal charge."[38]

In many other criminal circumstances, motive, in fact, plays no role in establishing criminal guilt; instead, the prosecutor must prove a requisite mental state. Lawyers distinguish these two by referring to "motive" as the purpose for which a person acts and "mental state" for the state of mind the criminal had during the commission of the act. In reality, such a distinction is more formulaic than it is real. Frederick M. Lawrence's two-tiered model is a better approach. In the context of a law passed under Congress's Thirteenth Amendment powers, the prosecution would first need to prove the *mens rea* of a crime, for instance vandalism, and, second, show that in committing that crime the defendant was motivated by bias associated with arbitrary intrusion into the victims' autonomy.[39]

Other critics, most prominently James B. Jacobs and Kimberly Potter, rhetorically question whether "punishing crimes motivated by politically unpopular beliefs more severely than crimes motivated by other factors itself violates our First Amendment traditions." Their worry is misplaced for two reasons. First, bias crime legislation does not increase punishment for persons who simply express their prejudices; it only increases punishment for those whose purpose was to intrude against a victim's life, liberty, or property interest. Second, even though perpetrating bias crime has some expressive component, First Amendment tradition incorporates the ideals of free speech with those of collateral freedom. Originally the

First Amendment was indifferent to violence perpetrated against blacks, the Constitution having been ratified partly to placate Southern slavocracy. Even after the passage of the First Amendment, governing majorities continued to tyrannize the black minority. The drafters of the Constitution did not incorporate any protections for their slaves' speech rights. Rather, they envisioned the First Amendment as a constraint against the censorship of the "political, scientific, and artistic discourse that they and their class enjoyed." But the Reconstruction amendments changed this dynamic. Both the Thirteenth and Fourteenth Amendments delegitimized bias motivated violence as a constitutional mode of self-expression. Taslitz has correctly pointed out that the constitutional right to free speech does not extend to "racially-subjugating expressive violence."[40]

By passing a bias crime law pursuant to its Thirteenth Amendment, section 2 power, Congress would take an important step to providing the physical security necessary for people to enjoy the boons of freedom. Moreover, such a statute would communicate the national aversion for bigotry and would send the message that bias crimes are a particularly egregious form of wrongdoing. As long as Congress determines that bias crimes are incidents or badges of servitude, it can promulgate a national law to punish their perpetration. Such a law promotes the message that all citizens will be treated decently and that the national government will help promote safety and security. Bias crime law, therefore, can improve intergroup respect.[41]

C. Contemporary Instances of Peonage

The Thirteenth Amendment protects citizens' right to make economically independent decisions. This significance belies the amendment's liberating effect in ending employment dependency. The amendment's provisions cover a broad range of labor issues. Domineering labor hierarchies, whether they are manifested through overt slavery, peonage, or inhumane working conditions, have from early colonial days until the present denied large segments of the population the benefits of freedom. Human rights abuses, such as those committed against persons exploited in the international sex trade, continue to impede the victims' autonomy and to stunt the forward progress of representative democracy. Such practices create economic relations that are more analogous to the aristocracy that the Thirteenth Amendment abolished than to a free market system where economic opportunities are open to all.

Peonage is a labor system directly related to slavery that is still perpetrated against some politically and economically disempowered workers. The Supreme Court's definition of peonage is "a status or condition of compulsory service based on indebtedness of the peon to the master." The practice first appeared in the United States after the acquisition of the New Mexican territory, where it was an established part of Spanish rule.

About the same time, the labor movement began comparing chattel slavery to wage slavery. It adopted the term "white slavery" to describe excessive working hours and oppressive factory conditions. A Philadelphia printer regarded coercive limits on the "option whether to labor or not" to be the "essence of slavery." The General Trades' Union in 1834 spoke against the widening differences between employers and workers to verge "toward a system of vassalage." The Republican Party from its ascent to national politics, in 1856, held "free labor" as a cornerstone of its political ideology. This meant providing wage earners the opportunity for upward economic mobility. And the Republican Party eventually drafted this principle into the Thirteenth Amendment.[42]

From its inception, the Republican party insisted that its vision for labor was colorblind; among those included in their vision were blacks, whites, and persons of Mexican heritage. Radical Republican senator Henry Wilson of Massachusetts explained that slavery degraded white and black working people: "I tell you, sir, that the man who is the enemy of the black laboring man is the enemy of the white laboring man the world over. The same influences that go to keep down and crush down the rights of the poor black man bear down and oppress the poor white laboring man."[43] Representative George Julian, an unflinching advocate of free labor, regarded corporate exploitation as a problem existing side by side with slavery: "The rights of men are sacred, whether trampled down by southern slave-drivers, the monopolists of the soil, the grinding power of corporate wealth, the legalized robbery of a protective tariff, or the power of concentrated capital in alliance with labor-saving machinery."[44]

The Republican critique of the South was not without sincerity because, for all the North's economic disparities, it forbade slavery. However, the circumstances of Northern free blacks were far from the ideals of free labor. As Eric Foner has pointed out, they were the prototypical wage slaves. Even after slavery was abolished in the North, blacks enjoyed a very limited form of economic liberty. In Philadelphia following the 1780 Abolition Act, for example, most of the black workforce was unskilled, with a smattering of educated professionals. Even though blacks were no longer enslaved, they and some of their indigent white counterparts were indentured servants, who were sold at their masters' behest. Some employment remained closed to blacks. For instance, the jobs of white craftsmen, like New York City cartmen, were protected by discriminatory laws. Blacks were also severely hampered from moving westward to take advantage of new economic prospects because many states, like Illinois and Oregon, denied them entrance.[45] After its ratification, the Thirteenth Amendment allowed Congress to end these and similar practices that forced the free labor force into subservience. Government regulations and private prejudices could no longer prevent peoples from working in the field of their choice, traveling freely to find employment, or obstructing them from choosing particular occupations.

Even after 1865, the South continued to use means for circumventing the amendment, including adhesion contracts, share-cropping agreements, child indenture, exclusionary employment practices, and violent protests. The limited successful use of the amendment for litigation during the late nineteenth and early twentieth centuries was in cases prohibiting peonage, which was one of the more prevalent forms of labor abuse. Congress used its Thirteenth Amendment, section 2, power to deal with the problem, passing the Anti-Peonage Act (1867). That statute provides a criminal penalty for holding or returning a person to a condition of peonage.[46]

In 1905, the Supreme Court heard its first case arising under the Anti-Peonage Act, *Clyatt v. United States*, finding that it prevented a creditor from binding a debtor to service. Neither could a law obligate such forced service nor could a debtor enter into a voluntary contract alienating the right to terminate employment. The Court held that the Anti-Peonage Act was constitutional. In *Bailey v. Alabama*, decided in 1911, the Court was even more forthcoming, finding that the Thirteenth Amendment "was a charter of universal civil freedom for all persons, of whatever race, color, or estate, under the flag."

The dominant judicial interpretation of *Clyatt* and *Bailey* has been that they secure workers no more than the right to quit. But this interpretation appears to significantly diminish the import of Supreme Court precedents. In fact, the amendment has a much broader application to worker autonomy. The Court made this abundantly clear in *Bailey*, determining that the amendment made "labor free by prohibiting that control by which the personal service of one man is disposed of or coerced for another's benefit."[47]

This reasoning differs widely from the traditional *laissez-faire* approach. This course of economic judicial making relies too much on an "individualist conception of justice, which exaggerates the importance of property and of contract." The Thirteenth Amendment was a move from the political theory that placed private property above the interest of human liberty. It mandated the federal government's involvement in the free labor movement. Unlike the *Lochner v. New York* era cases, the Thirteenth Amendment contains no illusion that coercive employers have the same bargaining power as the workers they contract for services.[48]

In fact, the Anti-Peonage Act provides a criminal penalty for anyone who "holds or returns any person to a condition of peonage." The U.S. Department of Justice, Civil Rights Division Trafficking in Persons and Worker Exploitation Task Force continues to specialize in prosecuting cases of trafficking and exploitation. These cases typically involve the exploitation of foreign nationals who are fraudulently, coercively, or forcefully brought to the United States. Congressional findings indicated that about 700,000 people a year are internationally trafficked, and most of them are women and children. In the United States, about 50,000 persons are trafficked yearly. Particularly common is the forceful recruitment of women into prostitution, domestic servitude, and sweatshop labor. Once here, employers often withhold wages, confiscate passports, and isolate workers. Most trafficking is from China, Vietnam, Thailand, Mexico, Russia, Ukraine, and the Czech Republic. In one case, women were recruited to be folk dancers, but when they arrived in the United States discovered that they would be forced to perform as exotic dancers. None of the women were permitted to quit their employment nor to keep their earnings. In a case of domestic servitude, an illiterate woman from Bangladesh, Marjina Khalifa, was enslaved as a domestic worker. For six months, her employers forced her to work six days a week, eighteen hours a day. At the end of that period, she was paid $695. The family kept Ms. Khalifa from leaving by confiscating her passport and threatening her with deportation.[49]

Congress recently recognized that the international trafficking market is similar to the institution that the Thirteenth Amendment abolished. In response, it passed the Victims of Trafficking and Violence Protection Act of 2000. Some of the key provisions of VTVPA prohibit persons from knowingly providing or obtaining services through "any scheme, plan, or pattern intended to cause the person to believe that, if the person did not perform such labor or services, that person or another person would suffer serious harm or physical restraint." The act further forbids anyone from knowingly destroying and removing another person's passport or other immigration documents as part of a scheme of peonage or involuntary servitude. This legislation potentially will decrease some of the international slave trade in the United States.[50]

In the past, Supreme Court peonage cases narrowly defined the Thirteenth Amendment's prohibition of involuntary servitude only to circumstances where the employer resorted to the use or threatened use of physical or legal coercion. Proof of psychological coercion was inadequate to establish liability. While the Court's reasoning may have been logical, it was not adequately based on history: some slaves, particular household hands, usually were not beaten or even threatened, but they were nevertheless unable to leave their work. Consequently, VTVPA has created a legal avenue of redress for exploited workers who previously lived in slavelike conditions without any avenues of redress. The VTVPA recognizes that some exploitative employers use subtle coercion that does not necessarily involve violence.[51]

Another pressing concern is the continued exploitation of migrant farmers. Even in the best circumstances, these agriculturalists usually work long hours for little remuneration. In a few cases, migrant workers who are foreign nationals are such an easy prey that exploitative employers either refuse to pay or keep them in a state of peonage. These circumstances typically occur when a farmer entices workers onto his farm promising to provide both a salary and low-cost living quarters. The employer then charges such an exorbitant amount for board and sales items that the employees wind up owing more than their salary. Workers are then forbidden from leaving without repaying the debt.[52]

There have recently been a number of such cases. In a 2001 district court case, three relatives were convicted for running a labor contracting business under the name R & A Harvesting, Inc. The company employed about seven hundred workers, most of whom were in the United States illegally. The company paid the laborers' transportation costs from Arizona to Florida. Then, the conspirators demanded that the workers not leave until they had repaid the $1,000 debt for transportation. Sometimes, the relatives threatened debtors at gunpoint. The court sentenced the men to between ten and twelve years' imprisonment and ordered the forfeiture of their real and personal property. In a similar circumstance, in 1999 Miguel A. Flores provided planters with agricultural workers near Manning, South Carolina. Flores recruited agricultural workers with low educational backgrounds who spoke little or no English. Once they arrived in Manning, the employees worked in remote areas surrounded by woods and marshes. Flores ingratiated himself by extending credit to new employees. They were then forced to work until they repaid the fee for smuggling them into the United States from Mexico. Workers were threatened with death or bodily harm if they chose to leave. The workers were also beaten to maintain discipline. On appeal, the Circuit Court affirmed Flores's six-year conviction.[53]

An earlier case concerned some migrant farmers who worked on Cecil Williams's farm, harvesting his cucumbers, sweet potatoes, and tobacco crops. Williams ran a store and charged workers for their meals, deducting these costs from wages. As a result, each laborer received only a $5.00 check at payday. To make sure that workers could not leave, by night guards were posted at their quarters, and those who did manage to get free were picked up and brought back. Williams even had a house that he used as a jail. These circumstances became known to law enforcement authorities when Williams's guards refused to get medical treatment for one of the workers, who died as a result of heatstroke. A similar situation occurred in a labor camp in Johnston County, North Carolina, where workers also ran up debts, which they were required to pay before they could leave, from retail purchases they made at a camp store. Severe beatings and assaults with firearms were commonly employed to keep workers in check. Prosecutors used Anti-Peonage provisions, as they did in the aforementioned cases, to end these crimes.[54]

With migrant farm abuse, VTVPA and traditional Anti-Peonage remedies are often more effective than ones based on the Commerce Clause. For instance, the Fair Labor Standards Act (the "FLSA") was passed pursuant to Congress's power to regulate interstate commerce. It prevents oppressive child labor, sets an overtime payment standard, and provides a minimum wage standard, all of which sometimes apply to migrant farm worker cases. One limitation of FLSA litigation is that it only protects workers within the context of an employer-employee relationship. Independent contractors do not fall under its provisions. This loophole is an easy one for employers to take advantage of in order to avoid complying with FLSA's substantive provisions. The Anti-Peonage Act makes no such limitation on law suits. Second, since FLSA relies on the Commerce

Clause for its constitutional authority, it is aimed at the incidental harms of slavery rather than making a direct attack on the human rights violation of abridging victims' liberty. Finally, FLSA is not applicable to all cases of peonage. For example, conditions involving enslaved persons who are neither underage nor paid below the minimum wage but whom employers nevertheless prevent from leaving or from whom they forcefully confiscate passports could seek redress under the Anti-Peonage Act or VTVPA but not FLSA.[55]

Another legal alternative for migrant farmers held in peonage is use of the Migrant and Seasonal Agricultural Worker Protection Act. This act, however, suffers from the same weakness as FLSA: it does not protect independent contractors, making it relatively easy for employers not to abide by its terms. Further, § 1803 of the AWPA contains a small business exemption, which exempts any agricultural business that did not employ over five hundred work hours of agricultural labor during any calendar quarter of the preceding year. Moreover, family businesses that exploit agricultural labor are under none of the "WPA's constraints because § 1803 also includes a family business exemption. Neither the Thirteenth Amendment nor the Federal Anti-Peonage Act have any such limitation, making them the more effective tool against servitude-like abuses committed against migrant agricultural workers.[56]

The Thirteenth Amendment ended all forms of labor subjugation just as it abolished involuntary servitude and provided a substantive right to freedom. Where employees' freedoms are limited through coercive means, whether that means limiting their movement, making their pay a practical nullity, or taking away their passports, the Thirteenth Amendment is a powerful alternative for ending the abuses. The amendment offers a way to safeguard freedom on a national level. It continues to be of central importance in the twenty-first century.

Conclusion

The Thirteenth Amendment provides a substantive right to freedom. During the congressional debates of 1864 and 1865, senators and representatives provided invaluable insights into the civil rights reforms they anticipated to effectuate. Their hopes for a free society were dashed by the Supreme Court's initial enfeeblement of the amendment. Only in 1968 did the Court find that the Amendment extended beyond cases of enforced compulsory services.

It contains principles originally established in the Declaration of Independence and then transmitted through the Preamble. Before the amendment's ratification, freedom was a hollow word for many people living and working in the United States. More than any segment of the population, slaves were given the least share of the American dream. But the same can be said in lesser degrees for free blacks, Native American and white indentured servants, and to some extent disempowered wage earners, all of whom were excluded from the enjoyment of the "unalienable right" to be free.

The Thirteenth Amendment created a substantive right to what had before only been a national aspiration. The amendment's second section grants Congress the power to pass any necessary and proper laws to end all remaining vestiges of subservience. That power is virtually plenary, but underused. In some circumstances, its breadth of potential extends beyond section 5 of the Fourteenth Amendment because the Thirteenth Amendment prohibits private and state discriminations. This means that a slew of discriminations that the Fourteenth Amendment does not cover fall under its parameters. Barring persons from public places of accommodations, for instance, is a vestige of slavocracy that is logically connected with the abolition amendment. This does not make it obsolete for courts and litigants to continue using the Commerce Clause for private and the Fourteenth Amendment against public discriminations, but it provides a viable alternative to current civil rights strategies. Further, the Thirteenth Amendment is not subject to the "economic enterprise" interpretation that the Court has recently associated with the Commerce Clause.

The amendment is more than a means for ending coercive domination, it is also one of the most important constitutional provisions requiring the government to assess and act to create laws for a country where everyone may live a good life. The freedom from arbitrary coercion requires that federal government enact laws for a civil society where people can achieve their goals. Those statutes should protect any fundamental liberties like the rights to family autonomy, free travel, and professional decision making.

A variety of limits to a free life harkening back to the days of slavery and involuntary servitude still call for congressional redress. Those I addressed here—state uses of Confederate symbols, hate crimes, and peonage—are only some of the pressing issues that await Thirteenth Amendment activism.

Notes

NOTES TO PREFACE

1. The Thirteenth Amendment consists of two sections. The first section is self-executing, and reads as follows: "Neither slavery nor involuntary servitude, except as a punishment for crime whereof the party shall have been duly convicted, shall exist within the United States, or any place subject to their jurisdiction." The second section grants Congress the power to enact any necessary and proper laws to make its substantive guarantees a reality, not merely a paper promise: "Congress shall have power to enforce this article by appropriate legislation."

2. While the original Constitution contained protections for slavery, it lacked a Bill of Rights, indicating the priority of delegates for adjusting property rights over other civil rights.

3. CONG. GLOBE, 36th Cong., 2d Sess. 1263 (1861); Michael J. Lynch, *The Other Amendments: Constitutional Amendments That Failed*, 93 L. LIBR. J. 303, 306 (2001); Pamela J. Smith, *Our Children's Burden: The Many-Headed Hydra of the Educational Disenfranchisement of Black Children*, 42 HOW. L.J. 133, 156–57 (1999); Erwin Chemerinsky, *Amending the Constitution*, 96 MICH. L. REV. 1561, 1563–64 (1998); Elai Katz, *On Amending Constitutions: The Legality & Legitimacy of Constitutional Entrenchment*, 29 COLUM. J.L. & SOC. PROBS. 251, 276 n. 103 (1996) (listing Ohio, Maryland, & Illinois as the ratifying states of the Corwin proposal). Michael Vorenberg argues that only Maryland's and Ohio's ratifications were valid. FINAL FREEDOM: THE CIVIL WAR, THE ABOLITION OF SLAVERY, & THE THIRTEENTH AMENDMENT 21 n. 43 (2001).

4. CONG. GLOBE, 38th Cong., 1st Sess. 19 (1863); CONG. GLOBE, 38th Cong., 1st Sess. 145 (1864).

5. HORACE WHITE, THE LIFE OF LYMAN TRUMBULL 224 (1913). The ordinance's prohibition of slavery on any land northwest of the Ohio River was counterbalanced by its ominous fugitive slave clause. *Ordinance of 1787, An Ordinance for the Government of the Territory of the United States Northwest of the River Ohio*, art. VI, *reprinted in* THE CONSTITUTIONS OF OHIO 52 (Isaac

F. Patterson ed., 1912). Thomas Jefferson drafted the Northwest Ordinance. On his contradictory statements about slaves and blacks, see ANTHONY F. C. WALLACE, JEFFERSON & THE INDIANS 78–79 (1999).

6. JAMES M. MCPHERSON, BATTLE CRY OF FREEDOM: THE CIVIL WAR ERA 706, 712–13 (1988).

7. Jones v. Alfred H. Mayer Co., 392 U.S. 409, 440–41 (1968). On the state action requirement, see United States v. Harris, 106 U.S. 629, 640 (1882); Civil Rights Cases, 109 U.S. 3, 11 (1883); United States v. Morrison, 529 U.S. 598, 620–21 (2000).

8. Akhil R. Amar & Daniel Widawsky, *Child Abuse as Slavery: A Thirteenth Amendment Response to Deshaney*, 105 Harv. L. Rev. 1359 (1992); Akhil R. Amar, *The Case of the Missing Amendment: R.A.V. v. City of St. Paul*, 106 HARV. L. REV. 124, 157 (1992); Douglas L. Colbert, *Liberating the Thirteenth Amendment*, 30 HARV. C.R.-C.L. L. REV. 1, 12 (1995); Douglas L. Colbert, *Affirming the Thirteenth Amendment*, 1995 ANN. SURV. AM. L. 403 (1995). Colbert has also pointed out the Thirteenth Amendment's applicability to peremptory challenge issues. *Challenging the Challenge: Thirteenth Amendment as a Prohibition against the Racial Use of Peremptory Challenges*, 76 CORNELL L. REV. 1 (1990); Jacobus tenBroek, *Thirteenth Amendment to the Constitution of the United States: Consummation to Abolition & Key to the Fourteenth Amendment*, 39 CAL. L. REV. 171 (1951).

9. *See* DAVID A. J. RICHARDS, CONSCIENCE & THE CONSTITUTION: HISTORY, THEORY, & LAW OF THE RECONSTRUCTION AMENDMENTS 109 (1993) (discussing the relevance of a historically based analysis of the Reconstruction amendments).

10. CONG. GLOBE, 38th Cong., 1st Sess. 1465 (Apr. 7, 1864).

11. PHILIP PETTIT, REPUBLICANISM: A THEORY OF FREEDOM AND GOVERNMENT 5 (1997).

12. DAVID A. J. RICHARDS, CONSCIENCE & THE CONSTITUTION: HISTORY, THEORY, & LAW OF THE RECONSTRUCTION AMENDMENTS 140–41 (1993); David A. J. Richards, *Constitutional Legitimacy & Constitutional Privacy*, 61 N.Y.U. L. Rev. 800, 823 (1986); David A. J. Richards, *Abolitionist Political & Constitutional Theory & the Reconstruction Amendments*, 25 Loy. L.A. L. Rev. 1187, 1200 (1992); GEORGE H. HOEMANN, WHAT GOD HATH WROUGHT: THE EMBODIMENT OF FREEDOM IN THE THIRTEENTH AMENDMENT 159 (1987).

13. United States v. Lopez, 514 U.S. 549, 563 (1995); United States v. Morrison, 529 U.S. 598 (2000).

14. James G. Pope, *The Thirteenth Amendment versus the Commerce Clause: Labor & the Shaping of American Constitutional Law, 1921–1957*, 102 COLUM. L. REV. 1 (2002); James G. Pope, *The First Amendment, The Thirteenth Amendment, & the Right to Organize in the Twenty-First Century*, 51 RUTGERS L. REV. 941 (1999); Lea S. Vandervelde, *The Labor Vision of the Thirteenth Amendment*, 138 U. PA. L. REV. 437 (1989).

NOTES TO CHAPTER I

1. Eric Foner, *The Meaning of Freedom in the Age of Emancipation*, 81 J. Am. Hist. 435, 439 (1994); FORREST MCDONALD, NOVUS ORDO SECLORUM: THE INTELLECTUAL ORIGINS OF THE CONSTITUTION 10 (1985); JAMES MACGREGOR BURNS, THE VINEYARD OF LIBERTY 23–25 (1982).

2. WINTHROP D. JORDAN, WHITE OVER BLACK: AMERICAN ATTITUDES TOWARD THE NEGRO, 1550–1812, at 291 (1968); Thomas J. Davis, *Emancipation Rhetoric, Natural Rights, & Revolutionary New England: A Note on Four Black Petitions in Massachusetts, 1773–1777*, 62 NEW ENG. Q. 248, 250–52, 255, 261 (1989). Lemuel Haynes, a racially mixed minister, wrote that "an *African,* or, in other terms, . . . *a Negro,* . . . *has an undeniable right to his Liberty.*" Quoted in Ruth Bogin, *"Liberty Further Extended": A 1776 Antislavery Manuscript by Lemuel Haynes*, 40 WM. AND MARY Q. 85, 92 (3 ser., 1983).

3. The founders relied on the theories of Enlightenment political philosophers other than John Locke as well. Among their other primary influences were Samuel Pufendorf and Jean-Jacques Burlamaqui. These theorists influenced the U.S. founders and their detractors, Whigs and anti-Federalists, with their republican tradition of freedom. That tradition concentrates on the liberty of persons living in social groups. Of all theorists on this issue, Locke had the greatest residual effect on U.S. foundational law. 1 J. BURLAMAQUI, THE PRINCIPLES OF NATURAL AND POLITIC LAW 69–70 (Thomas Nugent trans., Joseph H. Riley & Co. 7th ed. 1859); SAMUEL PUFENDORF, DE JURE NATURAE ET GENTIUM LIBRI OCTO (1688), *reprinted in* 2 THE CLASSICS OF INTERNATIONAL LAW 56, 158 (C. H. & W. A. Oldfather trans., James Brown Scott ed., 1934). On Locke's influence on revolutionary politics, see HERBERT FRIEDENWALD, THE DECLARATION OF INDEPENDENCE 201 (1904); MORTON WHITE, THE PHILOSOPHY OF THE AMERICAN REVOLUTION (1978); WILLARD S. RANDALL, THOMAS JEFFERSON: A LIFE 205 (1993); JEROME HUYLER, LOCKE IN AMERICA: THE MORAL PHILOSOPHY OF THE FOUNDING ERA (1995); Donald Doernberg, *"We the People": John Locke, Collective Constitutional Rights, and Standing to Challenge Government Action*, 73 Calif. L. Rev. 52, 65 (1985); Terry Kogan, *A New-Federalist Tale of Personal Jurisdiction*, 63 S. CAL. L. REV. 257, 307 (1990); *but see* GARRY WILLS, INVENTING AMERICA: JEFFERSON'S DECLARATION OF INDEPENDENCE 172–75 (1978) (arguing that Locke did not influence writing of the Declaration of Independence).

Locke's thoughts on freedom are as jumbled as the youthful nation that adopted much of his philosophical perspective. Locke's *Two Treatises of Government* are based on the premise that liberty is one of the inalienable rights, government must protect. People enter into a social contract to protect the "Natural Liberty of Man" and "to have only the Law of Nature for his Rule."

Persons "cannot" enslave themselves and thereby part from "[t]his Freedom from Absolute, Arbitrary Power." JOHN LOCKE, TWO TREATISES OF GOVERNMENT 2: § 22–23 (Peter Laslett ed., Mentor Press 1965) (1689). Life and property are also inalienable rights, according to Locke. As between these three rights, government's primary purpose is to protect property. His use of "property" is somewhat complicated because Locke extends the term for life, liberty, and estate; nevertheless, the right to material comfort remains foremost in his view. Indeed, people give up their natural liberty rights when they join political bodies because those sovereign entities can better preserve their property. JOHN LOCKE, TWO TREATISES OF GOVERNMENT 2: §§ 87, 95, 123 (Peter Laslett ed., Mentor Press 3d prtg. 1965) (1689); JAMES P. YOUNG, RECONSIDERING AMERICAN LIBERALISM: THE TROUBLED ODYSSEY OF THE LIBERAL IDEA 27, 32 (1996).

Locke's insistence on the primacy of property has had enormous consequences on American political thought. What is as surprising as it is contradictory is Locke's view on slavery, which American colonial aspirations influenced and which, in turn, he helped mold. Locke thought those slaves who were captured in "a just War" were naturally subject to the "Absolute Dominion and Arbitrary Power of their Masters," meaning that he did not envisage a universal right against arbitrary domination. Enslaved people could not participate in civil society because they "lost their Estates" and "being in the *State of Slavery*" could not possess any property. LOCKE, TWO TREATISES OF GOVERNMENT 2: § 85. His view had a practical component: Locke had a hand in drafting the 1669 Fundamental Constitutions of Carolina, which provided, in part, that regardless of religious affiliation, "[e]very freeman of Carolina shall have absolute power and authority over his negro slave." The document, which was never put into effect, was drafted in Locke's hand, and while this may only mean that he transcribed it, there are other indicators of his support of its provisions. For instance, Locke later became an investor in the Royal African Company, the British trading company that had a monopoly on the African slave trade between 1672 and 1697.

Locke became a primary philosophical source for the colonies both in legitimating natural liberty rights and the supposed natural right to own slaves. So too with other influential philosophers such as Pufendorf, Grotius, Montesquieu, and Hobbes, who also rationalized the institution of slavery. John Locke, *The Fundamental Constitutions of Carolina, in* 10 THE WORKS OF JOHN LOCKE 196 (1823); DAVID B. DAVIS, THE PROBLEM OF SLAVERY IN WESTERN CULTURE 118, 120–21 (1966); JOHN LOCKE, TWO TREATISES OF GOVERNMENT, A CRITICAL EDITION WITH AN INTRODUCTION AND APPARATUS CRITICUS 56 (1960); MAURICE CRANSTON, JOHN LOCKE: A BIOGRAPHY 119–20 (1957); BARON DE MONTESQUIEU, THE SPIRIT OF THE LAWS 238–39 (Thomas Nugent trans., 1949) (1748). This fact alone requires that we look beyond the founding generation's philosophical comprehension to understand the significance of liberty.

The ideas of later philosophers provide the rationale for comprehending autonomy as a human right that does not exclude any group, by virtue of its members' race, ethnicity, nationality, gender, wealth, or position of authority. My brief discussion is meant to show how the definition of freedom I am using helps understand both in what sense everyone has the right to live freely in a constitutional society and the role the Thirteenth Amendment should play to effectuate that circumstance.

4. *See e.g.* LOCKE, JOHN LOCKE, TWO TREATISES OF GOVERNMENT 2: § 22 (Peter Laslett ed., Mentor Press 1963) (1689).

5. *Quoted in* Tania Tetlow, *The Founders & Slavery: A Crisis of Conscience*, 3 LOY. J. PUB. INT. L. 1, 11 (2001) (quoting the excised clause on slave trade that Jefferson wrote for the Declaration of Independence); WILLIAM W. FREEHLING, THE REINTEGRATION OF AMERICAN HISTORY: SLAVERY AND THE CIVIL WAR 26, 187 (1994); JOHN HOPE FRANKLIN, FROM SLAVERY TO FREEDOM 129 (2d ed. 1956); ALEXANDER TSESIS, DESTRUCTIVE MESSAGES: HOW HATE SPEECH PAVES THE WAY FOR HARMFUL SOCIAL MOVEMENTS 43–44 (2002).

6. *Liberty Party Platform of 1844, reprinted in* NATIONAL PARTY PLATFORMS, 1840–1960, at 5–6 (Kirk H. Porter & Donald B. Johnson eds., 2d ed. 1961); *Republican Party Platform of 1860, reprinted in* NATIONAL PARTY PLATFORMS, 1840–1960, at 32 (Kirk H. Porter & Donald B. Johnson eds., 2d ed. 1961); for a similar political, antislavery perspective, see *Free Soil Platform of 1848, reprinted in* NATIONAL PARTY PLATFORMS, 1840–1960, at 13; *Republican Party Platform of 1856, reprinted in* NATIONAL PARTY PLATFORMS, 1840–1960, at 27. After ratification of the Thirteenth Amendment, Congressman Thaddeus Stevens, one of the Republican Party leaders, asserted that the founding fathers "had been compelled to postpone the principles of their great Declaration and wait for their full establishment till a more propitious time." CONG. GLOBE, 39th Cong., 1st Sess. 2459 (May 8, 1866). In this, Stevens was echoing the point of view of various antislavery parties before the Civil War.

7. Dred Scott v. Sandford, 60 U.S. (19 How.) 393, 450, 452 (1857); CONG. GLOBE, 33rd Cong., 1st Sess., Appendix 230 (Feb. 24, 1854).

8. JACOBUS TENBROEK, EQUAL UNDER THE LAW 56 (Collier Books 1965) (1951); Earl M. Maltz, *Fourteenth Amendment Concepts in Antebellum Era*, 32 AM. J.L. HIST. 305, 318–19 (1988) (discussing the proslavery reliance on Fifth Amendment rhetoric).

9. Ironically, George Mason, who delivered one of the most fiery antislavery speech at the Constitutional Convention, never freed his own slaves, bequeathing them to his children. Paul Finkelman, *Intentionalism, the Founders, & Constitutional Interpretation*, 75 TEX. L. REV. 435, 465–66 (1996); Thomas Jefferson, Letter to Jared Sparks (Feb. 4, 1824), *in* 12 THE WORKS OF THOMAS JEFFERSON 334–35 (Peterson, ed., 1984); *see also* 4 ALBERT J. BEVERIDGE, THE LIFE OF JOHN MARSHALL 473–79 (concerning Marshall's support for gradual,

compensated emancipation, and African colonization). James Madison believed in gradual emancipation compensated from national funds since the benefits of liberation would be national. ALLAN NEVINS, ORDEAL OF THE UNION, SELECTED CHAPTERS 19 (1973).

10. WILLIAM W. FREEHLING, THE REINTEGRATION OF AMERICAN HISTORY: SLAVERY AND THE CIVIL WAR 14, 16–18 (1994).

11. Frederick Douglass, *in* VOICES FROM THE GATHERING STORM: THE COMING OF THE AMERICAN CIVIL WAR 40–41 (Glenn M. Linden ed., 2001) (first published in *The North Star*, Apr. 5, 1850); Frederick Douglass, *The Revolution of 1848*, *in* 1 FREDERICK DOUGLASS, THE LIFE AND WRITINGS OF FREDERICK DOUGLASS (Philip S. Foner ed., 1950) (Aug. 1, 1848); Frederick Douglass, *The Constitution & Slavery*, *in* 1 FREDERICK DOUGLASS, THE LIFE AND WRITINGS OF FREDERICK DOUGLASS (Philip S. Foner ed., 1950) (first published in *The North Star*, Mar. 16, 1849).

12. Frederick Douglass, *The Constitution & Slavery*, *in* 1 FREDERICK DOUGLASS, THE LIFE AND WRITINGS OF FREDERICK DOUGLASS (Philip S. Foner ed., 1950) (first published in *The North Star*, Mar. 16, 1849); Paul Finkelman, *The Color of Law*, 87 Nw. U. L. Rev. 937, 971 (1993); WILLIAM M. WIECEK, SOURCES OF ANTISLAVERY CONSTITUTIONALISM, 1760–1848, at 62–63 (1977); HENRY H. SIMMS, A DECADE OF SECTIONAL CONTROVERSY, 1851–1861, at 33–34 (Greenwood Press 1978) (1942); P. L. Rainwater, *Economic Benefits of Secession: Opinions in Mississippi in the 1850's*, 1 J. S. HIST. 459, 467 (1935); Harvey Wish, *The Revival of the African Slave Trade in the United States, 1856–1860*, 27 MISS. VALLEY HIST. REV. 569, 569, 572 (1941); Frederick Douglass, *Farewell Speech to the British People*, *in* 1 FREDERICK DOUGLASS, THE LIFE AND WRITINGS OF FREDERICK DOUGLASS (Philip S. Foner ed., 1950) (Mar. 30, 1847).

13. MARK E. BRANDON, FREE IN THE WORLD: AMERICAN SLAVERY & CONSTITUTIONAL FAILURE 54 (1998).

14. Thurgood Marshall, *Reflections on the Bicentennial of the United States Constitution*, 101 HARV. L. REV. 1, 2 (1987).

15. JAMES OAKES, SLAVERY & FREEDOM: AN INTERPRETATION OF THE OLD SOUTH 40 (1990); DAVID M. POTTER, THE IMPENDING CRISIS, 1848–1861, at 455 (1976).

16. JAMES F. RHODES, HISTORY OF THE UNITED STATES FROM THE COMPROMISE OF 1850 TO THE FINAL RESTORATION OF HOME RULE AT THE SOUTH IN 1877, at 344–45 (1892); KENNETH M. STAMPP, THE PECULIAR INSTITUTION: SLAVERY IN THE ANTE-BELLUM SOUTH 426 (1956).

17. THOMAS JEFFERSON, NOTES ON THE STATE OF VIRGINIA 162–63 (William Peden ed., 1982) (1782); FANNY KEMBLE, JOURNAL OF A RESIDENCE ON A GEORGIAN PLANTATION IN 1838–1839, at 57–58 (1864); *Narrative of James Curry*, LIBERATOR, Jan. 10, 1840, *reprinted in* SLAVE TESTIMONY: TWO

CENTURIES OF LETTERS, SPEECHES, INTERVIEWS, AND AUTOBIOGRAPHIES 132–33 (John W. Blassingame ed., 1977).

18. Allen C. Guelzo, *Apple of Gold in a Picture of Silver: The Constitution & Liberty, in* THE LINCOLN ENIGMA 125–26 (Gabor Boritt ed., 2001); 1 ALLAN NEVINS, ORDEAL OF THE UNION 449–50 (1947); Mary Beth Norton *et al.*, *Afro-American Family in the Age of Revolution, in* SLAVERY & FREEDOM IN THE AGE OF THE AMERICAN REVOLUTION 186–87 (Ira Berlin & Ronald Hoffman eds., 1983); FREDERIC BANCROFT, SLAVE-TRADING IN THE OLD SOUTH 197, 199, 202, 208 (1931); 1 FREDERICK L. OLMSTED, COTTON KINGDOM: A TRAVELLER'S OBSERVATIONS OF COTTON & SLAVERY IN THE AMERICAN SLAVE STATES 51–52 (1861); ETHAN A. ANDREWS, SLAVERY AND THE DOMESTIC SLAVE TRADE IN THE UNITED STATES 147 (1836).

19. JAMES OAKES, SLAVERY & FREEDOM: AN INTERPRETATION OF THE OLD SOUTH 4–5 (1990).

20. JOHN HOPE FRANKLIN, FROM SLAVERY TO FREEDOM 216–17 (2d ed. 1956).

21. JOHN C. HURD, THE LAW OF FREEDOM AND BONDAGE IN THE UNITED STATES 20–21, 23–24, 40–41, 43 (Ohio); 177 (Iowa); 217 (Oregon) (Negro University Press 1968) (1862) (providing the text of state laws and constitutions); FRANK U. QUILLIN, THE COLOR LINE IN OHIO: A HISTORY OF RACE PREJUDICE IN A TYPICAL NORTHERN STATE 20–24, 38–40, 88 (1913) (Ohio); ALLAN NEVINS, ORDEAL OF THE UNION, SELECTED CHAPTERS 38–40, 44 (1973) (Illinois, Iowa, and Indiana); HENRY H. SIMMS, A DECADE OF SECTIONAL CONTROVERSY, 1851–1861, at 127–29 (1942) (New England states, Ohio, Illinois, Iowa, and Oregon); N. DWIGHT HARRIS, THE HISTORY OF NEGRO SERVITUDE IN ILLINOIS & OF THE SLAVERY AGITATION IN THAT STATE, 1719–1864, at 235–36, 239 (1904) (Illinois).

22. Allan Nevins, *The Ordeal of the Union, in* THE CAUSES OF THE AMERICAN CIVIL WAR 224, 238–39, 241 (Edwin C. Rozwenc ed., 2d ed. 1972).

23. Act of March 6, 1820, ch. 22, § 8, 3 Stat. 545, 548 (1820).

24. ANNALS OF CONG., 15th Cong., 2d Sess. 1166, 1169–70, 1214–15, 1272–73 (1819); LAWRENCE R. TENZER, THE FORGOTTEN CAUSE OF THE CIVIL WAR: A NEW LOOK AT THE SLAVERY ISSUE 89 (1997); GLOVER MOORE, THE MISSOURI CONTROVERSY 1819–1821, at 54 (1953).

25. Thomas Jefferson, *Kentucky Resolution, in* THE LIFE & WRITINGS OF THOMAS JEFFERSON 287 (S. E. Forman ed., 2d ed. 1900) (1798); WILLIAM W. FREEHLING, PRELUDE TO CIVIL WAR: THE NULLIFICATION CONTROVERSY IN SOUTH CAROLINA, 1816–1836, at 258, 292, 296–97 (1965); SAMUEL F. BEMIS, JOHN QUINCY ADAMS & THE UNION 260 (Easton Press 1984) (1956).

26. Eugene Portlette Southall, *Arthur Tappan & the Anti-Slavery Movement*, 15 J. NEGRO HIST. 162, 189, 191 (1930); Louis Fuller, *Liberalism, Anti-Slavery,*

& the Founders of the Independent, 27 NEW ENG. Q. 291, 296 (1954); Letter from James G. Birney to Gerrit Smith (Mar. 21, 1835), *in* 1 LETTERS OF JAMES GILLESPIE BIRNEY, 1831–1857, at 190 (Dwight L. Dumond ed., 1938); William L. Garrison, LIBERATOR, Feb. 10, 1865, at 2; THEODORE D. WELD, AMERICAN SLAVERY AS IT IS: TESTIMONY OF A THOUSAND WITNESSES, *in* SLAVERY IN AMERICA: THEODORE WELD'S AMERICAN SLAVERY AS IT IS 5 (Richard O. Curry & Joanna Dunlap Cowden eds., F. E. Peacock Publishers, Inc., 1972) (1839); Letter from Theodore D. Weld to Ray Potter (June 11, 1836), *in* 1 LETTERS OF THEODORE DWIGHT WELD, ANGELINA GRIMKÉ WELD, & SARAH GRIMKÉ, 1822–1844, at 309–10 (Gilbert H. Barnes & Dwight L. Dumond eds., 1934); 1 WILLIAM W. FREEHLING, THE ROAD TO DISUNION: SECESSIONISTS AT BAY, 1776–1854 (1990).

27. Cong. Globe 31st Cong., 1st Sess. 99–100 (Jan. 4, 1850) (Senator Foote's proposal on organizing three territories without restrictions on slavery); CONG. GLOBE 31st Cong., 1st Sess. 86 (Dec. 27, 1849) (Senator Douglas proposing a Utah constitution with a petition for admission into the Union); CONG. GLOBE 31st Cong., 1st Sess. 165–66 (Jan. 16, 1850) (Senator Thomas Hart proposing to split Texas into two with slavery forbidden in the Northern and Northwestern portions of the territory); CONG. GLOBE 31st Cong., 1st Sess. 166–71 (Jan. 16, 1850) (Senator Foote on the creation of a new slave state, Jacinto, out of a portion of Texas); CONG. GLOBE 31st Cong., 1st Sess. 103 (Jan. 4, 1850) (Senator Mason proposing a more effective fugitive slave law).

28. *Reminiscences of Washington*, 47 ATLANTIC MONTHLY 234, 241 (Feb. 1881).

29. GEORGE TICHNOR CURTIS, LIFE OF DANIEL WEBSTER 397–98 (1870). The Compromise of 1850 consisted of five statutes providing that (1) California be admitted with a free constitution; (2) the territorial governments gained from Mexico be established without any preconditions on slavery, the borders between Texas and New Mexico be reconciled, and the federal government take on any *bona fide* debt Texas incurred before annexation; (3) the Utah territory be organized; (4) slavery trade, but not slavery, be abolished in the District of Columbia; (5) a Fugitive Slave Act be passed. *See generally* HOLMAN HAMILTON, PROLOGUE TO CONFLICT: THE COMPROMISE OF 1850 (1964).

30. WILLIAM E. DODD, JEFFERSON DAVIS 118–19 (1907); 1 BEN PERLEY POORE, PERLEY'S REMINISCENCES OF SIXTY YEARS IN THE NATIONAL METROPOLIS 377–78 (1886); 1 JAMES F. RHODES, HISTORY OF THE UNITED STATES FROM THE COMPROMISE OF 1850 TO THE FINAL RESTORATION OF HOME RULE AT THE SOUTH IN 1877, at 193–94 (1892).

31. Allen Johnson, *The Constitutionality of the Fugitive Slave Acts*, 31 YALE L.J. 161, 168–69 (1921–22); DWIGHT L. DUMOND, ANTISLAVERY ORIGINS OF THE CIVIL WAR IN THE UNITED STATES 65 (1939).

32. Prigg v. Pennsylvania, 41 U.S. (16 Pet.) 539 (1842); JAMES M. McPHER-

SON, BATTLE CRY OF FREEDOM: THE CIVIL WAR ERA 78–79 (1988). LAWRENCE R. TENZER, THE FORGOTTEN CAUSE OF THE CIVIL WAR: A NEW LOOK AT THE SLAVERY ISSUE 83 (1997). Tenzer also lists eleven states, including Pennsylvania, which had laws protecting personal liberty and outlawing kidnapping prior to the *Prigg* decision. 2 JAMES F. RHODES, HISTORY OF THE UNITED STATES FROM THE COMPROMISE OF 1850 TO THE FINAL RESTORATION OF HOME RULE AT THE SOUTH IN 1877, at 73–74 (1892).

33. ARTHUR CHARLES COLE, THE IRREPRESSIBLE CONFLICT 1850–1865, at 268 (1934).

34. MARION G. McDOUGALL, FUGITIVE SLAVES 112–15 (1969) (giving the text of the Fugitive Slave Act of 1850).

35. Ableman v. Booth, 62 U.S. (21 How.) 506, 524, 526 (1858).

36. WENDELL P. & FRANCIS J. GARRISON, WILLIAM LLOYD GARRISON, 1805–1879, at 412 (1889).

37. Abraham Lincoln, *Speech at Peoria, Illinois*, Oct. 16, 1854, *in* 2 THE COLLECTED WORKS OF ABRAHAM LINCOLN 254–55 (Roy P. Basler ed., 1953); CONG. GLOBE, 36th Cong., 1st Sess., 559 (Jan. 23, 1860); CONG. GLOBE, 36th Cong., 1st Sess., 915 (Feb. 29, 1860).

38. The text of the *Appeal* is found in CONG. GLOBE, 33d Cong., 1st Sess. 281–82 (Jan. 30, 1854); CONG. GLOBE, 33d Cong., 1st Sess., Appendix 447 (Mar. 28, 1854) (Yates); CONG. GLOBE, 33d Cong., 1st Sess., Appendix 155 (Feb. 17, 1854) (Seward); CONG. GLOBE, 33rd Cong., 1st Sess., Appendix 268 (Feb. 24, 1854) (Sumner).

39. Dred Scott v. Sandford, 60 U.S. (19 How.) 393, 450, 590–94 (1857); DAVID M. POTTER, THE IMPENDING CRISIS, 1848–1861, at 267–68, 275–78, 292–93 (1976). The relationship between Taney and Curtis deteriorated because of their differing views of the case. On a small scale, the justices' brake reflected the rift *Dred Scott* caused in the country at large. 1 BENJAMIN R. CURTIS, A MEMOIR OF BENJAMIN ROBBINS CURTIS 211 *et seq.* (1879).

40. REPUBLICAN PARTY PLATFORM OF 1860, *reprinted in* NATIONAL PARTY PLATFORMS, 1840–1960, at 32 (Kirk H. Porter & Donald B. Johnson eds., 2d ed. 1961); Eric Foner, *Politics, Ideology, & the Origins of the American Civil War*, *in* A NATION DIVIDED: PROBLEMS & ISSUES OF THE CIVIL WAR & RECONSTRUCTION 30 (George M. Fredrickson ed., 1975).

41. *A Declaration of the Causes Which Induced the Secession of South Carolina*, *in* SLAVERY AS A CAUSE OF THE CIVIL WAR 29–30 (Edwin C. Rozwenc ed., 1963).

NOTES TO CHAPTER 2

1. STATUTES AT LARGE, TREATIES, AND PROCLAMATIONS OF THE UNITED STATES OF AMERICA 589–92 (George P. Sanger ed., Dec. 5, 1859–Mar. 3, 1863)

(July 1862); 12 *Id.* 597, 599; IRA BERLIN ET AL., SLAVES NO MORE: THREE ESSAYS ON EMANCIPATION & THE CIVIL WAR 40–41 (1992).

2. Abraham Lincoln, *Speech at Peoria, Illinois, in Reply to Senator Douglas, in* THE WORKS OF ABRAHAM LINCOLN 191 (Arthur B. Lapsley ed., 1905) (Oct. 16, 1854); Abraham Lincoln, *Appeal to Border State Representatives to Favor Compensated Emancipation, in* 5 THE COLLECTED WORKS OF ABRAHAM LINCOLN 317–19 (Roy P. Basler *et al.* ed., 1953) (July 12, 1862); Abraham Lincoln, *Address on Colonization to a Deputation of Negroes, in* 5 THE COLLECTED WORKS OF ABRAHAM LINCOLN 371–73 (Roy P. Basler *et al.* ed., 1953) (first published in *New York Tribune*, Aug. 15, 1862).

3. Gideon Welles, *The History of Emancipation*, 14 THE GALAXY 842–43 (Dec. 1872); SALMON P. CHASE, INSIDE LINCOLN'S CABINET: THE CIVIL WAR DIARIES OF SALMON P. CHASE 149–52 (David Donald ed., 1954).

4. In pertinent part the proclamation states:

[A]ll persons held as slaves within any State or designated part of a State the people whereof shall then be in rebellion against the United States shall be then, thenceforward, and forever free; and the executive government of the United States, including the military and naval authority thereof, will recognize and maintain the freedom of such persons and will do no act or acts to repress such persons, or any of them, in any efforts they may make for their actual freedom.

President Abraham Lincoln, *The Emancipation Proclamation, reprinted in* THE UNIVERSAL ALMANAC 62 (John W. Wright ed., 2000); David P. Tedhams, *The Reincarnation of "Jim Crow": A Thirteenth Amendment Analysis of Colorado's Amendment 2*, 4 TEMP. POL. & CIV. RTS. L. REV. 133, 137 (1994); Kenneth L. Karst, *The Pursuit of Manhood & the Desegregation of the Armed Forces*, 38 UCLA L. REV. 499, 512 (1991); Ira Berlin, *Emancipation & Its Meaning, in* UNION & EMANCIPATION: ESSAYS ON POLITICS & RACE IN THE CIVIL WAR ERA 109 (David W. Blight & Brooks D. Simpson eds., 1997).

5. DONALD G. NIEMAN, PROMISES TO KEEP: AFRICAN-AMERICANS & THE CONSTITUTIONAL ORDER, 1776 TO THE PRESENT 55 (1991); JOHN HOPE FRANKLIN, FROM SLAVERY TO FREEDOM 278–79 (2d ed. 1956); JAMES M. MCPHERSON, THE STRUGGLE FOR EQUALITY 118–19, 125–26 (2d ed. 1995); CONG. GLOBE, 38th Cong., 1st Sess. 536 (Feb. 9, 1864).

6. *See Concerning the Loyalty of Slaves in North Louisiana in 1863: Letters from John H. Ransdell to Governor Thomas O. Moore, Dated 1863*, 14 LOUISIANA HIST. Q. 487, 494, 501 (1931); Don E. Fehrenbacher, *Only His Stepchildren: Lincoln & the Negro, in* A NATION DIVIDED: PROBLEMS & ISSUES OF THE CIVIL WAR & RECONSTRUCTION 51 (George M. Fredrickson ed., 1975); Frederick Douglass, Speech at Cooper Institute, February 1863, *quoted in* LINCOLN ON BLACK AND WHITE 133, 135 (Arthur Zilversmit ed., 1971).

7. CONG. GLOBE, 38th Cong., 1st Sess. 19 (Dec. 14, 1863); *Id.* at 21; *Id.* at 521 (Feb. 8, 1864); *Id.* at 522; *Id.* at 1483 (Apr. 8, 1864).

8. CONG. GLOBE, 38th Cong., 1st Sess. 2995 (June 15, 1864—ninety-three yeas; sixty-five nays; and twenty-three representatives not voting); CONG. GLOBE, 38th Cong., 2d Sess. 531 (Jan. 31, 1865—119 yeas, 56 yeas, and 8 representatives not voting); ISAAC N. ARNOLD, THE LIFE OF ABRAHAM LINCOLN 346 (1887).

9. *See e.g.* CONG. GLOBE, 38th Cong., 2d Sess. 222 (Jan. 11, 1865) (stating that preamble is the repository of moral and political truths that should guide the formulation to any amendments); CONG. GLOBE, 38th Cong., 1st Sess. 1199 (Mar. 19, 1864).

10. *See* CONG. GLOBE, 38th Cong., 1st Sess. 104 (Jan. 6, 1864) (statement of Senator Garrett Davis of Kentucky on state rights); *Id.* at 2962 (June 15, 1864); *Id.* at 2991 (June 15, 1864).

11. CONG. GLOBE, 38th Cong., 1st Sess. 1483, 1488, 1490 (Apr. 8, 1864); Xi Wang, *Black Suffrage & the Redefining of American Freedom, 1860–1870*, 17 CARDOZO L. REV. 2153, 2177 (1996); MICHAEL VORENBERG, FINAL FREEDOM: THE CIVIL WAR, THE ABOLITION OF SLAVERY, & THE THIRTEENTH AMENDMENT 106–7 (2001).

12. F. Michael Higginbotham, *Affirmative Action in the United States & South Africa: Lessons from the Other Side*, 13 TEMP. INT'L & COMP. L.J. 187, 191 (1999); Corinne E. Anderson, *A Current Perspective: The Erosion of Affirmative Action in University Admissions* 32 AKRON L. REV. 181, 191 n.48 (1999). Congress created the first section of the Fourteenth Amendment when it became evident that the Thirteenth Amendment was not clear enough to unequivocally direct states to grant blacks civil equality. *See* John Marquez Lundin, *The Law of Equality before Equality Was the Law*, 49 SYRACUSE L. REV. 1137, 1181 (1999).

13. JAMES F. RHODES, HISTORY OF THE UNITED STATES FROM THE COMPROMISE OF 1850 TO THE FINAL RESTORATION OF HOME RULE AT THE SOUTH IN 1877, at 227–28 (1892); WILLIAM L. RICHTER, AMERICAN RECONSTRUCTION, 1862–1877, at 374 (1996); W. R. BROCK, AN AMERICAN CRISIS 1865–1867, at 76–79 (1963).

14. *See* CONG. GLOBE, 38th Cong., 2d Sess. 265 (Jan. 13, 1865).

15. James F. Rhodes, 5 HISTORY OF THE UNITED STATES FROM THE COMPROMISE OF 1850, 541–44 (1904); 1 JAMES G. BLAINE, TWENTY YEARS OF CONGRESS: FROM LINCOLN TO GARFIELD WITH A REVIEW OF THE EVENTS WHICH LED TO THE POLITICAL REVOLUTION OF 1860, at 25 (1884); WILLIAM L. RICHTER, AMERICAN RECONSTRUCTION, 1862–1877, at 371–72 (1996).

16. Thaddeus Stevens's proposal appears at CONG. GLOBE, 40th Cong., 1st Sess. 203 (Mar. 19, 1867); CONG. GLOBE, 39th Cong., 1st Sess. 74 (Dec. 18,

1865); Lance S. Hamilton, Note, *Ethnomiseducationalization: A Legal Challenge*, 100 YALE L.J. 1815, 1820 n.18 (1991). Under President Andrew Johnson's Proclamation of Amnesty, former slave owners reclaimed the plots of land that had been given to blacks by personnel from the Union Army and Freedmen's Bureau. Derrick Bell, *The Civil Rights Chronicles*, 99 HARV. L. REV. 4, 9 n.20 (1985).

17. CONG. GLOBE, 38th Cong., 1st Sess., Appendix 118 (Apr. 15, 1864).

18. Jones v. Alfred H. Mayer, 392 U.S. 409 (1968); CONG. GLOBE, 38th Cong., 1st Sess. 1439–40 (Apr. 6, 1864); CONG. GLOBE, 38th Cong., 1st Sess. 1324 (1864) (emphasis added). Many antebellum Southern states made it a criminal offense to educate blacks. James W. Fox Jr., *Citizenship, Poverty, & Federalism: 1787–1882*, 60 U. PITT. L. REV. 421, 487 (1999).

19. ALLAN NEVINS, ORDEAL OF THE UNION 412–13 (1947); W. R. BROCK, AN AMERICAN CRISIS 1865–1867, at 83–84 (1963).

20. *See e.g.* DAVID COOPER, A SERIOUS ADDRESS TO THE RULERS OF AMERICA, ON THE INCONSISTENCY OF THEIR CONDUCT RESPECTING SLAVERY (1783); CONG. GLOBE, 27th Cong., 2nd Sess., Appendix 337–38 (1842); CONG. GLOBE, 33rd Cong., 1st Sess., Appendix 230 (Feb. 24, 1854).

21. CONG. GLOBE, 38th Cong., 2d Sess. 142 (Jan. 6, 1865); *Id.*, 38th Cong., 1st Sess. 2955 (June 14, 1864).

22. CONG. GLOBE, 38th Cong., 2d Sess. 142 (Jan. 6, 1865); CONG. GLOBE, 38th Cong., 1st Sess. 1199 (Mar. 19, 1864); *Id.* at 2955 (June 14, 1864); *Id.* at 2990 (June 15, 1864); *Id.* at 1324 (Mar. 28, 1864); *Id.* at 1439 (Apr. 6, 1864). Even a Democratic supporter of the proposal, Representative James S. Rollins, who was himself a Missouri slave owner, used the Declaration to argue that race was an accidental circumstance, and all men are created equal. CONG. GLOBE, 38th Cong. 2d Sess. 260 (Jan. 13, 1865).

23. CONG. GLOBE, 38th Cong., 2d Sess. 154 (Jan. 7, 1865). Likewise, during the Senate debate Reverdy Johnson, who had represented one of Dred Scott's owners, argued that had the framers known how much sectional strife would result from slavery, they would have opposed it. N.Y. TIMES, Apr. 6, 1864, at 1; CONG. GLOBE, 38th Cong., 1st Sess. 2978 (June 15, 1864); *Id.* at 2983 (June 15, 1864).

24. CONG. GLOBE, 38th Cong., 2d Sess. 244 (Jan. 12, 1865).

25. CONG. GLOBE, 39th Cong., 1st Sess. 1151 (Mar. 2, 1866).

26. CONG. GLOBE, 39th Cong., 1st Sess. 1151 (Mar. 2, 1866); *Id.* at 39 (Dec. 13, 1865); CONG. GLOBE, 39th Cong., 1st Sess. 46 (Dec. 13, 1865).

27. CONG. GLOBE, 38th Cong., 1st Sess. 1439 (Apr. 6, 1864); CONG. GLOBE, 38th Cong., 2d Sess. 154 (Jan. 10, 1865).

28. Jacobus tenBroek, *Thirteenth Amendment to the Constitution of the United States: Consummation to Abolition & Key to the Fourteenth Amend-*

ment, 39 CAL. L. REV. 171, 175–76 (1951); CONG. GLOBE, 38th Cong., 1st Sess. 2982 (June 15, 1864); CONG. GLOBE, 38th Cong., 2nd Sess. 179 (Jan. 9, 1865).

29. CONG. GLOBE, 38th Cong., 2d Sess. 257 (Jan. 13, 1865); Representative James Rollins, *quoted in* ISAAC N. ARNOLD, THE LIFE OF ABRAHAM LINCOLN, 358–59 (1887); *Id.* at 469; Abraham Lincoln, *Annual Message to Congress, in* 8 THE COLLECTED WORKS OF ABRAHAM LINCOLN 149 (Roy P. Basler *et al.* ed., 1953) (Dec. 6, 1864); NOAH BROOKS, WASHINGTON IN LINCOLN'S TIME 141–42 (Herbert Mitgang ed., Rinehart & Company, Inc. 1958) (1895); 7 *Reply to the Committee Notifying Lincoln of His Renomination,* 7; *Id.* at 380 (June 9, 1864); LAWANDA & JOHN H. COX, POLITICS, PRINCIPLE, & PREJUDICE 1865–1866, 30 (1969).

30. ISAAC N. ARNOLD, THE HISTORY OF ABRAHAM LINCOLN, & THE OVERTHROW OF SLAVERY 587–88 (1866).

31. MICHAEL VORENBERG, FINAL FREEDOM: THE CIVIL WAR, THE ABOLITION OF SLAVERY, & THE THIRTEENTH AMENDMENT 212–27 (2001); 2 DOCUMENTARY HISTORY OF THE CONSTITUTION OF THE UNITED STATES OF AMERICA, 1786–1870, at 520–635 (1894); Howard D. Hamilton, *The Legislative & Judicial History of the Thirteenth Amendment,* 9 NAT'L B.J. 26, 44 (1951); 3 FRANCIS N. THORPE, CONSTITUTIONAL HISTORY OF THE UNITED STATES 158–232 (1901); CONG. GLOBE, 38th Cong., 2d Sess. 588 (Feb. 4, 1865); Abraham Lincoln, *Last Public Address, in* 8 THE COLLECTED WORKS OF ABRAHAM LINCOLN 404–5 (Roy P. Basler *et al.* ed., 1953) (Apr. 11, 1865).

32. Executive Proclamation Appointing William W. Holden Provisional Governor of North Carolina, May 29, 1865, *in* E. MCPHERSON, POLITICAL MANUAL FOR 1866 & 1867, at 11 (1867); Robert L. Kohl, *The Civil Rights Act of 1866, Its Hour Come Round at Last:* Jones v. Alfred H. Mayer Co., 55 VA. L. REV. 272, 276–77 (1969), *citing to* C. Wood, A Complete History of the United States 344 (1941); *Journal of the Mississippi Constitutional Convention of 1865,* 137–38, *quoted in* Howard D. Hamilton, *The Legislative & Judicial History of the Thirteenth Amendment,* 9 NAT'L B.J. 26, 45–46 (1951); 39th Cong., 1st sess., *Ex. Doc. No. 26,* 254, *cited in* Howard D. Hamilton, *The Legislative & Judicial History of the Thirteenth Amendment,* 9 NAT'L B.J. 26, 45–46 (1951); HERMAN BELZ, A NEW BIRTH OF FREEDOM: THE REPUBLICAN PARTY & FREEDMEN'S RIGHTS, 1861 TO 1866, at 159 (1976); 2 DOCUMENTARY HISTORY OF THE CONSTITUTION OF THE UNITED STATES OF AMERICA, 1786–1870, at 636–37 (1894).

33. WEEVILS IN THE WHEAT: INTERVIEWS WITH VIRGINIA EX-SLAVES 58–59 (Perdue *et al.* eds., 1976); LEON F. LITWACK, BEEN IN THE STORM SO LONG: THE AFTERMATH OF SLAVERY 373–74 (1979); PETER KOLCHIN, AMERICAN SLAVERY, 1619–1877, at 216–18 (1993).

34. PETER KOLCHIN, AMERICAN SLAVERY, 1619–1877, 216–22 (1993); WHITELAW REID, AFTER THE WAR: A TOUR OF THE SOUTHERN STATES, MAY 1,

1865–May 1, 1866, at 387, 389 (1866); 5 AMERICAN SLAVE: A COMPOSITE AUTOBIOGRAPHY 153 (George Rawick ed., 1972).

35. WILLIAM PRESTON VAUGHN, SCHOOLS FOR ALL: THE BLACKS & PUBLIC EDUCATION IN THE SOUTH, 1865–1877, 1 (1974); ERIC FONER, RECONSTRUCTION: AMERICA'S UNFINISHED REVOLUTION, 1863–1877 96 (Perennial Library 1989) (1988); Letter from Edmonia G. Highgate to M. E. Strieby, Dec. 17, 1866, *in* WE ARE YOUR SISTERS: BLACK WOMEN IN THE NINETEENTH CENTURY 298–99 (Dorothy Sterling ed., 1984).

36. PETER KOLCHIN, AMERICAN SLAVERY, 1619–1877, at 63–67, 220–21 (1993); LEON F. LITWACK, BEEN IN THE STORM SO LONG: THE AFTERMATH OF SLAVERY 191, 237–38 (1979); PETER KOLCHIN, FIRST FREEDOM: THE RESPONSES OF ALABAMA'S BLACKS TO EMANCIPATION AND RECONSTRUCTION 65–67 (1972); James Hammond, *Letter to an English Abolitionist, in* THE IDEOLOGY OF SLAVERY 191–92 (1981); AVERY CRAVEN, RECONSTRUCTION: THE ENDING OF THE CIVIL WAR 119–20 (1969).

37. HERBERT G. GUTMAN, BLACK FAMILY IN SLAVERY & FREEDOM, 1750–1925, at 207–9 (1976).

38. Eventually states curtailed these rights. South Carolina infringed on them when they became the first state to make a separate criminal court system for blacks and whites. RANDALL KENNEDY, RACE, CRIME, & THE LAW 85 (1997).

39. Andrew E. Taslitz, *Slaves No More! The Implications of the Informed Citizen Ideal for Discovery before Fourth Amendment Suppression Hearings*, 15 GA. ST. U. L. REV. 709, 747 (1999); DONALD G. NIEMAN, TO SET THE LAW IN MOTION: THE FREEDMEN'S BUREAU & THE LEGAL RIGHTS OF BLACKS, 1865–68, at 98 (1979); CONG. GLOBE, 39th Cong., 1st Sess. 111 (1865).

40. Slaughterhouse Cases, 83 U.S. (16 Wall.) 36, 70 (1872); RANDALL KENNEDY, RACE, CRIME, & THE LAW 84–85 (1997); AVERY CRAVEN, RECONSTRUCTION, THE ENDING OF THE CIVIL WAR 119–20 (1969).

41. CONG. GLOBE, 39th Cong., 1st Sess. 39 (1865); W. E. B. DU BOIS, BLACK RECONSTRUCTION 167 (Kraus-Thomson Org. Ltd. 1973) (1935); DAVID OSHINSKY, WORSE THAN SLAVERY (1996).

42. Congressmen disseminated their constituents' testimonials. For example, a woman in New Orleans wrote her congressman about persons who shot at her because they opposed her educating black children. CONG. GLOBE, 39th Cong., 1st Sess. 95 (Dec. 20, 1865). A "loyal Texan" wrote that any abolitionists who traveled to the South ran the risk of being shot and that juries were unlikely to convict violent perpetrators. *Id.*

43. HERBERT SHAPIRO, WHITE VIOLENCE AND BLACK RESPONSE: FROM RECONSTRUCTION TO MONTGOMERY 5 (1988); ERIC FONER, A SHORT HISTORY OF RECONSTRUCTION 189–90 (1990).

44. CONG. GLOBE, 39th Cong., 1st Sess. 322–23 (Jan. 19, 1866); CONG. GLOBE, 39th Cong., 1st Sess. 503–4 (Jan. 30, 1866).

45. CONG. GLOBE, 38th Cong., 2d Sess. 589 (Feb. 4, 1865); S. 427, 38th Cong. (1865).

46. CONG. GLOBE, 39th Cong., 1st Sess. 111 (Dec. 21, 1865); Senate Bill No. 345, Senate Joint Resolution No. 28, *cited in* Howard D. Hamilton, *The Legislative & Judicial History of the Thirteenth Amendment,* 9 NAT'L B.J. 26, 59 (1951); CONG. GLOBE, 39th Cong., 1st Sess. 472 (Jan. 29, 1866); ch. 31, 14 Stat. 27 (1866) (Civil Rights Act of 1866); ch. 86, 14 Stat. 50 (1866) (Slave Kidnaping Act); ch. 187, 14 Stat. 546 (1867) (Peonage Act of 1867); ch. 27, 14 Stat. 385 (Act of Feb. 5, 1867, expanding the scope of habeas corpus statutes).

47. JAMES Z. GEORGE, THE POLITICAL HISTORY OF SLAVERY IN THE UNITED STATES 114 (Negro University Press 1969) (1915).

48. CONG. GLOBE, 39th Cong., 1st Sess. 211–12 (Jan. 12, 1866); Civil Rights Act, 14 Stat. 27 (1866).

49. Letter from Jacob D. Cox to Andrew Johnson, *in* 10 THE PAPERS OF ANDREW JOHNSON 287 (Paul H. Bergeron *et al.* ed., 1992) (Mar. 22, 1866). The note from Seward is filed under date of March 27, 1866, in ANDREW JOHNSON PAPERS Reel 21 and at the Library of Congress; ANDREW JOHNSON, 8 COMPILATION OF THE MESSAGES & PAPERS OF THE PRESIDENTS 3603 (James D. Richardson ed., 1897).

50. DONALD G. NIEMAN, PROMISES TO KEEP: AFRICAN-AMERICANS & THE CONSTITUTIONAL ORDER, 1776 TO THE PRESENT 69 (1991).

NOTES TO CHAPTER 3

1. W. R. BROCK, AN AMERICAN CRISIS 1865–1867, at 33–34 (1963); ERIC FONER, RECONSTRUCTION: AMERICA'S UNFINISHED REVOLUTION 1863–1877, at 421 (Perennial Library 1989) (1988); 13 DELAWARE HISTORY 64–65 (1968); Cong. Globe, 41st Cong., 3d Sess. 1039 (Feb. 7, 1871); Walter J. Fraser, Jr., *William Henry Ruffner & the Establishment of Virginia's Public School System, 1870–1874,* 79 VA. MAG. OF HIST. & BIOGRAPHY 272–74 (1971).

2. KENNETH M. STAMPP, THE ERA OF RECONSTRUCTION, 1865–1877, at 189 (1966).

3. James M. McPherson, *Coercion or Conciliation? Abolitionists Debate President Hayes' Southern Policy,* 39 NEW ENG. Q. 476 (1966) (Dec. 17, 1874); WILLIAM GILLETTE, RETREAT FROM RECONSTRUCTION 1869–1879, at 238 (1979).

4. *Quoted in* VINCENT P. DE SANTIS, REPUBLICANS FACE THE SOUTHERN QUESTION: THE NEW DEPARTURE YEARS, 1877–1897, at 100–101 (1959).

5. G. Sidney Buchanan, *The Quest for Freedom: A Legal History of the Thirteenth Amendment,* 12 HOUSTON L. REV. 357, 367 (1974).

6. United States v. Rhodes, 27 F. Cas. 785 (C.C.D. Ky. 1866). Kentucky did not extend the right of blacks to testify against whites until 1872. Victor B.

Howard, *The Black Testimony Controversy in Kentucky, 1866–1872*, 58 J. NEGRO HIST. 140, 141, 146–48, 165 (1973). The Kentucky supreme court held that the Thirteenth Amendment did nothing more than free slaves, but gave them no social or political rights. Bowlin v. Commonwealth, 65 Ky. (2 Bush) 5 (1867).

7. Ex parte Warren, 31 Tex. 143 (1868) (finding that the Civil Rights Act of 1866 gave blacks the equal right to testify in judicial proceedings); Kelley v. State, 25 Ark. 392 (1869) (finding unconstitutional an Arkansas law forbidding blacks to testify against white persons); People v. Washington, 36 Cal. 658 (1869) (affirming the federal government's authority to enforce the rights of various ethnic groups to give evidence and finding that the Civil Rights Act affirmed peoples equality before the laws); Bowlin v. Commonwealth, 65 Ky. (2 Bush) 5 (1867) (holding that the Civil Rights Act of 1866 violated state sovereignty and therefore rejecting Congress's authority to strike a state law that forbade blacks from testifying against whites).

8. The Judiciary Act of 1789 required justices to ride to circuits and hear cases there. Act of Mar. 2, 1793, ch. 22, 1 Stat. 333. The Circuit Court of Appeals Act of 1891 ended the practice. Act of Mar. 3, 1891, ch. 517, 26 Stat. 826. In re Turner, 24 F. Cas. 337, 339 (C.C.D. Md. 1867) (No. 14,247).

9. United States v. Given, 25 F. Cas. 1324, 1325 (C.C.D. Del. 1873).

10. Blyew v. United States, 80 U.S. (13 Wall.) 581 (1872).

11. *Murder: Particulars of the Late Tragedy in Lewis County*, LOUISVILLE (KY.) DAILY J., Sept. 9, 1868, at 3.

12. *Blyew*, 80 U.S. at 581, *citing* 1860 Ky. Acts, § 1, ch. 104, vol. 2, at 470. The law only permitted blacks and Native Americans to act as "competent witnesses" in civil suits to which the only parties were blacks or Native Americans. *Blyew*, 80 U.S. at 581.

13. Slaughterhouse Cases, 83 U.S. (16 Wall.) 36 (1873); JOHN HART ELY, DEMOCRACY AND DISTRUST 24 (1980); John Harrison, *Reconstructing the Privileges or Immunities Clause*, 101 YALE L.J. 1385, 1387 (1992) ("the main point of the clause is to require that every state give the same privileges and immunities of state citizenship—the same positive law rights of property, contract, and so forth—to all of its citizens"). See Saenz v. Roe, 526 U.S. 489, 501–4 (1999) (determining that the privileges and immunities of state citizenship are protected by U.S. Const. Art. IV, § 2, cl. 1).

14. United States v. Cruikshank, 25 F. Cas. 707 (C.C.D. La. 1874) (No. 14,897), aff'd, 92 U.S. 542 (1875); PETER IRONS, A PEOPLE'S HISTORY OF THE SUPREME COURT 202–3 (1999); ROBERT KACZOROWSKI, THE POLITICS OF JUDICIAL INTERPRETATION: THE FEDERAL COURTS, DEPARTMENT OF JUSTICE AND CIVIL RIGHTS, 1866–1876, at 176 (1985); ERIC FONER, RECONSTRUCTION: AMERICA'S UNFINISHED REVOLUTION 1863–1877, at 530–31 (Perennial Library

1989) (1988); TED TUNNELL, CRUCIBLE OF RECONSTRUCTION: WAR, RADICAL-ISM, AND RACE IN LOUISIANA, 1862–1877, at 189–93 (1984).

15. Arthur Kinoy, *The Constitutional Right of Negro Freedom*, 21 RUTGERS L. REV. 387 (1967).

16. The full name of the Civil Rights Act of 1875 was "An act to protect all citizens in their civil and legal rights." 18 Stat. 335; JAMES M. MCPHERSON, THE ABOLITIONIST LEGACY: FROM RECONSTRUCTION TO THE NAACP 16, 20–21 (2d ed. 1995); WILLIAM B. HESSELTINE, ULYSSES S. GRANT, POLITICIAN 368–71 (1935).

17. Sumner and Butler are quoted in ERIC FONER, A SHORT HISTORY OF RE-CONSTRUCTION 226 (1990).

18. George Curtis is quoted in JAMES M. MCPHERSON, THE ABOLITIONIST LEGACY: FROM RECONSTRUCTION TO THE NAACP 18 (1975).

19. Civil Rights Act of 1875, ch. 114, §§ 1–2, 18 Stat. 335.

20. Civil Rights Cases, 109 U.S. 3 (1883).

21. Hall v. Decuir, 95 U.S. 485 (1877).

22. FRANK B. LATHAM, THE GREAT DISSENTER: JOHN MARSHALL HARLAN 1833–1911, at 27 (1970); LOREN P. BETH, JOHN MARSHALL HARLAN 74 (1992).

23. Alan F. Westin, *John Marshall Harlan & the Constitutional Rights of Negroes: The Transformation of a Southerner*, 66 YALE L.J. 637, 698 (1957).

24. MALVINA S. HARLAN, SOME MEMORIES OF A LONG LIFE, 1854–1911, at 112–13 (2002).

25. Alan F. Westin, *John Marshall Harlan & the Constitutional Rights of Negroes: The Transformation of a Southerner*, 66 YALE L.J. 637, 681–82 (1957).

26. *See* Heart of Atlanta Motel, Inc. v. United States, 379 U.S. 241, 250–51 (1964); Katzenbach v. McClung, 379 U.S. 294, 303–4 (1964). If not for Justice Bradley's majority decision in the *Civil Rights Cases*, the Court could have prohibited public place discrimination on the basis of basic liberty interests rather than commercial interests.

27. *Address to the Colored People of Louisville*, ARK. MANSION, Oct. 27, 1883, at 1; *Arkansaw [sic] Dispatch*, ARK. MANSION, Nov. 17, 1883, at 1; *Washington Letter*, ARK. MANSION, Dec. 1, 1883, at 1; *Galveston News*, ARK. MANSION, Nov. 17, 1883, at 1.

28. Owen Fiss, *Troubled Beginnings of the Modern State, 1888–1910*, in 8 HISTORY OF THE SUPREME COURT OF THE UNITED STATES 352–85 (1993) (discussing Supreme Court case law about the time of *Plessy v. Ferguson*); *Plessy v. Ferguson*, 163 U.S. 537 (1896).

29. CHARLES A. LOFGREN, THE PLESSY CASE: A LEGAL-HISTORICAL INTER-PRETATION 41 (1987).

30. The Louisiana legislature found authority to enact the 1890 law from a

case mentioned earlier in this chapter. *Hall v. DeCuir*, decided in 1877, had found a very different Louisiana law unconstitutional, one that required the desegregation of public conveyance.

31. *Homer Adolph Plessy*, AFRO-AMERICAN ALMANAC, http://www.toptags .com/aama/bio/men/hplessy.htm (visited on Mar. 9, 2003).

32. *A Fool's Errand. By One of the Fools*, Electronic Version http://docsouth.unc.edu/church/tourgee/tourgee.html 163, 172–74 (visited Mar. 9, 2003).

33. C. Vann Woodward, *The Case of the Louisiana Traveler, in* QUARRELS THAT HAVE SHAPED THE CONSTITUTION 164 (John A. Garraty ed., 1987); CHARLES A. LOFGREN, THE PLESSY CASE: A LEGAL-HISTORICAL INTERPRETATION 34 (1987); John M. Wisdom, *Plessy v. Ferguson—100 Years Later*, 53 WASH. & LEE L. REV. 9, 14 (1996).

34. Brook Thomas, *Plessy v. Ferguson & the Literary Imagination*, 9 CARDOZO STUD. L. & LITERATURE 45, 46 (1997); PETER IRONS, A PEOPLE'S HISTORY OF THE SUPREME COURT 225–26 (1999); *Ex Parte Plessy*, 11 So. 948 (1892).

35. LOFGREN, *supra*, at 50; John C. Duncan, Jr., *The American "Legal" Dilemma: Colorblind I/Colorblind II—The Rules Have Changed Again: A Semantic Apothegmatic Permutation*, 7 VA. J. SOC. POL'Y & L. 315, 384 (2000); *Brief for Plaintiff in Error* at 7–8, Plessy v. Ferguson, 163 U.S. 537 (1896), *reprinted in* 13 LANDMARK BRIEFS AND ARGUMENTS OF THE SUPREME COURT OF THE UNITED STATES 10–11 (Brief of S. F. Phillips and F. D. McKenney).

36. Howard D. Hamilton, *The Legislative & Judicial History of the Thirteenth Amendment*, 9 NAT'L B.J. 26, 75 (1951).

37. United States v. Morris, 125 F. 322 (E.D. Ark. 1903).

38. Hodges v. United States, 203 U.S. 1 (1906), *rev'd*, Jones v. Alfred H. Mayer Co., 392 U.S. 409 (1968).

39. The majority was explicit in its abandonment of African Americans to the whim of the several states, and couched its argument in benevolent terms: "It is for us to accept the decision, which declined to constitute them wards of the nation or leave them in a condition of alienage where they would be subject to the jurisdiction of Congress, but gave them citizenship, doubtless believing that thereby in the long run their best interests would be subserved, they taking their chances with other citizens in the states where they should make their homes." *Id.* at 20.

40. Corrigan v. Buckley, 271 U.S. 323 (1926).

41. James G. Pope, *The Thirteenth Amendment versus the Commerce Clause*, 102 COLUM. L. REV. 1, 3–4 (2002).

42. The decision's far-reaching potentials have not gone uncriticized. Some early criticisms include Louis Henkin, *The Supreme Court—1967 Term—Foreword: On Drawing Lines*, 82 HARV. L. REV. 63, 82–87 (1968), and Sam J. Ervin, Jr., Jones v. Alfred H. Mayer Co.: *Judicial Activism Run Riot*, 22 VAND. L. REV. 485 (1969).

43. *See* Tobias B. Wolff, *The Thirteenth Amendment & Slavery in the Global Economy*, 102 COLUM. L. REV. 973, 1040 (2002) (stating that since the Thirteenth Amendment "contains no state action requirement, the Amendment both restrains the actions of the State and regulates the activities of private individuals").

44. The Supreme Court case may be found at Jones v. Alfred H. Mayer Co., 392 U.S. 409, 440–41 (1968). I take some facts from Jones v. Mayer, 379 F.2d 33, 35 (8th Cir. 1967).

45. After the Civil War, former Confederate leaders were permitted to join governmental bodies even though many of them continued to maintain racist attitudes. ERIC FONER, A SHORT HISTORY OF RECONSTRUCTION 213, 248 (1990) (discussing how at the end of Reconstruction Southern governments emerged committed to black subordination).

46. The dissent recognized that the Fair Housing Act, Title VIII of the Civil Rights Act of 1968, was passed too late for the Joneses to rely on it, but thought further housing discrimination should fall under it. The Fair Housing Act was amended in 1974, Pub. L. No. 93-265, 88 Stat. 84 (codified in 25 U.S.C. § 1341 [1994]), to include sex discrimination.

47. Runyon v. McCrary, 427 U.S. 160 (1976).

48. Tillman v. Wheaton-Haven Recreation Assn., 410 U.S. 431 (1973).

49. Johnson v. Railway Express Agency, 421 U.S. 454 (1975). Title VII ordinarily requires an aggrieved party to file a charge with the EEOC within a 180 days of the alleged unlawful employment practice or three hundred days after the unlawful practice if the aggrieved party filed a discrimination complaint in a state or local agency. 42 USCA s 2000e-5(11) (2003). Filing a Title VII action with the EEOC does not toll the statute of limitations on § 1981 claims. *Johnson*, 421 U.S. at 465. The Court further bolstered *Johnson* in a footnote to a 1994 case. *See* Rivers v. Roadway Express, Inc., 511 U.S. 298, 304 n.3 (1994) ("[e]ven in the employment context, § 1981's coverage is broader than Title VII's, for Title VII applies only to employers with 15 or more employees, see 42 U.S.C. s 2000e(b), whereas § 1981 has no such limitation"). Alexander v. Fulton County Georgia, 207 F.3d 1303, 1346 (11th Cir. 2000) (applying a two-year personal injury statute of limitations to both § 1981 and § 1983 claims); Rogers v. Barkin, 20 Fed.Appx. 630, 631, 2001 WL 1218413, at 1 (9th Cir.) (unpublished opinion) (finding that Nevada's two-year personal injury statute of limitations applied to § 1981 claims); Thomas v. Denny's, Inc., 111 F.3d 1506, 1514 (7th Cir. 1997) (recognizing that based on damages awarded for a § 1981 claim were limited by the state's two personal injury statutes). Some courts have also applied three-year personal injury statutes of limitations. *See e.g.* King v. American Airlines, Inc., 284 F.3d 352, 356 (2d Cir. 2002); Carney v. American University, 151 F.3d 1090, 1096 (D.C. Cir. 1998). The Eleventh Circuit even found a four-year statute of limitations

applied to a § 1981 claim. Baker v. Gulf & Western Indus., Inc., 850 F.2d 1480, 1481 (11th Cir. 1988).

50. Patterson v. McLean Credit Union, 491 U.S. 164 (1989).

51. U.S.C. Section 1981.

52. The Fifth Circuit noted in 1997 that "while it is true that suits attacking the 'badges and incidents of slavery' must be based on a statute enacted under § 2, suits attacking compulsory labor arise directly under prohibition of § 1, which is 'undoubtedly self-executing without any ancillary legislation.'" Channer v. Hall, 112 F.3d 214, 217 n.5. Likewise, the Fourth Circuit stated that "while Congress may arguably have some discretion in determining what kind of protective legislation to enact pursuant to the thirteenth amendment, it appears that the amendment's independent scope is limited to the eradication of the incidents or badges of slavery and does not reach other acts of discrimination." Washington v. Finlay, 664 F.2d 913, 927 (1981).

53. Palmer v. Thompson, 403 U.S. 217 (1971).

54. Washington v. Davis, 426 U.S. 229, 242–43 (explaining the Court's holding in *Palmer*). The Court's reliance on the City's good faith purposes for closing the pools was dubious. *See* Paul Brest, Palmer v. Thompson: *An Approach to the Problem of Unconstitutional Legislative Motive*, 1971 Sup. Ct. Rev. 95, 95.

55. *Memphis v. Greene*, 451 U.S. 100 (1981).

NOTES TO CHAPTER 4

1. Michael Vorenberg, Final Freedom: The Civil War, the Abolition of Slavery, & the Thirteenth Amendment 90–92, 191 (2001).

2. Isaac N. Arnold, The History of Abraham Lincoln, & the Overthrow of Slavery 590 (1866); Herman Belz, A New Birth of Freedom: The Republican Party & Freedmen's Rights, 1861–1866, at 133–34 (1976).

3. Ch. 31, 14 Stat. 27 (1866); An Act to Establish a Bureau for the Relief of Freedmen and Refugees, ch. 90, 13 Stat. 507 (1865); An Act to Continue in Force and to Amend "An Act to Establish a Bureau for the Relief of Freedmen and Refugees," ch. 200, 14 Stat. 173 (1866). While slavery was outlawed throughout the North, many persons and entities located there continued abridging black rights. *See* Leon F. Litwack, North of Slavery 64–187 (1961) (discussing political, educational, and economic repressions in the North). Abolitionists did make significant inroads against discriminatory practices in the North. By 1861, New England had numerous desegregated public schools, but many private schools continued to be segregated. *See* James McPherson, Struggle for Equality 223, 227–28 (1964). Thanks to Charles Sumner and Sojourner Truth, the public transportation system in Washington, D.C., was desegregated in 1865. *See id.* at 230. There was even a move toward black suffrage in states like Rhode Island, where a state constitutional provision that allowed

for only white manhood suffrage was revoked. *See id.* at 223. And by 1860 blacks throughout New England, except Connecticut, enjoyed equal political rights. *See id.* at 223.

4. GEORGE H. HOEMANN, WHAT GOD HATH WROUGHT: THE EMBODIMENT OF FREEDOM IN THE THIRTEENTH AMENDMENT 160 (1987).

5. Aviam Soifer, *Status, Contract, and Promises Unkept,* 96 YALE L.J. 1916, 1938 (1987) (concluding that the Thirteenth Amendment granted Congress the power to "protect fundamental rights throughout the nation"); Howard D. Hamilton, *The Legislative & Judicial History of the Thirteenth Amendment,* 9 NAT'L B.J. 26, 80 (1951).

6. John Locke, one of the natural-rights theory's chief proponents, drafted a constitution for the South Carolina colony in 1669. The provisions of that constitution indicate that even Locke viewed natural rights in a light that excluded blacks from their enjoyment. His South Carolina constitution contains provisions against interference with black slavery. Jonathan A. Bush, *Free to Enslave: The Foundations of Colonial American Slave Law,* 5 YALE J.L. & HUMAN. 417, 421 (1993); *see* Paul Finkelman, *The Crime of Color,* 67 TUL. L. REV. 2063, 2075 (1993) (discussing the development of South Carolina's slave laws from Locke's constitution to later emendations).

7. Larry J. Pittman, *Physician Assisted Suicide in the Dark Ward: The Intersection of the Thirteenth Amendment & Health Care Treatments Having Disproportionate Impacts on Disfavored Groups,* 28 SETON HALL L. REV. 774, 858–59 (1998). For a detailed discussion on fundamental rights, *see* ALEXANDER TSESIS, DESTRUCTIVE MESSAGES: HOW HATE SPEECH PAVES THE WAY FOR HARMFUL SOCIAL MOVEMENTS ch. 10 (2002). Fundamental rights are those that persons have before joining political societies. Among them is the liberty of movement and expression. Persons give up some of these natural or essential rights when they form a state to increase social welfare; however, civil laws do not violate fundamental rights. *See* Philip A. Hamburger, *Natural Rights, Natural Law, & the American Constitutions,* 102 YALE L.J. 907, 908–9 (1993).

8. Jones v. Alfred H. Mayer Co., 392 U.S. 409, 445 (1968) (Douglas, J., concurring) (stating that while slavery has been abolished as an institution, "badges of slavery" were still prevalent).

9. *See* HAROLD M. HYMAN & WILLIAM M. WIECEK, EQUAL JUSTICE UNDER LAW: CONSTITUTIONAL DEVELOPMENT 1835–1875, at 391–92 (1982) (discussing the usefulness of an organic concept of liberty for understanding the Thirteenth Amendment).

NOTES TO CHAPTER 5

1. Olmstead v. United States, 277 U.S. 438, 478 (1928) (Brandeis, J., dissenting).

2. The American Anti-Slavery Society's 1833 Declaration of Sentiments was an early example. http://www.etsu.edu/cas/history/docs/antislavery.htm (visited Apr. 7, 2003); WILLIAM E. CHANNING, SLAVERY 47–48, 51 (Arno Press 1969) (3d ed. 1835).

3. DAVID A. J. RICHARDS, CONSCIENCE & THE CONSTITUTION: HISTORY, THEORY, & LAW OF THE RECONSTRUCTION AMENDMENTS 98–99 (1993); Abraham Lincoln, *Speech at Peoria, Illinois, in Reply to Senator Douglas, in* THE WORKS OF ABRAHAM LINCOLN 209 (Arthur B. Lapsley ed., 1905) (Oct. 16, 1854).

4. THE DECLARATION OF INDEPENDENCE para. 2 (U.S. 1776). The Declaration recognizes the existence of three natural rights: life, liberty, and the pursuit of happiness. ALLEN C. GUELZO, ABRAHAM LINCOLN: REDEEMER PRESIDENT 224 (1999); 1 BERNARD BAILYN ET AL., THE GREAT REPUBLIC: A HISTORY OF THE AMERICAN PEOPLE 576–77 (4th ed. 1992).

5. CONG. GLOBE, 38th Cong., 2d Sess. 200 (1865) (Representative Farnsworth).

6. CONG. GLOBE, 38th Cong., 2d Sess. 200 (Jan. 10, 1865); CONG. GLOBE, 38th Cong., 1St Sess. 1482 (Apr. 8, 1864); W. R. BROCK, AN AMERICAN CRISIS: CONGRESS & RECONSTRUCTION 1865–1867, at 267–68 (1963); STAUGHTON LYND, CLASS CONFLICT, SLAVERY, AND THE UNITED STATES CONSTITUTION 185–213 (1967) (concerning the question of slavery and the Constitutional Convention); Charles L. Black, Jr., *Further Reflections on the Constitutional Justice of Livelihood*, 86 COLUM. L. REV. 1103, 1103 (1986); CONG. GLOBE, 38th Cong., 1st Sess. 142 (1864) (Godlove S. Orth of Indiana) (arguing for a practical application via the Thirteenth Amendment of natural-rights principles).

7. CONG. GLOBE, 39th Cong., 1st Sess. 1152 (Mar. 2, 1866).

8. CONG. GLOBE, 39th Cong., 1st Sess. 5 (Dec. 4, 1865).

9. CONG. GLOBE, 38th Cong., 1st Sess. 2990 (1864).

10. CONG. GLOBE, 39th Cong., 1st Sess. 588 (Feb. 1, 1866); CONG. GLOBE, 39th Cong., 1st Sess. 41 (Dec. 13, 1865).

11. *See* James E. Fleming, *Fidelity to Our Imperfect Constitution*, 65 FORDHAM LAW REVIEW 1335, 1350–51 (1997) (discussing the importance of aspirational principles to constitutional fidelity).

12. *See* SANFORD LEVINSON, CONSTITUTIONAL FAITH 139 (1988) ("the conflict of 1861, among other things, divides our constitutional history, and some historians refer to the 'first' and 'second' Constitutions. The first Constitution—that of 1787—was predicated, among other things, on federalism and recognition of slavery, and the second Constitution, on an enhanced national government and individual liberty").

13. The Republican Party's decision after the Civil War to use the language of the patriarchal family structure helped maintain some of the unequal civil structure that existed in the antebellum United States. *See* LAURA F. EDWARDS, GENDER STRIFE & CONFUSION: THE POLITICAL CULTURE OF RECONSTRUCTION

184–85 (1997). On the decision of the women's rights movements to alter from joining race and gender issues to an insistence of specific gender rights, see Ellen C. DuBois, *Outgrowing the Compact of the Fathers: Equal Rights, Woman Suffrage, and the United States Constitution, 1820–1878*, 74 J. AM. HIST. 846 (1987).

14. Poe v. Ullman, 367 U.S. 497, 542–43 (1961) (Harlan, J. dissenting). Compare Harlan's statement from *Poe* to his grandfather's other dissents: "[T]he power conferred by the thirteenth amendment does not rest upon implication or inference. Those who framed it were not ignorant of the discussion, covering many years of the country's history, as to the constitutional power of congress to enact the fugitive slave laws of 1793 and 1850. When, therefore, it was determined, by a change in the fundamental law, to uproot the institution of slavery wherever it existed in this land, and to establish *universal freedom*, there was a fixed purpose to place the power of congress in the premises beyond the possibility of doubt." *Civil Rights Cases*, 109 U.S. at 33–34 (emphasis added). "The thirteenth amendment does not permit the withholding or the deprivation of any right necessarily inhering in freedom. It not only struck down the institution of slavery as previously existing in the United States, but it prevents the imposition of any burdens or disabilities that constitute badges of slavery or servitude. It decreed universal civil freedom in this country. . . . The sure guaranty of the peace and security of each race is the clear, distinct, unconditional recognition by our governments, national and state, of every right that inheres in civil freedom, and of the equality before the law of all citizens of the United States, without regard to race." *Plessy v. Ferguson*, 163 U.S. 537, 555, 560 (1896). The Thirteenth Amendment "conferred upon every person within the jurisdiction of the United States (except those legally imprisoned for crime) the right, without discrimination against them on account of their race, to enjoy all the privileges that inhere in freedom. It went further, however, and by its second section, invested Congress with power, by appropriate legislation, to enforce its provisions. . . . It may be also observed that the freedom created and established by the Thirteenth Amendment was further protected against assault when the Fourteenth Amendment became a part of the supreme law of the land; for that Amendment provided that no state shall deprive any person of life, liberty, or property without due process of law. To deprive any person of a privilege inhering in the freedom ordained and established by the Thirteenth Amendment is to deprive him of a privilege inhering in the liberty recognized by the Fourteenth Amendment." *United States v. Hodges*, 203 U.S. 1, 27–28 (1905).

15. *See* Robert J. Kaczorowski, *Revolutionary Constitutionalism in the Era of the Civil War & Reconstruction*, 61 N.Y.U. L. REV. 863, 878 (stating that postbellum civil rights legislation was intended to protect blacks and whites).

16. Slaughterhouse Cases, 83 U.S. (16 Wall.) 36, 72 (1873); Shaare Tefila

Congregation v. Cobb, 481 U.S. 615, 617–18 (1987); *see also* St. Francis Coll. v. Al-Khazraji, 481 U.S. 604, 611 (1987).

17. The Abolition Amendment freed slaves from much more than their obligation to engage in unrequited labor. It ended all incidents of servitude such as the forced limitations on slaves' rights to practice religion, hire out their labor, and leave their plantations without permission. KENNETH M. STAMPP, THE PECULIAR INSTITUTION: SLAVERY IN THE ANTE-BELLUM SOUTH 208 (1956).

18. As is already clear, I accept as axiomatic that persons have the right to live as happy, autonomous agents within a diverse polity. The Thirteenth Amendment requires the federal legislature and judiciary to provide the security necessary for citizens to direct their lives pursuant to unique plans, relationships, and interests. Slavery denies persons the opportunity to creatively engage with the world by restricting their right to pursue professions, choose how to raise their children, and make reasonable choices among varying options. A free society allows persons to make plans about their lives rather than externally necessitating them to act on undesired alternatives. Becoming a cobbler because of an interest in the craft is significantly different from having no option but to choose that trade. Living in a predominantly black neighborhood by choice is different, under the Thirteenth Amendment, than being foreclosed from living elsewhere.

19. ISAIAH BERLIN, FOUR ESSAYS ON LIBERTY 121–22 (1969); David Miller, *Introduction* to LIBERTY 4 (David Miller ed., 1991) (discussing the idealist view of freedom). Berlin claimed his analysis was built on centuries of thought. Protagonists of the positive theory of freedom included Plato, who discussed it in the context of virtue and the state; Spinoza, who considered it a limited virtue; Rousseau, who thought freedom for people living in a sate was embodied in the general will determined by laws, and who also influenced Kant's ideas on the subject. While the negative theory of liberty is linked to Hobbes and Bentham, who respectively regard freedom as an absence of external impediments and a lack of coercion existing in the absence of law. PLATO, REPUBLIC *in* THE DIALOGUES OF PLATO 875 (10. 617E) (562–66) (B. Jowett trans., Random House 1937) (5th or 4th century B.C.E.), PLATO, LAWS, *in Id.* 475 (3. 701); BARUCH SPINOZA, A POLITICAL TREATISE, *in* A THEOLOGICO-POLITICAL TREATISE & A POLITICAL TREATISE 294 (II. 7) (H. M. Elwes trans., 1951) (1670); JEAN JACQUES ROUSSEAU, THE SOCIAL CONTRACT 26 (Willmoore Kendall trans., 1954); THOMAS HOBBES, LEVIATHAN, ch. 21 (C. B. MacPherson ed., 1981) (1651); Jeremy Bentham, *quoted in* DOUGLAS G. LONG, BENTHAM ON LIBERTY 74 (1977).

20. ERIC FONER, THE STORY OF AMERICAN FREEDOM 277 (1998).

21. My distinction between "license" and "independent" action derives from RONALD DWORKIN, TAKING RIGHTS SERIOUSLY 262–63 (1977).

22. On making neutral decisions about how to best benefit society, see FRIEDRICH A. HAYEK, THE CONSTITUTION OF LIBERTY 32 (1960).

NOTES TO CHAPTER 6

1. City of Boerne v. Flores, 521 U.S. 507, 532 (1997); Kimel v. Florida Board of Regents, 528 U.S. 62, 86 (2000).

2. City of Cleburne v. Cleburne Living Center, 473 U.S. 432, 440 (1985); Wygant v. Jackson Bd. of Ed., 476 U.S. 267, 280 (1986); Shaw v. Hunt, 517 U.S. 899, 908 (1996); McLaughlin v. Florida, 379 U.S. 184, 196 (1964).

3. Washington v. Glucksberg, 521 U.S. 702, 721 (1997).

4. City of Boerne v. Flores, 521 U.S. 507, 520, 532 (1997); Kimel v. Florida Board of Regents, 528 U.S. 62, 86 (2000) (*quoting Boerne*, 521 U.S. at 532) ("[j]udged against the backdrop of our equal protection jurisprudence, it is clear that the ADEA is 'so out of proportion to a supposed remedial or preventive object that it cannot be understood as responsive to, or designed to prevent, unconstitutional behavior'").

5. *Boerne*, 521 U.S. at 519–20, 533. Both *Boerne* and *Morrison* failed to evaluate the Court's interpretation of "enforce" in Thirteenth Amendment cases, relying, instead, on the *Civil Rights Cases*' "niggardly" interpretation of that term. Jed Rubenfeld, *The Anti-Antidiscrimination Agenda*, 111 YALE L.J. 1141, 1155–56 (2002). Ruth Colker, *The Supreme Court's Historical Errors in City of Boerne v. Flores*, 43 B.C. L. REV. 783, 797–817 (2002).

6. Jones v. Alfred H. Mayer Co., 392 U.S. 409, 440 (1968).

7. U.S. CONST. PMBL. ("We the People of the United States, in Order to form a more perfect Union, establish Justice, insure domestic Tranquility, provide for the common defence, promote the general Welfare, and secure the Blessings of Liberty to ourselves and our Posterity, do ordain and establish this Constitution for the United States of America"). The Court first connected governmental interference with the Privileges and Immunities Clause in the *Slaughterhouse Cases*, 83 U.S. 36 (1872), finding that the clause protected citizens only from state interference with the privileges and immunities of enjoying national, but not state, citizenship. *Id.* at 61–62. Likewise, the Equal Protection Clause prevents the interference with the exercise of fundamental rights "unless it is supported by sufficiently important state interests and is closely tailored to effectuate only those interests." *See, e.g.*, Zablocki v. Redhail, 434 U.S. 374, 388 (1978). "The Fourteenth Amendment's Due Process Clause has a substantive component that 'provides heightened protection against government interference with certain fundamental rights and liberty interests.'" Troxel v. Granville, 530 U.S. 57, 57 (2000), *quoting* Washington v. Glucksberg, 521 U.S. 702, 720 (1997).

8. Civil Rights Cases, 109 U.S. 3, 11–12 (1883).

9. *Morrison*, 529 U.S. at 621, 626–27; James W. Fox Jr., *Re-Readings & Misreadings: Slaughter-House, Privileges or Immunities, & Section Five Enforcement Powers*, 91 KY. L.J. 67, 159 (2002–2003). From that year, the Court began

using the Constitution to avoid the enforcement of antidiscrimination laws. *See Hall v. DeCuir*, 95 U.S. 485 (1877) (finding Louisiana violated the Commerce Clause by requiring the desegregation of public conveyance).

10. Jones, 392 U.S. at 416–20, 438–39. Even the *Civil Rights Cases* recognized that the Thirteenth Amendment does not contain a state action requirement. 109 U.S. 19–20. In spite of this finding, the Court held that discrimination in public accommodations did not amount to a badge of servitude. *Id.* at 20. *See* Tobias B. Wolff, *The Thirteenth Amendment and Slavery in the Global Economy*, 102 COLUM. L. REV. 973, 1040 (2002) (stating that since Thirteenth Amendment "contains no state action requirement, the Amendment both restrains the actions of the State and regulates the activities of private individuals").

11. HAROLD M. HYMAN & WILLIAM M. WIECEK, EQUAL JUSTICE UNDER LAW: CONSTITUTIONAL DEVELOPMENT 1835–1875, at 408–9 (1982).

12. Antonin Scalia, *Common-Law Courts in a Civil-Law System: The Role of United States Federal Courts in Interpreting the Constitution and Laws, in* A MATTER OF INTERPRETATION: FEDERAL COURTS AND THE LAW 25, 47 (Amy Gutmann ed., 1997).

13. Robert H. Bork, *Neutral Principles and Some First Amendment Problems*, 47 IND. L.J. 1, 7–12 (1971); John Hart Ely, *The Wages of Crying Wolf: A Comment on Roe v. Wade*, 82 YALE L.J. 920, 949 (1973).

14. Washington v. Glucksberg, 521 U.S. 702, 720–22 (1997).

15. My approach is analogous to the Supreme Court's analytic two-tiered method in substantive due process cases: "First, we have regularly observed that the Due Process Clause specially protects those fundamental rights and liberties which are, objectively, 'deeply rooted in this Nation's history and tradition,' . . . and 'implicit in the concept of ordered liberty.' . . . Second, we have required in substantive due-process cases a 'careful description' of the asserted fundamental liberty interest. . . . Our Nation's history, legal traditions, and practices thus provide the crucial 'guideposts for responsible decisionmaking.' . . . This approach tends to rein in the subjective elements that are necessarily present in due process judicial review." Washington v. Glucksberg, 521 U.S. 702, 720–22 (1997). Unlike the Thirteenth Amendment, substantive due process only comes in to play when the controversy involves a state action.

16. RICHARD HOFSTADTER, SOCIAL DARWINISM IN AMERICAN THOUGHT 32, 34, 41, 50 (Beacon Press 1955) (1944); *In re* Jacobs, 98 N.Y. 98 (1885); William E. Forbath, *The Ambiguities of Free Labor: Labor & the Law in the Gilded Age*, 1985 WIS. L. REV. 767, 795; HARRY A. MILLIS AND ROYAL E. MONTGORNERY, ORGANIZED LABOR 630–31 (New York, 1945).

17. LAURENCE H. TRIBE, AMERICAN CONSTITUTIONAL LAW § 5–15, at 926–27 (3d ed. 2000).

18. For instance, in Shapiro v. Thompson, the Court ascribed the right to travel to "a particular constitutional provision." 394 U.S. 618, 630 (1969).

19. U.S. 113, 153 (1973).

20. *See* Adam B. Wolf, *Fundamentally Flawed: Tradition & Fundamental Rights*, 57 U. MIAMI L. REV. 101, 131 (2002) ("While the majority opinion in Roe never explicitly stated that it was relying on tradition to find the fundamental right to an abortion, its nearly twenty-page discussion of the history of abortion precedes its finding that there is such a fundamental right").

21. Andrew Koppelman argued that "[w]hen women are compelled to carry and bear children, they are subjected to 'involuntary servitude' in violation of the thirteenth amendment." *Forced Labor: A Thirteenth Amendment Analysis*, 84 Nw. U. L. REV. 480, 484 (1990).

22. CONG. GLOBE, 38th Cong., 1st Sess. 1439 (Apr. 6, 1864); Poe v. Ullman, 367 U.S. 497, 517 (1961).

23. Poe v. Ullman, 367 U.S. 497, 542–43 (1961) (Douglas, J., dissenting) (regarding a Connecticut law against the use of contraceptives which the Court dismissed for lack of standing).

24. JOHN H. RUSSELL, THE FREE NEGRO IN VIRGINIA, 1619–1865, at 126 (Negro University Press 1969) (1913); CARL N. DEGLER, OUT OF OUR PAST: THE FORCES THAT SHAPED MODERN AMERICA 167 (1959).

25. Loving v. Virginia, 388 U.S. 1, 12 (1967).

26. Vanessa B. M. Vergara, *Abusive Mail-Order Bride Marriage and the Thirteenth Amendment*, 94 Nw. U. L. REV. 1547 (2000).

27. JOHN HOPE FRANKLIN, FROM SLAVERY TO FREEDOM 201–2 (2d ed. 1956); Jo Ann Manfra & Robert R. Dykstra, *Serial Marriage & the Origins of the Black Stepfamily: The Rowanty Evidence*, 72 J. AM. HIST. 18, 34–35 (1985).

28. LAURA S. HAVILAND, A WOMAN'S LIFE-WORK 463 (Arno Press & The New York Times 1969) (1881); THE AMERICAN SLAVE: A COMPOSITE AUTOBIOGRAPHY 274 (George P. Rawick ed., 1975) (*Unwritten History of Slavery*); Letter from Lucy Chase to Miss Lowell, Nov. 29, 1863, *in* DEAR ONES AT HOME 99 (Henry L. Swint ed., 1966).

29. PETER KOLCHIN, AMERICAN SLAVERY 1619–1877, at 125–26 (1993).

30. Moore v. City of E. Cleveland, 431 U.S. 494, 499, 503–4 (1977).

31. The Supreme Court has never addressed the question of whether § 1982 applies to housing that is exempt from the Fair Housing Act of 1968. A couple of lower courts have held that such housing is covered by § 1982. See Morris v. Cizek, 503 F.2d 1303 (7th Cir. 1974); Johnson v. Zaremba, 381 F. Supp. 165 (N.D. Ill. 1973).

32. Griswold v. Connecticut, 381 U.S. 479, 482, 485–86 (1965); Laurence H. Tribe, *In Memoriam: William J. Brennan, Jr.*, 111 HARV. L. REV. 41, 45 (1997).

33. HUGO L. BLACK, A CONSTITUTIONAL FAITH 9 (1968); Robert H. Bork, *Neutral Principles and Some First Amendment Problems*, 47 IND. L.J. 1, 9 (1971).

34. Laurence H. Tribe, *The Puzzling Persistence of Process-Based Constitutional Theories*, 89 YALE L.J. 1063, 1065 (1980) (arguing that there is a "stubbornly substantive character of so many of the Constitution's most crucial commitments: commitments defining the values that we as a society, acting politically, must respect. Plainly, the First Amendment's guarantee of religious liberty and its prohibition of religious establishment are substantive in this sense. So, too, is the Thirteenth Amendment, in its abolition of slavery").

35. FELIX FRANKFURTER, THE COMMERCE CLAUSE UNDER MARSHALL, TANEY AND WAITE 2 (1937); Felix Frankfurter, *Taft and the Supreme Court, in* FELIX FRANKFURTER ON THE SUPREME COURT: EXTRAJUDICIAL ESSAYS ON THE COURT AND THE CONSTITUTION 49, 61 (Philip B. Kurland ed., 1970).

36. United States v. Virginia, 518 U.S. 514, 557 (1996) (*citing* RICHARD MORRIS, THE FORGING OF THE UNION, 1781–1789, at 193 (1987)).

37. THEODORE WELD, AMERICAN SLAVERY AS IT IS 56 (Arno Press 1968) (1839).

38. Runyon v. McCrary, 427 U.S. 160 (1976).

39. Meyer v. Nebraska, 262 U.S. 390, 399 (1923); Wisconsin v. Yoder, 406 U.S. 205, 232 (1972); Santosky v. Kramer, 455 U.S. 745, 753 (1982); *see also* Pierce v. Soc'y of Sisters, 268 U.S. 510, 534–35 (1925)

40. The Court recently held that sovereign immunity does not shield a state from complying with the Family Medical Leave Act. *Nev. Dept Human Resources v. Hibbs*, 123 S.Ct. 1972 (2003). The Court determined that Congress's use of its Fourteenth Amendment section 5, power to prevent gender discrimination under the FMLA was congruent or proportional to the injury it sought to prevent and the means adopted to that end. *Id.* at 1974. "Unlike the statutes at issue in *City of Boerne, Kimel*, and *Garrett*, which applied broadly to every aspect of state employers' operations, the FMLA is narrowly targeted at the fault line between work and family—precisely where sex-based overgeneralization has been and remains strongest—and affects only one aspect of the employment relationship. Also significant are the many other limitations that Congress placed on the FMLA's scope." *Id.* at 1975. The FMLA "applies only to employees who have worked for the employer for at least one year and provided 1,250 hours of service within the last 12 months, § 2611(2)(A); and does not apply to employees in high-ranking or sensitive positions, including state elected officials, their staffs, and appointed policymakers, §§ 2611(2)(B)(I) and (3), 203(e)(2)(c))." *Id.* No such restriction is applicable to the Thirteenth Amendment since it prohibits all incidents and badges of servitude, regardless of the perpetrator's characteristics or the time for which a victim was exploited.

41. Skinner v. Oklahoma, 316 U.S. 535, 541 (1942); ROBERT H. BORK, THE TEMPTING OF AMERICA: THE POLITICAL SEDUCTION OF THE LAW 63–64 (1990).

42. Barbara L. Bernier, *Class, Race, and Poverty: Medical Technologies & Sociopolitical Choices*, 11 HARV. BLACKLETTER L.J. 115, 121 (1994); WINTHROP D. JORDAN, WHITE OVER BLACK: AMERICAN ATTITUDES TOWARD THE NEGRO, 1550–1812, at 154, 156, 473 (1968).

43. Kent v. Dulles, 357 U.S. 116, 126 (1958).

44. Christopher Morris, *The Articulation of Two Worlds: The Master-Slave Relationship Reconsidered*, 85 J. AM. HIST. 982, 1000 (1998); Robert Starobin, *Disciplining Industrial Slaves in the Old South*, 53 J. NEGRO HIST. 111, 114 (1968); David Waldstreicher, *Reading the Runaways: Self-Fashioned, Print, Culture, & Confidence in Slavery in the Eighteenth-Century Mid-Atlantic*, 56 WILLIAM & MARY Q. 243, 263 (1999).

45. SIDNEY ANDREWS, THE SOUTH SINCE THE WAR 350–52 (1866); OCTAVIA V. ROGERS ALBERT, HOUSE OF BONDAGE 134–35 (1891).

46. CONG. GLOBE, 39th Cong., 1st Sess. 43 (Dec. 13, 1866).

47. William Cohen, *Negro Involuntary Servitude in the South, 1865–1940: A Preliminary Analysis*, 42 J. SOUTHERN HIST. 31, 47 (1976); LEON F. LITWACK, BEEN IN THE STORM SO LONG: THE AFTERMATH OF SLAVERY 318–19, 321 (1979); Amy Dru Stanley, *Beggars Can't Be Choosers: Compulsion & Contract in Postbellum America*, 78 J. AM. HIST. 1265, 1293 (1992).

48. City of Chicago v. Morales, 527 U.S. 41, 53–54 (1999) (plurality opinion) (holding that gang loitering ordinance was unconstitutionally vague and violated personal liberty of the Due Process Clause of the Fourteenth Amendment). *See also* Papachristou v. City of Jacksonville, 405 U.S. 156, 164 (1972) (stating that wandering is "historically part of the amenities of life as we know them. They are not mentioned in the Constitution or in the Bill of Rights. These unwritten amenities have been in part responsible for giving our people the feeling of independence and self-confidence, the feeling of creativity"). Alexander Tsesis, *Eliminating the Destitution of America's Homeless: A Fair, Federal Approach*, 10 TEMPLE POL. & CIV. RTS. L. REV. 103, 113–17 (2000).

49. United States v. Guest, 383 U.S. 745, 757, 758–59 (1966); Saenz v. Roe, 526 U.S. 489, 501 (1999); Shapiro v. Thompson, 394 U.S. 618, 629–30, 634 (1969); *Id.* at 666 (Harlan, J., dissenting); Edwards v. California, 314 U.S. 160, 173–74 (1941); *Id.* at 178 (Douglas, J., concurring). Earlier cases were just as unspecific about the source of liberty rights. Zemel v. Rusk, 381 U.S. 1, 14 (1965) found the right to travel in the Fifth Amendment; Twining v. New Jersey, 211 U.S. 78, 97 (1908) located the right in the Fourteenth Amendment; and Paul v. Virginia, 8 Wall. (75 U.S.) 168, 180 (1869) found that it derived from the Privileges and Immunities Clause of Article IV.

50. Griffin v. Breckenridge, 403 U.S. 88, 102, 105–6 (1971); United Brotherhood of Carpenters v. Scott, 463 U.S. 825, 832 (1983).

51. Heart of Atlanta Motel, Inc. v. United States, 379 U.S. 241, 243, 253 (1964).

52. *Id.*, 379 U.S. 241, 258, 261–62, 270 n.4, 278 n.12 (1964); Civil Rights Cases, 109 U.S. 3, 25 (1883).

53. Katzenbach v. McClung, 379 U.S. 294 (1964).

54. United States v. Lopez, 514 U.S. 549, 561, 563 (1995). 18 U.S.C. § 922(q). The Act forbade persons who "knowingly . . . possess a firearm at a place that the individual knows, or has reasonable cause to believe, is a school zone." 18 U.S.C. § 922(q)(2)(A).

55. United States v. Morrison, 529 U.S. 598, 608–9, 610, 613, 617 (2000); 42 U.S.C. § 13,981 (1994). The Thirteenth Amendment emerged as one of Congress's stated bases for enacting the VAWA, but the district court discounted it as "the straw grasping in which Congress engaged. The Thirteenth Amendment applies to racial, not gender, discrimination." S.Rep. No. 197, 102d Cong., 1st Sess. 53 (1991); Brzonkala v. Va. Polytechnic Inst. & State Univ., 935 F. Supp. 779, 796 n.3 (W.D. Va. 1996). The Thirteenth Amendment rationale does not appear in the appellate decision. Brzonkala v. Va. Polytechnic Inst. & State Univ., 132 F.3d 949 (4th Cir. 1997); 169 F.3d 820 (4th Cir. 1999) (en banc).

56. Andrew Koppelman, *Forced Labor: A Thirteenth Amendment Analysis*, 84 Nw. U. L. Rev. 480 (1990).

57. Jones v. Alfred H. Mayer Co., 392 U.S. 409, 440 (1968); Heart of Atlanta Motel, Inc. v. United States, 379 U.S. 241, 262 (1964) (explaining, in the context of Commerce Clause, the use of the rational basis test).

58. Gibbons v. Ogden, 22 U.S. 1 (1824); PAUL FINKELMAN, AN IMPERFECT UNION: SLAVERY, FEDERALISM, AND COMITY 24 (1981); Robert J. Pushaw, Jr. & Grant S. Nelson, *A Critique of the Narrow Interpretation of the Commerce Clause*, 96 Nw. U. L. Rev. 695, 702 n.54 (2002) (stating that even if Congress could not regulate intrastate slave trade it certainly could have done so on an interstate level); Charles H. Cosgrove, *The Declaration of Independence in Constitutional Interpretation: A Selective History & Analysis*, 32 U. RICH. L. REV. 107, 123 (1998) (stating that Congress had power under the Commerce Clause to regulate "incoming slave trade" and failure to do so was a sign of "bad faith of the American people").

59. U.S.C. s 2000e(b) (2002); Theodore Eisenberg & Stewart Schwab, *The Importance of Section 1981*, 73 CORNELL L. REV. 596, 602 (1988); Johnson v. Railway Express Agency, Inc., 421 U.S. 454, 461 (1975); Rivers v. Roadway Express, Inc., 511 U.S. 298, 304 n.3 (1994) (concerning § 101 of Civil Rights Act of 1991).

60. James G. Pope, *The Thirteenth Amendment versus the Commerce Clause: Labor & the Shaping of American Constitutional Law, 1921-1957*, 102 COLUM. L. REV. 1, 119–20 (2002); STUART A. SCHEINGOLD, THE POLITICS OF RIGHTS: LAWYERS, PUBLIC POLICY, & POLITICAL CHANGE 131–35 (1974);

Frances Kahn Zemans, *Legal Mobilization: The Neglected Role of Law in the Political System*, 77 AM. POL. SCI. REV. 690, 697 (1983); Elizabeth S. Anderson & Richard H. Pildes, *Expressive Theories of Law: A General Restatement*, 148 U. PA. L. REV. 1503, 1529 (2000).

NOTES TO CHAPTER 7

1. GEORGE SCHEDLER, RACIST SYMBOLS & REPARATIONS 9 (1998); Robert J. Bein, *Stained Flags: Public Symbols & Equal Protection*, 28 SETON HALL L. REV. 897, 917 (1998).

2. PIERRE BOURDIEU, LANGUAGE & SYMBOLIC POWER 106 (Gino Raymond & Matthew Adamson trans., 1991); HOWARD J. EHRLICH, SOCIAL PSYCHOLOGY OF PREJUDICE 39 (1973); WALTER LIPPMANN, PUBLIC OPINION 85 (16th prtg. 1957); SCHEDLER, *supra*, at 8–9.

3. Lawrence Lessig, *The Regulations of Social Meaning*, 62 U. CHI. L. REV. 943, 957–58 (1995); Joel Kovel, WHITE RACISM: A PSYCHOHISTORY 96–97 (1970); Akhil R. Amar, *The Case of the Missing Amendment: R.A.V. v. City of St. Paul*, 106 HARV. L. REV. 124, 157 (arguing that Thirteenth Amendment permits some regulation of racist speech).

4. WILLIAM L. SHIRER, THE RISE & FALL OF THE THIRD REICH 43–44 (1960) (explaining how Hitler developed the swastika from ancient sources and surrounded it with the colors of imperial Germany); RAYMOND W. FIRTH, SYMBOLS: PUBLIC & PRIVATE 142 (1973); Bronislaw Malinowski, The Group & The Individual in Functional Analysis, 44 Amer. J. Soc. 958 (1939); Andrew Lass, *Romantic Documents and Political Monuments: The Meaning-Fulfillment of History in 19th-Century Czech Nationalism*, 15 AM. ETHNOLOGIST 456, 457 (1988); Eric Hobsbawm, *Inventing Traditions, in* THE INVENTION OF TRADITION 1–3 (Eric Hobsbawm & Terence Ranger eds., 1983); Lessig, *supra*, at 978.

5. LIPPMANN, *supra*, at 83–84, 90; BOURDIEU, *supra*, at 166–67. In highlighting the importance of a nation's flag to its people, Justice Stevens pointed out that "in times of national crisis, [the flag] inspires and motivates the average citizen to make personal sacrifices in order to achieve societal goals of overriding importance; at all times, it serves as a reminder of the paramount importance of pursuing the ideals that characterize our society." United States v. Eichman, 496 U.S. 310, 319–20 (1990) (Stevens, J., dissenting); Texas v. Johnson, 491 U.S. 397, 405 (1989).

6. DAVID MILNER, CHILDREN AND RACE 75–76 (1983); GORDON W. ALLPORT, THE NATURE OF PREJUDICE 15 (3d ed. 1979) (1954) (concerning the gradual development of prejudice through expressive acts); GEORGE E. SIMPSON & J. MILTON YINGER, RACIAL & CULTURAL MINORITIES 143 (3d ed. 1972).

7. MILNER, *supra*, at 75–76; TEUN A. VAN DIJK, COMMUNICATING RACISM 40 (1987); *Face-Off with Hatred; KKK Visit Is Met by Police Presence,*

Thousands Praying for Peace, PITTSBURGH POST-GAZETTE, Apr. 6, 1997, at A-1; David Treadwell, *Southern Communities Uniting against Klan*, THE RECORD, May 4, 1986, at A45 (noting display of statue of Confederate soldier in town square of Gainesville, Georgia).

8. WILLIAM SUMNER JENKINS, PRO-SLAVERY THOUGHT IN THE OLD SOUTH 244 (1935). Albert G. Brown of Mississippi summed up Southern ideology on the Declaration during a speech in the Senate well, during a debate on the Kansas and Nebraska Bill: "In the South all men are equal. I mean, of course, white men; Negroes are not men, within the meaning of the Declaration. If they were, Madison, and Jefferson, and Washington, all of whom lived and died slaveholders, never could have made it, for they never regarded Negroes as their equals, in any respect." CONG. GLOBE, 33d Cong., 1st Sess., app. 230 (1854).

9. Fundamental U.S. ideals in the Declaration of Independence opposed slavery even while it was practiced in this country. William Lee Miller, a historian, has explained that "the use of elaborate euphemisms and circumlocutory verbal devices to avoid the words 'slave' and 'slavery,' at considerable cost at least to brevity and possibly to clarity, had an important purpose. It was explicitly designed to keep the Constitution from recognizing, as James Madison put it, that there could be 'property in men.'" WILLIAM LEE MILLER, ARGUING ABOUT SLAVERY 20–21 (1996). The Confederate Constitution, which was adopted in 1861, is reprinted in EMORY M. THOMAS, THE CONFEDERATE NATION, 1861–1865, at 307–22 (1979). CONFEDERATE CONST. art. I, § 9, cl. 4; *Id.* at art. IV, § 2, cl. 1; *Id.* at art. IV, § 2, cl. 3; *Id.* at art. IV, § 3, cl. 3.

10. The Confederate Constitution's prohibition against any laws abridging property in the Negro slave seems to have precluded any amendment to the Confederate Constitution abolishing slavery. CONFEDERATE CONST. art. I, § 9, cl. 4.

11. JAMES MCPHERSON, STRUGGLE FOR EQUALITY 47–48 (1964).

12. The Middle Passage was the harrowing transatlantic voyage by which enslaved Africans were taken to European countries and their colonies. *See generally Gustavus Vassa, The Life of Olaudah Equiano, the African, in* GREAT DOCUMENTS IN BLACK AMERICAN HISTORY 47 (George Ducas, Charles Van Doren, eds., Praeger Publishers 1970) (1789) (describing the stifling and often deathly journey); ALEXANDER FALCONBRIDGE, BLACK VOYAGE — ACCOUNT OF THE SLAVE TRADE ON THE COAST OF AFRICA (1788), available at http://web-cro5.pbs.org/wgbh/aia/part1/1h281t.html (same); JOHN C. CALHOUN, CALHOUN: BASIC DOCUMENTS 63–64 (John M. Anderson ed., 1952); John E. Mulligan, *A Tourist's Guide to D.C.—Memorials, Museums, More Govern a Visit to the Capital*, THE PROVIDENCE J.-BULL., Apr. 9, 2000, at 18A.

13. Gloria Johnson Powell, *Self-Concept in White & Black Children, in* RACISM & MENTAL HEALTH 300–301 (Charles V. Willie *et al.* eds., 2d ed.); Mary J. Matsuda, *Public Response to Racist Speech: Considering the Victim's Story*, 87 MICH. L. REV. 2320, 2378 (1989).

14. Lessig, *supra*, at 954; James Forman Jr., Note, *Driving Dixie Down: Removing the Confederate Flag from Southern State Capitols*, 101 YALE L.J. 505, 514–15 (1991); Martin D. Carcieri, *Democracy and Education in the Thought of Jefferson and Madison*, 26 J.L. & EDUC. 1, 6 (1997); Cynthia Vaughn, Editorial, *Theory Comparing Flag to Cross Misses the Mark*, GREENSBORO NEWS & RECORD, Jan. 29, 2000.

15. CONG. GLOBE, 38th Cong., 1st Sess. 2618 (May 31, 1864); *Id.* at 1324 (Mar. 28, 1864); *Id.* at 2984–85 (June 15, 1864); CONG. GLOBE, 38th Cong., 2d Sess. 176 (Jan. 9, 1865); CONG. GLOBE, 39th Cong., 1st Sess. 503 (Jan. 30, 1865) (discussing statement of Senator Jacob M. Howard of Michigan describing murder of man in Texas for raising Union flag).

16. Chris Springer, *The Troubled Resurgence of the Confederate Flag*, 43 HISTORY TODAY 7, 8–9 (1993).

17. Miss. Laws 154; EDWARD L. AYERS, THE PROMISE OF THE NEW SOUTH: LIFE AFTER RECONSTRUCTION 146–49 (1972); 2 A HISTORY OF MISSISSIPPI 13–14 (Richard A. McLemore ed., 1973); Miss. Code Ann. §§ 3-3-15, 37-13-5, 37-13-5 (1), (3), 37-13-7 (2) (2001).

18. Robert Tait, *Mississippi's Racial Divide Widens with Vote to Keep Rebel Yell Flying*, THE SCOTSMAN Apr. 19, 2001, at 11; Daniels v. Harrison County Bd. of Sup'rs, 722 So. 2d 136, 138 (Miss. 1998); Mississippi Div. of United Sons of Confederate Veterans v. Mississippi State, Conference of NAACP Branches, 774 So. 2d 388, 389 (Miss. 2000).

19. H.B. 16, Gen. Assem., Reg. Sess. (Ga. 2001) (amending Ga. Code Ann. § 50-3-1 (1994 & Supp. 1997)); Ga. Code Ann. §§ 50-3-3, 50-3-10, 50-3-5 (2000).

20. Brown v. Board of Education, 347 U.S. 483 (1954); Eric Harrison, *Georgia Flag's Rebel Emblem Assumes Olympian Proportions*, L.A. TIMES, Feb. 11, 1993, at A5; Coleman v. Miller, 117 F.3d 527, 528–31 (11th Cir. 1997). The appellant in *Coleman* also argued that the flag violated his First Amendment rights, but the Court turned that aside, finding nothing compelled appellant to affirm the ideals of the state flag by carrying or displaying it. *Id.* at 531.

21. The Supreme Court has recognized that there are private interests in equal protection. Adarand Constructors, Inc. v. Pena, 515 U.S. 200, 227 (1995); Erwin Chemerinsky, *Making the Right Case for a Constitutional Right to Minimum Entitlements*, 44 MERCER L. REV. 525, 538 (1993) (stating that Supreme Court has "repeatedly . . . used the Fourteenth Amendment to protect rights from state interference, and it is widely accepted that the Amendment does safeguard individual rights from state interference"). The traditional Supreme Court view, however, is that since the Fourteenth Amendment states "No state shall . . . ," the implication is that the amendment's provisions apply to state but not private actions. Consequently, as best stated by Paul Berman, "the state cannot constitutionally exclude African-Americans from a government housing facility,

but the Constitution is silent with regard to an individual's choice to exclude African-Americans from his or her home." Paul Schiff Berman, *Cyberspace and the State Action Debate: The Cultural Value of Applying Constitutional Norms to "Private" Regulation*, 71 U. COLO. L. REV. 1263, 1266 (2000).

22. Civil rights organizations threatened to boycott Georgian industries if the state flag's Confederate design remained unchanged. David Pendered, *Boycott by SCLC Threatened If Georgia Flag Not Changed*, COX NEWS SERVICE, Apr. 4, 2000; *Georgia House Passes Bill to Reduce Confederate Emblem on State Flag*, ST. LOUIS POST-DISPATCH, Jan. 25, 2001, at A2; Patricia M. LaHay, *Senate Resolution Encourages Flying of Former Georgia Flags*, ASSOCIATED PRESS STATE & LOCAL WIRE, Mar. 20, 2001.

23. Rick Freeman, *S. Carolina's Allegiance to the Flag; State Is a Sports Outcast Because of Confederate Link*, WASH. POST, May 20, 2000, at D1; Jim Davenport, *S.C. Legislature Approves Moving Confederate Flag from Statehouse Dome*, ASSOCIATED PRESS STATE & LOCAL WIRE, May 18, 2000. As in Mississippi, two years after Brown, state congressmen showed their contempt for civil rights reform by embracing the Confederate flag. Following the lead of South Carolina senator John D. Long, they raised the Confederate flag above the Senate chambers. Tim Smith, *Banner Traced to One Man, Work of Single Racially Motivated Lawmaker Brought Rise of Confederate Flag to Chambers*, AUGUSTA CHRON., Jan. 30, 2000, at B2; Kevin Sack, *Battle Lines Form Again on the Battle Flag*, N.Y. TIMES, Aug. 4, 2001, at A12; *Tennessee Flag*, at http://www.ultimateflags.com/states/tennessee.htm (last visited Oct. 11, 2001); Charles A. Spain, Jr., *The Flags & Seals of Texas*, 33 S. Tex. L. Rev. 215, 252–53 (1992); NAACP v. Hunt, 891 F.2d 1555 (11th Cir. 1990), the Eleventh Circuit Court of Appeals found that flying the Confederate flag above the Alabama capital building was neither a "badge of servitude," under the Thirteenth Amendment, nor a violation of the Equal Protection Clause. Id. at 1562. Some of the flaws of that case include the court's failure to investigate whether the flag is at all connected to slavery, and its history indicates that it is, and that the court's strict reading of the Equal Protection Clause is unlikely to withstand strict scrutiny. Weeden, *supra* note 26, at 535–36; Ronald J. Krotoszynski, Jr., *Equal Justice under Law: The Jurisprudential Legacy of Judge Frank M. Johnson, Jr.*, 109 YALE L.J. 1237, 1240 n.14 (2000).

24. Telephone interview with Barbara McMillan, Office of the White House Curator (Sept. 27, 2001); WILLIAM A. DEGREGORIO, THE COMPLETE BOOK OF U.S. PRESIDENTS 158 (5th ed. 1993 with 1996 update by Connie Jo Dickerson); Tyler propelled the drive to annex Texas in order to spread slavery into western territories. Id. at 157; George B. Tindall, *America: A Narrative History* 519–20 (1984).

25. Annals of Cong. 934 (1794).

26. Randall P. Bezanson & William G. Buss, *The Many Faces of Government*

Speech, 86 Iowa L. Rev. 1377, 1502, 1508–9 (2001); Akhil R. Amar, *The Case of the Missing Amendment: R.A.V. v. City of St. Paul,* 106 Harv. L. Rev. 124, 155–61 (1992); Frederick Schauer, *Is Government Speech a Problem?* 35 Stan. L. Rev. 373, 386 (1983); Andrew E. Taslitz, *Hate Crimes, Free Speech, & the Contract of Mutual Indifference,* 80 B.U. L. Rev. 1283, 1391 (2000).

27. Patterson v. McLean Credit Union, 491 U.S. 190, 192–93 (1989) (Brennan, J., concurring and dissenting in part); Larry J. Pittman, *Physician Assisted Suicide in the Dark Ward: The Intersection of the Thirteenth Amendment & Health Care Treatments Having Disproportionate Impacts on Disfavored Groups,* 28 Seton Hall L. Rev. 774, 853, 859–60 (1998) (analogizing private causes of action under Thirteenth Amendment to enslaved persons individually suing slave owners); Laurence H. Tribe, American Constitutional Law § 5–13 (2d ed. 1988).

28. In Coleman, appellant relied only on his own testimony "to demonstrate a disproportionate racial effect." *Coleman,* 117 F.3d at 530. The appellant in Hunt also presented insufficient factual evidence to prove his claim. *Hunt,* 891 F. 2d at 1563.

29. Valerie Jenness & Ryken Grattet, Making Hate a Crime 73–101 (2001); James B. Jacobs & Kimberly Potter, Hate Crimes: Criminal Law & Identity Politics 29–44 (1998). For a list of current federal criminal civil rights statutes see Frederick M. Lawrence, *Civil Rights & Criminal Wrongs: The Mens Rea of Federal Civil Rights Crime,* 67 Tul. L. Rev. 2113, 2229 (1993). Those statutes, which are still good law, include 18 U.S.C. 241 (conspiracy to violate civil rights), 18 U.S.C. § 242 (deprivation of rights under color of law), 18 U.S.C. § 245 (intimidation, interference, or injury of federally protected activities).

30. Sara Sun Beale, *Federalizing Hate Crimes: Symbolic Politics, Expressive Law, or Tool for Criminal Enforcement?,* 80 B.U. L. Rev. 1227 (2000); Dan Hasenstab, Comment, *Is Hate a Form of Commerce? The Questionable Constitutionality of Federal "Hate Crime" Legislation,* 45 St. Louis U. L.J. 973, 1016 (2001); Christopher Chorba, Note, *The Danger of Federalizing Hate Crimes: Congressional Misconceptions & the Unintended of the Hate Crimes Prevention Act,* 87 Va. L. Rev. 319 (2001).

31. Andrew E. Taslitz, *Hate Crimes, Free Speech, and the Contract of Mutual Indifference,* 80 Boston U. L. Rev. 1283, 1304 (2000).

32. The measure was reintroduced by Congresswoman Sheila Jackson Lee under the title "Hate Crimes Prevention Act of 2001" (Introduced in the House), HR 74 IH, 107th Cong., 1st Sess., H.R. 74. Congress never voted on the 2001 Bill.

33. S. 19, 107th Cong., § 102, at 10 (2001); see also H.R. 74, 107th Cong., § 2, at 8 (2001) (determining that "violence motivated by bias that is a relic of slavery can constitute badges and incidents of slavery").

34. S. 966, 108th Cong., 1st Sess. (2003).

35. Shaare Tefila Congregation v. Cobb, 481 U.S. 615, 617–18 (1987); St. Francis Coll. v. Al-Khazraji, 481 U.S. 604, 611 (1987); Gregory M. Herek, *Hate Crimes against Lesbians and Gay Men: Issues for Research and Policy*, 44 AM. PSYCHOLOGIST 948, 948 (1989).

36. MILTON KLEG, HATE, PREJUDICE & RACISM 155 (1993); Frederick M. Lawrence, *The Punishment of Hate: Toward a Normative Theory of Bias-Motivated Crimes*, 93 MICH. L. REV. 320, 343 (1994); Craig L. Uhrich, *Hate Crime Legislation: A Policy Analysis*, 36 HOUS. L. REV. 1467, 1506–7 (1999); Joan C. Weiss, Howard J. Ehrlich, & Barbara E. K. Larcom, *Ethnoviolence at Work*, 18 J. INTERGROUP RELATIONS 21, 27 (Winter 1991–92).

37. Joan C. Weiss, *Violence Motivated by Bigotry: "Ethnoviolence," in* ENCYCLOPEDIA OF SOCIAL WORK 307, 314 (Leon Ginsberg *et al.* eds., 18th ed. 1990 Supp.); Chuck Wexler & Gary T. Marx, *When Law and Order Works: Boston's Innovative Approach to the Problem of Racial Violence*, 32 CRIME & DELINQ. 205, 210 (1986); Lu-in Wang, *The Transforming Power of "Hate": Social Cognition Theory & the Harms of Bias-Related Crime*, 71 S. CAL. L. REV. 47, 123 (1997); FRANTZ FANON, BLACK SKIN, WHITE MASKS 50–51, 191–93 (Grove Press, Inc. 1967) (1952); JEAN-PAUL SARTRE, ANTI-SEMITE AND JEW (1948); Troy A. Scotting, Comment, *Hate Crimes & the Need for Stronger Federal Legislation*, 34 AKRON L. REV. 853, 862–66 (2001).

38. Steven G. Gey, *What If Wisconsin v. Mitchell Had Involved Martin Luther King Jr.? The Constitutional Flaws of Hate Crime Enhancement Statutes*, 65 GEO. WASH. L. REV. 1014, 1069–70 (1997); JAMES B. JACOBS & KIMBERLY POTTER, HATE CRIMES: CRIMINAL LAW & IDENTITY POLITICS 111–29 (1998); Susan Gellman, *Sticks and Stones Can Put You in Jail, but Can Words Increase Your Sentence? Constitutional and Policy Dilemmas of Ethnic Intimidation Laws*, 39 UCLA L. REV. 333, 333–34 (1991).

39. FREDERICK M. LAWRENCE, PUNISHING HATE: BIAS CRIMES UNDER AMERICAN LAW 95 (1999). Motive is not an unheard-of factor in criminal law; for instance, burglary requires the mental state to enter a house and the purpose to commit a felony therein. Similarly, treason requires supplying aid in order to help the enemy. Claire Finkelstein, *The Inefficiency of Mens Rea*, 88 CALIF. L. REV. 895, 911 (2000); SANFORD H. KADISH & STEPHEN J. SCHULHOFER, CRIMINAL LAW AND ITS PROCESSES: CASES AND MATERIALS 218 (6th ed. 1995); Andrew E. Taslitz, *Condemning the Racist Personality: Why the Critics of Hate Crimes Legislation Are Wrong*, 40 B.C. L. REV. 739, 754 (1999); 18 USCA § 2381 (2001); H. L. A. HART, PUNISHMENT & RESPONSIBILITY 125 (1968).

40. JACOBS & POTTER, *supra*, at 129; Scott Phillips & Ryken Grattet, *Judicial Rhetoric, Meaning-Making, & the Institutionalization of Hate Crime Law*, 34 L. & SOC'Y REV. 567, 580 (2000); Richard Delgado & David H. Yun, *Pressure Valves and Bloodied Chickens: An Analysis of Paternalistic Objections to Hate*

Speech Regulation, 82 CAL. L. REV. 871, 881–82 (1994); Andrew E. Taslitz, *Hate Crimes, Free Speech, & the Contract of Mutual Indifference*, 80 B.U. L. REV. 1283, 1379–98 (2000).

41. FREDERICK LAWRENCE, PUNISHING HATE: BIAS CRIMES UNDER AMERICAN LAW 154 (1999); Andrew E. Taslitz, *Condemning the Racist Personality: Why the Critics of Hate Crimes Legislation Are Wrong*, 40 B.C. L. Rev. 739, 746 (1999); Charles H. Jones, *Proscribing Hate: Distinctions between Criminal Harm & Protected Expression*, 18 WM. MITCHELL L. REV. 935, 959 (1992).

42. Clyatt v. United States, 197 U.S. 207, 215 (1905); James Henry Haag, *Involuntary Servitude: An Eighteenth-Century Concept in Search of a Twentieth-Century Definition*, 19 Pac. L.J. 873, 877–78 and n.5 (1988); MARCUS CUNLIFFE, CHATTEL SLAVERY AND WAGE SLAVERY: THE ANGLO-AMERICAN CONTEXT 1830–1860, at 10–11 (1979); CHRISTOPHER LASCH, THE TRUE AND ONLY HEAVEN: PROGRESS AND ITS CRITICS 203 (1991); ERIC FONER, FREE SOIL, FREE LABOR, FREE MEN: THE IDEOLOGY OF THE REPUBLICAN PARTY BEFORE THE CIVIL WAR 11–17, 27 (1970); Abraham Lincoln, Speech at Kalamazoo, Michigan, *in* 2 THE COLLECTED WORKS OF ABRAHAM LINCOLN 361, 364 (1953) (Aug. 27, 1856).

43. Lea S. Vandervelde, *The Labor Vision of the Thirteenth Amendment*, 138 U. PA. L. REV. 437, 445–46 (1989); CONG. GLOBE, 39th Cong., 1st Sess. 343 (Jan. 22, 1866).

44. GEORGE W. JULIAN, POLITICAL RECOLLECTIONS, 1840–1872, at 322 (1884).

45. ERIC FONER, THE STORY OF AMERICAN FREEDOM 76–77 (1998); GARY B. NASH, FORGING FREEDOM: THE FORMATION OF PHILADELPHIA'S BLACK COMMUNITY 1720–1840, at 146–47 (1988); GARY B. NASH & JEAN R. SODELUND, FREEDOM BY DEGREES: EMANCIPATION IN PENNSYLVANIA & ITS AFTERMATH 170, 175 (1991); GRAHAM R. HODGES, NEW YORK CITY CARTMEN, 1667–1850, at 158–59 (1986).

46. Peonage Act of 1867, 14 Stat. 546, ch. 187, § 1 (1867) *as amended* 18 U.S.C. § 1581 (2002).

47. Clyatt v. United States, 197 U.S. 207 (1905); Bailey v. State, 219 U.S. 219, 240–41 (1911); James Gray Pope, *The First Amendment, The Thirteenth Amendment, & the Right to Organize in the Twenty-First Century*, 51 RUTGERS L. REV. 941, 962 (1999); Lea S. Vandervelde, *The Labor Vision of the Thirteenth Amendment*, 138 U. PA. L. REV. 437, 438 (1989).

48. Roscoe Pound, *Liberty of Contract*, 18 YALE L.J. 454, 456–57 (1909); Lochner v. New York, 198 U.S. 45, 57 (1905) (holding that "[t]here is no reasonable ground for interfering with the liberty of person or the right of free contract, by determining the hours of labor, in the occupation of a baker. There is no contention that bakers as a class are not equal in intelligence and capacity to men in other trades or manual occupations, or that they are not able to assert

their rights and care for themselves without the protecting arm of the state, interfering with their independence of judgment and of action. They are in no sense
wards of the State").

49. 42 U.S.C. § 2000e(b) (2002); U.S. v. Booker, 655 F.2d 562, 564 (4th Cir.
1981); 18 U.S.C. § 1581 (2002) (twenty years of imprisonment is the maximum
penalty); Baher Azmy, *Unshackling the Thirteenth Amendment: Modern Slavery
and a Reconstructed Civil Rights Agenda*, 71 FORDHAM L. REV. 981, 983, 987–
88 (2002); AMY O. RICHARD, AN INTELLIGENCE MONOGRAPH. INTERNATIONAL
TRAFFICKING IN WOMEN TO THE UNITED STATES: A CONTEMPORARY MANIFES-
TATION OF SLAVERY AND ORGANIZED CRIME 3, 5 (1999); 22 U.S.C. §
7101(b)(1).

50. Victims of Trafficking and Violence Protection Act of 2000 (VTVPA),
Pub. L. 106–386, 114 Stat. 1164 (codified as amended at 22 U.S.C. § 7101–10
(2000); VTVPA § 102(b)(22), 22 U.S.C. § 7101(b)(22); 18 U.S.C. § 1589,
amended by VTVPA, § 112; 18 U.S.C. § 1592, amended by VTVPA, § 112.

51. United States v. Kozminski, 487 U.S. 931, 944, 949 (1988); Michael R.
Candes, *The Victims of Trafficking & Violence Protection Act of 2000: Will It
Become the Thirteenth Amendment of the Twenty-First Century?* 32 U. MIAMI
INTER-AM. L. REV. 571, 588 (2001).

52. Michael H. LeRoy, *Farm Labor Contractors & Agricultural Producers as
Joint Employers under the Migrant & Seasonal Agricultural Work Protection
Act: An Empirical Public Policy Analysis*, 19 BERKELEY J. EMP. & LAB. L. 175,
177 (1998); Andrew Koppelman, *Forced Labor: A Thirteenth Amendment Defense of Abortion*, 84 NW. U. L. REV. 480, 533 (1990).

53. *Three Men Jailed in Human Trafficking Conspiracy—Illegal Migrants
Forced into Indentured Servitude*, Nov. 21, 2002, 2002 WL 25973396; United
States v. Flores, 1999 WL 982041, at 1 (4th Cir. 1999).

54. United States v. Harris, 701 F.2d 1095, 1097–98 (4th Cir. 1983); United
States v. Booker, 655 F.2d 562, 563–66 (4th Cir. 1981); *see also* United States v.
Bibbs, 564 F.2d 1165, 1167–68 (5th Cir. 1977), *cert. denied*, 437 U.S. 1007
(1978).

55. 29 U.S.C. §§ 201–19. In Bureerong v. Uvawas, the Asian Pacific Ameri-
can Legal Center filed a suit under FLSA alleging operators of the El Monte
Compound in California and manufacturers enslaved Thai textile workers. The
District Court refused to reach the merits of the FLSA claim; instead, it dismissed
the case without prejudice on other grounds. Bureerong v. Uvawas, 959 F. Supp.
1231 (C.D. Cal. 1997). Azmy, *supra*, at 1035–36; Becki Young, Note,
*Trafficking of Humans across United States Borders: How United States Laws
Can Be Used to Punish Traffickers & Protect Victims*, 13 GEO. IMMIGR. L.J. 73,
85 (1998); Jennifer T. Manion, Note, *Cultivating Farmworker Injustice: The
Resurgence of Sharecropping*, 621 Ohio St. L.J. 1665, 1678 (2001).

56. 29 U.S.C. § 1803.

Select Bibliography

Ackerman, Bruce, *Constitutional Politics/Constitutional Law*, 99 YALE LAW JOURNAL 453 (1989).

———, *Discovering the Constitution*, 93 YALE LAW JOURNAL 1013 (1984).

———, 1 WE THE PEOPLE: FOUNDATIONS (1991).

AGRICULTURE OF THE UNITED STATES IN 1860; COMPILED FROM THE ORIGINAL RETURNS OF THE EIGHTH CENSUS (1864).

ALBERT, OCTAVIA V. ROGERS, HOUSE OF BONDAGE (1891).

Aleinikoff, T. Alexander, *Re-Reading Justice Harlan's Dissent in Plessy v. Ferguson: Freedom, Antiracism, and Citizenship*, 1992 UNIVERSITY OF ILLINOIS LAW REVIEW 961.

Alexy, Robert, *Individual Rights and Collective Goods, in* RIGHTS (Carlos Nino ed., 1992).

ALLPORT, GORDON W., THE NATURE OF PREJUDICE (1954).

Amar, Akhil Reed, *The Case of the Missing Amendment: R.A.V. v. City of St. Paul*, 106 HARVARD LAW REVIEW 124 (1992).

———, *Intratextualism*, 112 HARVARD LAW REVIEW 747 (1999).

AMERICAN SLAVE: A COMPOSITE AUTOBIOGRAPHY (George Rawick ed., 1972).

ANASTAPLO, GEORGE, THE CONSTITUTIONALIST: NOTES ON THE FIRST AMENDMENT (1971).

Anderson, Elizabeth S., and Richard H. Pildes, *Expressive Theories of Law: A General Restatement*, 148 UNIVERSITY OF PENNSYLVANIA LAW REVIEW 1503 (2000).

ANDREWS, ETHAN A., SLAVERY AND THE DOMESTIC SLAVE-TRADE IN THE UNITED STATES (1836).

ANDREWS, SIDNEY, THE SOUTH SINCE THE WAR: AS SHOWN BY FOURTEEN WEEKS OF TRAVEL AND OBSERVATION IN GEORGIA AND CAROLINAS (1866).

ARNOLD, ISAAC N., THE LIFE OF ABRAHAM LINCOLN (1887).

———, THE HISTORY OF ABRAHAM LINCOLN, AND THE OVERTHROW OF SLAVERY (1866).

AYERS, EDWARD L., THE PROMISE OF THE NEW SOUTH: LIFE AFTER RECONSTRUCTION (1972).

Azmy, Baher, *Unshackling the Thirteenth Amendment: Modern Slavery and a Reconstructed Civil Rights Agenda*, 71 FORDHAM LAW REVIEW 981 (2002).

BANCROFT, FREDERIC, CALHOUN AND THE SOUTH CAROLINA NULLIFICATION MOVEMENT (1928).

———, SLAVE TRADING IN THE OLD SOUTH (1959).

Banning, Lance, *Jeffersonian Ideology Revisited: Liberal & Classical Ideas in the New American Republic*, 43 WILLIAM AND MARY QUARTERLY 3 (3 ser., 1986).

BARNES, GILBERT H., THE ANTI-SLAVERY IMPULSE, 1830–1844 (1933).

BECKER, CARL L., THE DECLARATION OF INDEPENDENCE: A STUDY IN THE HISTORY OF POLITICAL IDEAS (1922).

Beermann, Jack M., *The Unhappy History of Civil Rights Legislation, Fifty Years Later*, 34 CONNECTICUT LAW REVIEW 981 (2002).

Bein, Robert J., *Stained Flags: Public Symbols & Equal Protection*, 28 SETON HALL LAW REVIEW 897 (1998).

BELZ, HERMAN, A NEW BIRTH OF FREEDOM: THE REPUBLICAN PARTY & FREEDMEN'S RIGHTS, 1861–1866 (1976).

———, RECONSTRUCTING THE UNION: THEORY & POLICY DURING THE CIVIL WAR (1969).

BEMIS, SAMUEL F., JOHN QUINCY ADAMS & THE UNION (1956).

BENN, STANLEY I., A THEORY OF FREEDOM (1988).

BERLIN, ISAIAH, FOUR ESSAYS ON LIBERTY (1969).

Berlin, Ira, *Emancipation & Its Meaning, in* UNION & EMANCIPATION: ESSAYS ON POLITICS & RACE IN THE CIVIL WAR ERA (David W. Blight and Brooks D. Simpson eds., 1997).

———, SLAVES NO MORE: THREE ESSAYS ON EMANCIPATION & THE CIVIL WAR (1992).

BICKEL, ALEXANDER M., THE LEAST DANGEROUS BRANCH: THE SUPREME COURT AT THE BAR OF POLITICS (1962).

Binder, Guyora, *Did the Slaves Author the Thirteenth Amendment? An Essay in Redemptive History*, 5 YALE JOURNAL OF LAW AND THE HUMANITIES 471 (1993).

Black, Jr., Charles L., *Further Reflections on the Constitutional Justice of Livelihood*, 86 COLUMBIA LAW REVIEW 1103 (1986).

———, *The Unfinished Business of the Warren Court*, 46 WASHINGTON LAW REVIEW 2 (1970).

BLAINE, JAMES G., TWENTY YEARS OF CONGRESS: FROM LINCOLN TO GARFIELD (1884–1886).

Blake, Michael, *Distributive Justice, State Coercion, and Autonomy*, 30 PHILOSOPHY & PUBLIC AFFAIRS 257 (2002).

BLEDSOE, ALBERT T., AN ESSAY ON LIBERTY & SLAVERY (1857).

Bogin, Ruth, *"Liberty Further Extended": A 1776 Antislavery Manuscript by Lemuel Haynes*, 40 WILLIAM AND MARY QUARTERLY 85 (3 ser., 1983).

Bork, Robert H., *Neutral Principles & Some First Amendment Problems*, 47 IN-
DIANA LAW JOURNAL 1 (1971).
———, THE TEMPTING OF AMERICA: THE POLITICAL SEDUCTION OF THE LAW
(1990).
BOURDIEU, PIERRE, LANGUAGE & SYMBOLIC POWER (Gino Raymond and
Matthew Adamson trans., 1991).
BOWLES, SAMUEL, AND HERBERT GINTIS, DEMOCRACY & CAPITALISM: PROPERTY,
COMMUNITY, & THE CONTRADICTIONS OF MODERN SOCIAL THOUGHT
(1986).
BRADEN, WALDO W., ABRAHAM LINCOLN, PUBLIC SPEAKER (1988).
BRANDON, MARK E., FREE IN THE WORLD: AMERICAN SLAVERY & CONSTITU-
TIONAL FAILURE (1998).
BRANDWEIN, PAMELA T., RECONSTRUCTING RECONSTRUCTION: THE SUPREME
COURT & THE PRODUCTION OF HISTORICAL KNOWLEDGE (1999).
———, *Slavery as an Interpretive Issue in the Reconstruction Congresses*, 34
LAW & SOCIETY REVIEW 315 (2000).
Brest, Paul, *The Conscientious Legislator's Guide to Constitutional Interpreta-
tion*, 27 STANFORD LAW REVIEW 585 (1975).
———, *The Misconceived Quest for the Original Understanding*, 60 BOSTON
UNIVERSITY LAW REVIEW 204 (1980).
Bridgewater, Pamela D., *Reproductive Freedom as Civil Freedom: The Thir-
teenth Amendment's Role in the Struggle for Reproductive Rights*, 3 JOURNAL
OF GENDER, RACE AND JUSTICE 401 (2000).
BROCK, WILLIAM R., AN AMERICAN CRISIS: CONGRESS & RECONSTRUCTION,
1865–1867 (1963).
BROOKS, NOAH, WASHINGTON IN LINCOLN'S TIME (Herbert Mitgang ed., Rine-
hart & Co., Inc. 1958) (1895).
Buchanan, G. Sidney, *The Quest for Freedom: A Legal History of the Thirteenth
Amendment*, 12 HOUSTON LAW REVIEW 1 et seq. (1974).
BURNS, JAMES M., THE VINEYARD OF LIBERTY (1982).
CALABRESI, GUIDO, AND PHILIP BOBBITT, TRAGIC CHOICES (1978).
CALHOUN, JOHN C., CALHOUN: BASIC DOCUMENTS (John M. Anderson ed.,
1952).
———, Letter to Virgil Maxcy (Sept. 11, 1830) (on file with Galloway-Maxcy-
Markoe Papers).
Carcieri, Martin D., *Democracy and Education in the Thought of Jefferson and
Madison*, 26 JOURNAL OF LAW AND EDUCATION 1 (1997).
CARPENTER, FRANCIS B., SIX MONTHS AT THE WHITE HOUSE WITH ABRAHAM
LINCOLN (1867).
THE CAUSES OF THE CIVIL WAR (Kenneth M. Stampp ed., 1974).
CHASE, SALMON P., INSIDE LINCOLN'S CABINET: THE CIVIL WAR DIARIES OF
SALMON P. CHASE (David Donald ed., 1954).

———, Letter to Gerrit Smith (Mar. 2, 1864) *in* JACOB W. SCHUCKERS, THE LIFE AND PUBLIC SERVICE OF SALMON PORTLAND CHASE (1874).

CHASTELLUX, FRANÇOIS J., TRAVELS IN NORTH-AMERICA IN THE YEARS 1780, 1781, & 1782 (1787).

Chemerinsky, Erwin, *Making the Right Case for a Constitutional Right to Minimum Entitlements*, 44 MERCER LAW REVIEW 525 (1993).

Christman, John, *Constructing the Inner Citadel: Recent Work on the Concept of Autonomy*, 99 ETHICS 109 (1988).

CLEVELAND, HENRY, ALEXANDER H. STEPHENS IN PUBLIC AND PRIVATE (1866).

Cohen, William, *Negro Involuntary Servitude in the South, 1865–1940: A Preliminary Analysis*, 42 JOURNAL OF SOUTHERN HISTORY 31 (1976).

Colbert, Douglas L., *Affirming the Thirteenth Amendment*, 1995 ANNUAL SURVEY OF AMERICAN LAW 403 (1995).

———, *Challenging the Challenge: Thirteenth Amendment as a Prohibition against the Racial Use of Peremptory Challenges*, 76 CORNELL LAW REVIEW 1 (1990).

———, *Liberating the Thirteenth Amendment*, 30 HARVARD CIVIL RIGHTS–CIVIL LIBERTIES LAW REVIEW 1 (1995).

COLE, ARTHUR CHARLES, THE ERA OF THE CIVIL WAR, 1848–1870 (1919).

———, THE IRREPRESSIBLE CONFLICT, 1850–1865 (1934).

CONWAY, MONCURE D., TESTIMONIES CONCERNING SLAVERY (1864).

Corwin, Edward S., *The Doctrine of Due Process of Law before the Civil War*, 24 HARVARD LAW REVIEW 460 (1911).

Cosgrove, Charles H., *The Declaration of Independence in Constitutional Interpretation: A Selective History & Analysis*, 32 UNIVERSITY OF RICHMOND LAW REVIEW 107 (1998).

Cox, Archibald, *Constitutional Adjudication and the Promotion of Human Rights*, 80 HARVARD LAW REVIEW 91 (1966).

COX, LAWANDA C., FREEDOM, RACISM, & RECONSTRUCTION: COLLECTED WRITINGS OF LAWANDA COX (Donald G. Nieman ed., 1997).

COX, LAWANDA, AND JOHN H. COX, POLITICS, PRINCIPLE, & PREJUDICE, 1865–1866 (1969).

Crane, Elaine F., *Dependence in the Era of Independence: The Role of Women in a Republican Society, in* THE AMERICAN REVOLUTION: ITS CHARACTER AND LIMITS (Jack P. Greene ed., 1987).

CRAVEN, AVERY O., THE COMING OF THE CIVIL WAR (1942).

———, RECONSTRUCTION: THE ENDING OF THE CIVIL WAR (1969).

CROCKER, LAWRENCE, POSITIVE LIBERTY: AN ESSAY IN NORMATIVE POLITICAL PHILOSOPHY (1980).

Cruz, David B., *"Just Don't Call It Marriage": The First Amendment and Marriage as an Expressive Resource*, 74 SOUTHERN CALIFORNIA LAW REVIEW 925 (2001).

CUNLIFFE, MARCUS, CHATTEL SLAVERY AND WAGE SLAVERY: THE ANGLO-AMERI-CAN CONTEXT, 1830–1860 (1979).

CURRY, LEONARD P., THE FREE BLACK IN URBAN AMERICA, 1800–1850 (1981).

CURTIS, BENJAMIN R., A MEMOIR OF BENJAMIN ROBBINS CURTIS: WITH SOME PROFESSIONAL AND MISCELLANEOUS WRITINGS (1879).

CURTIS, GEORGE T., LIFE OF DANIEL WEBSTER (1870).

DAHL, ROBERT A., DEMOCRACY AND ITS CRITICS (1989).

DAVIS, DAVID BRION, THE PROBLEM OF SLAVERY IN THE AGE OF REVOLUTION, 1770–1823 (1975).

——, THE PROBLEM OF SLAVERY IN WESTERN CULTURE (1966).

Davis, Thomas J., *Emancipation Rhetoric, Natural Rights, & Revolutionary New England: A Note on Four Black Petitions in Massachusetts, 1773–1777*, 62 NEW ENGLAND QUARTERLY 248 (1989).

Degler, Carl N., *Irony of American Negro Slavery, in* PERSPECTIVES & IRONY IN AMERICAN SLAVERY: ESSAYS (Harry P. Owens ed., 1976).

——, OUT OF OUR PAST: THE FORCES THAT SHAPED MODERN AMERICA (1959).

DEGREGORIO, WILLIAM A., THE COMPLETE BOOK OF U.S. PRESIDENTS (5th ed. 1993).

DePauw, Linda G., *Land of the Unfree: Legal Limitations on Liberty in Pre-Revolutionary America*, 68 MARYLAND HISTORICAL MAGAZINE 355 (1973).

DE SANTIS, VINCENT P., REPUBLICANS FACE THE SOUTHERN QUESTION: THE NEW DEPARTURE YEARS, 1877–1897 (1959).

DODD, WILLIAM E., JEFFERSON DAVIS (1907).

DOUGLASS, FREDERICK, THE LIFE AND WRITINGS OF FREDERICK DOUGLASS (Philip S. Foner ed., 1950–1955).

Drake, Richard B., *Freedmen's Aid Societies and Sectional Compromise*, 29 JOURNAL OF SOUTHERN HISTORY 175 (1963).

DUMOND, DWIGHT L., ANTISLAVERY ORIGINS OF THE CIVIL WAR IN THE UNITED STATES (1939).

DWORKIN, GERALD, THE THEORY AND PRACTICE OF AUTONOMY (1988).

DWORKIN, RONALD M., FREEDOM'S LAW: THE MORAL READING OF THE AMERI-CAN CONSTITUTION (1996).

——, TAKING RIGHTS SERIOUSLY (1977).

EHRLICH, HOWARD J., THE SOCIAL PSYCHOLOGY OF PREJUDICE: A SYSTEMATIC THEORETICAL REVIEW AND PROPOSITIONAL INVENTORY OF THE AMERICAN SOCIAL PSYCHOLOGICAL STUDY OF PREJUDICE (1973).

Eisenberg, Theodore, and Stewart Schwab, Note, *The Importance of Section 1981*, 73 CORNELL LAW REVIEW 596 (1988).

Ely, John Hart, *The Wages of Crying Wolf: A Comment on* Roe v. Wade, 82 YALE LAW JOURNAL 920 (1973).

Engel, Steven A., Note, *The* McCulloch *Theory of the Fourteenth Amendment: City of Boerne v. Flores & the Original Understanding of Section 5*, 109 YALE LAW JOURNAL 115 (1999).

Engelman Lado, Marianne L., *A Question of a Question of Justice: African-American Legal Perspectives on the 1883 Civil Rights Cases*, 70 CHICAGO-KENT LAW REVIEW 1123 (1995).

Epstein, Richard A., *The Proper Scope of the Commerce Clause*, 73 VIRGINIA LAW REVIEW 1387 (1987).

ESCOTT, PAUL D., SLAVERY REMEMBERED: A RECORD OF TWENTIETH-CENTURY SLAVE NARRATIVES (1979).

FALKNER, LEONARD, THE PRESIDENT WHO WOULDN'T RETIRE (1967).

Fallon, Jr., Richard H., *How to Choose a Constitutional Theory*, 87 CALIFORNIA LAW REVIEW 535 (1999).

———, *"The Rule of Law" as a Concept in Constitutional Discourse*, 97 COLUM. L. REV. 1 (1997).

———, *Two Senses of Autonomy*, 46 STANFORD LAW REVIEW 875 (1994).

FEHRENBACHER, DON E., CONSTITUTIONS & CONSTITUTIONALISM IN THE SLAVE-HOLDING SOUTH (1989).

———, *Only His Stepchildren: Lincoln & the Negro, in* A NATION DIVIDED: PROBLEMS & ISSUES OF THE CIVIL WAR & RECONSTRUCTION (George M. Fredrickson ed., 1975).

FEINBERG, JOEL, RIGHTS, JUSTICE, & THE BOUNDS OF LIBERTY: ESSAYS IN SOCIAL PHILOSOPHY (1980).

———, SOCIAL PHILOSOPHY (1973).

FILLER, LOUIS, RISE & FALL OF SLAVERY IN AMERICA (1980).

FINE, SIDNEY, LAISSEZ FAIRE AND THE GENERAL-WELFARE STATE: A STUDY OF CONFLICT IN AMERICAN THOUGHT, 1865–1901 (1956).

Fink, Leon, *Labor, Liberty, and the Law: Trade Unionism and the Problem of the American Constitutional Order*, 74 JOURNAL OF AMERICAN HISTORY 904 (1987).

Finkelman, Paul, *The Color of Law*, 87 NORTHWESTERN UNIVERSITY LAW REVIEW 937 (1993).

———, *The Crime of Color*, 67 TULANE LAW REVIEW 2063 (1993).

———, AN IMPERFECT UNION: SLAVERY, FEDERALISM, AND COMITY (1981).

FINNIS, JOHN, NATURAL LAW AND NATURAL RIGHTS (1980).

FIRTH, RAYMOND W., SYMBOLS: PUBLIC AND PRIVATE (1973).

FISCH, GEORGES, NINE MONTHS IN THE UNITED STATES DURING THE CRISIS (1863).

Fiss, Owen M., *The Forms of Justice*, 93 HARVARD LAW REVIEW 1 (1979).

FITZHUGH, GEORGE, CANNIBALS ALL!, OR SLAVES WITHOUT MASTERS (1857).

———, SOCIOLOGY FOR THE SOUTH, OR, THE FAILURE OF FREE SOCIETY (1854).

Fleming, James E., *Constructing the Substantive Constitution*, 72 TEXAS LAW REVIEW 211 (1993).

———, *Fidelity to Our Imperfect Constitution*, 65 FORDHAM LAW REVIEW 1335 (1997).

———, *Securing Deliberative Autonomy*, 48 STANFORD LAW REVIEW 1 (1995).

Foner, Eric, *From Free Soil, Free Labor, Free Men: The Ideology of the Republican Party, in* THE CAUSES OF THE AMERICAN CIVIL WAR (Edwin C. Rozwenc ed., 1972).

———, *The Meaning of Freedom in the Age of Emancipation*, 81 JOURNAL OF AMERICAN HISTORY 435 (1994).

———, *Politics, Ideology, & the Origins of the American Civil War, in* A NATION DIVIDED: PROBLEMS & ISSUES OF THE CIVIL WAR AND RECONSTRUCTION (George M. Fredrickson ed., 1975).

———, RECONSTRUCTION: AMERICA'S UNFINISHED REVOLUTION, 1863–1877 (1988).

———, THE STORY OF AMERICAN FREEDOM (1998).

———, TOM PAINE AND REVOLUTIONARY AMERICA (1976).

Forbath, William E., *The Ambiguities of Free Labor: Labor & the Law in the Gilded Age*, 1985 WISCONSIN LAW REVIEW 767.

———, *Caste, Class, and Equal Citizenship*, 98 MICHIGAN LAW REVIEW 1 (1999).

Forman, Jr., James, *Driving Dixie Down: Removing the Confederate Flag from Southern State Capitols*, 101 YALE LAW JOURNAL 505 (1991).

FRANKFURTER, FELIX, THE COMMERCE CLAUSE UNDER MARSHALL, TANEY AND WAITE (1937).

———, *Taft and the Supreme Court, in* FELIX FRANKFURTER ON THE SUPREME COURT: EXTRAJUDICIAL ESSAYS ON THE COURT AND THE CONSTITUTION (Philip B. Kurland ed., 1970).

FRANKLIN, JOHN HOPE, THE EMANCIPATION PROCLAMATION (1963).

———, FROM SLAVERY TO FREEDOM (1956).

Fraser, Jr., Walter J., *William Henry Ruffner and the Establishment of Virginia's Public School System, 1870–1874*, 79 VIRGINIA MAGAZINE OF HISTORY AND BIOGRAPHY 259 (1971).

FREEHLING, WILLIAM W., PRELUDE TO CIVIL WAR: THE NULLIFICATION CONTROVERSY IN SOUTH CAROLINA, 1816–1836 (1965).

———, THE REINTEGRATION OF AMERICAN HISTORY: SLAVERY AND THE CIVIL WAR (1994).

———, THE ROAD TO DISUNION: SECESSIONISTS AT BAY 1776–1854 (1990).

Friedman, Barry, and Scott B. Smith, *The Sedimentary Constitution*, 147 UNIVERSITY OF PENNSYLVANIA LAW REVIEW 1 (1998).

FROMM, ERICH, ESCAPE FROM FREEDOM (1965).

GARRISON, FRANCIS J., AND WENDELL P. GARRISON, WILLIAM LLOYD GARRISON 1805–1879 (1889).

GEORGE, JAMES Z., THE POLITICAL HISTORY OF SLAVERY IN THE UNITED STATES (1915).

GIENAPP, WILLIAM E., THE ORIGINS OF THE REPUBLICAN PARTY, 1852–1856 (1987).

Gillette, William, *Noah H. Swayne, in* THE JUSTICES OF THE UNITED STATES SUPREME COURT 1789–1978: THEIR LIVES & MAJOR OPINIONS (Leon Friedman and Fred L. Israel eds., 1980).

———, RETREAT FROM RECONSTRUCTION 1869–1879 (1979).

Goldstein, Robert D., *Blyew: Variations on a Jurisdictional Theme,* 41 STANFORD LAW REVIEW 469 (1989).

Goluboff, Risa L., *The Thirteenth Amendment & the Lost Origins of Civil Rights,* 50 DUKE LAW JOURNAL 1609 (2001).

GOODELL, WILLIAM, THE AMERICAN SLAVE CODE IN THEORY & PRACTICE (1853).

———, SLAVERY AND ANTISLAVERY (1853).

GRAY, TIM, FREEDOM (1991).

Green, F., *Some Aspects of the Convict Lease System in the Southern States, The James Sprunt Studies, in* HISTORY AND POLITICAL SCIENCE: ESSAYS IN SOUTHERN HISTORY (1949).

Grey, Thomas C., *Do We Have an Unwritten Constitution?* 27 STANFORD LAW REVIEW 703 (1975).

Griffin, James, *The Human Good & the Ambitions of Consequentialism,* 9 SOCIAL PHILOSOPHY AND POLICY 118 (1992).

GUNTHER, GERALD, AND KATHLEEN M. SULLIVAN, CONSTITUTIONAL LAW (1997).

GUTMAN, HERBERT G., BLACK FAMILY IN SLAVERY & FREEDOM, 1750–1925 (1976).

HAMILTON, ALEXANDER, JAMES MADISON, AND JOHN JAY, THE FEDERALIST (Benjamin Fletcher Wright ed., 1961).

Hamilton, Howard D., *The Legislative & Judicial History of the Thirteenth Amendment,* 9 NATIONAL BAR JOURNAL 26 (1951).

HARLAN, MALVINA S., SOME MEMORIES OF A LONG LIFE, 1854–1911 (2002).

Harris, Carl V., *Reforms in Government Control of Negroes in Birmingham, Alabama, 1890–1920,* 38 JOURNAL OF SOUTHERN HISTORY 567 (1972).

HARRIS, N. DWIGHT, THE HISTORY OF NEGRO SERVITUDE IN ILLINOIS AND OF THE SLAVERY AGITATION IN THAT STATE, 1719–1864 (1904).

HART, H. L. A., POLITICAL PHILOSOPHY (Anthony Quinton ed., 1967).

HAVILAND, LAURA S., A WOMAN'S LIFE-WORK (1889).

HAYEK, FRIEDRICH A., THE CONSTITUTION OF LIBERTY (1960).

HERTZ, EMANUEL, ABRAHAM LINCOLN: A NEW PORTRAIT (1931).

HESSELTINE, WILLIAM B., ULYSSES S. GRANT, POLITICIAN (1935).

HIGGINSON, THOMAS W., ARMY LIFE IN A BLACK REGIMENT (1870).

Hill, John Lawrence, *A Third Theory of Liberty: The Evolution of Our Conception of Freedom in American Constitutional Thought*, 29 HASTINGS CONSTITUTIONAL LAW QUARTERLY 115 (2002).

HIRSHSON, STANLEY P., FAREWELL TO THE BLOODY SHIRT (1962) .

HOAR, GEORGE F., AUTOBIOGRAPHY OF SEVENTY YEARS (1903).

HOBHOUSE, L. T., THE ELEMENTS OF SOCIAL JUSTICE (1922).

Hobsbawm, Eric, *Inventing Traditions, in* THE INVENTION OF TRADITION (Eric Hobsbawm and Terence Ranger eds., 1983).

HODGES, GRAHAM R., NEW YORK CITY CARTMEN, 1667–1850 (1986).

HOEMANN, GEORGE H., WHAT GOD HATH WROUGHT: THE EMBODIMENT OF FREEDOM IN THE THIRTEENTH AMENDMENT (1987).

HOFSTADTER, RICHARD, SOCIAL DARWINISM IN AMERICAN THOUGHT (1955).

HOLCOMBE, W. H., THE ALTERNATIVE: A SEPARATE NATIONALITY OR THE AFRICANIZATION OF THE SOUTH (1860).

HOLLISTER, O., LIFE OF SCHUYLER COLFAX (1886).

HOPKINS, VINCENT C., DRED SCOTT'S CASE (1951).

HOROWITZ, ROBERT F., THE GREAT IMPEACHER: A POLITICAL BIOGRAPHY OF JAMES M. ASHLEY (1979).

HORWITZ, MORTON J., THE TRANSFORMATION OF AMERICAN LAW 1870–1960: THE CRISIS OF LEGAL ORTHODOXY (1992).

Howard, Victor B., *The Black Testimony Controversy in Kentucky, 1866–1872*, 58 JOURNAL NEGRO HISTORY 140 (1973).

———, *The Civil War in Kentucky: The Slave Claims His Freedom*, 67 JOURNAL NEGRO HISTORY 245 (1982).

HUME, DAVID, ENQUIRIES CONCERNING THE HUMAN UNDERSTANDING AND CONCERNING THE PRINCIPLES OF MORALS (L. A. Selby-Bigge and P. H. Nidditch III eds., reprinted, 1975) (1748).

Huq, Aziz Z., Note, *Peonage & Contractual Liberty*, 101 COLUMBIA LAW REVIEW 351 (2001).

HURD, JOHN C., THE LAW OF FREEDOM AND BONDAGE IN THE UNITED STATES (1858–1862).

Hyde, Alan, *A Theory of Labor Legislation*, 38 BUFFALO LAW REVIEW 383 (1990).

HYMAN, HAROLD M., THE RADICAL REPUBLICANS & RECONSTRUCTION 1861–1870 (1967).

HYMAN, HAROLD M. AND WILLIAM M. WIECEK, EQUAL JUSTICE UNDER LAW: CONSTITUTIONAL DEVELOPMENT 1835–1875 (1982).

IRONS, PETER, A PEOPLE'S HISTORY OF THE SUPREME COURT (1999).

Jefferson, Thomas, *Kentucky Resolution, in* THE LIFE & WRITINGS OF THOMAS JEFFERSON (S. E. Forman ed., 1900).

———, THE WORKS OF THOMAS JEFFERSON (Paul L. Ford ed., 1904–05).

———, NOTES ON THE STATE OF VIRGINIA (William Peden ed., 1982) (1782).

JENKINS, WILLIAM S., PRO-SLAVERY THOUGHT IN THE OLD SOUTH (1935).

JOHANNSEN, ROBERT W., THE LINCOLN-DOUGLAS DEBATES OF 1858 (1965).

Johnson, Allen, *The Constitutionality of the Fugitive Slave Acts*, 31 YALE LAW JOURNAL 161 (1921–22).

JORDAN, WINTHROP D., WHITE OVER BLACK: AMERICAN ATTITUDES TOWARD THE NEGRO, 1550–1812 (1968).

JULIAN, GEORGE W., POLITICAL RECOLLECTIONS, 1840–1872 (1884).

———, SPEECHES ON POLITICAL QUESTIONS (1872).

Kaczorowski, Robert J., *To Begin the Nation Anew: Congress, Citizenship, & Civil Rights after the Civil War*, 92 AMERICAN HISTORICAL REVIEW 45 (1987).

———. *Revolutionary Constitutionalism In the Era of the Civil War & Reconstruction*, 61 NEW YORK UNIVERSITY LAW REVIEW 863 (1986).

Kant, Immanuel, *Groundwork of the Metaphysic of Morals, in* THE MORAL LAW (H. J. Paton ed. & trans., 3d ed. 1958).

KEMBLE, FANNY, JOURNAL OF A RESIDENCE ON A GEORGIAN PLANTATION IN 1838–1839 (1864).

KENDRICK, BENJAMIN B., THE JOURNAL OF THE JOINT COMMITTEE OF FIFTEEN ON RECONSTRUCTION, 39TH CONGRESS, 1865–1867 (1914).

KING, RICHARD H., CIVIL RIGHTS AND THE IDEA OF FREEDOM (1992).

KOLCHIN, PETER, AMERICAN SLAVERY, 1619–1877 (1993).

———, FIRST FREEDOM: THE RESPONSES OF ALABAMA'S BLACKS TO EMANCIPATION AND RECONSTRUCTION (1972).

Koppelman, Andrew, *Forced Labor: A Thirteenth Amendment Defense of Abortion*, 84 NORTHWESTERN UNIVERSITY LAW REVIEW 480 (1990).

KOVEL, JOEL, WHITE RACISM: A PSYCHOHISTORY (1970).

Krotoszynski, Jr., Ronald J., *Equal Justice under Law: The Jurisprudential Legacy of Judge Frank M. Johnson, Jr.*, 109 YALE LAW JOURNAL 1237 (2000).

KULL, ANDREW, THE COLOR-BLIND CONSTITUTION (1992).

Ladenson, Robert F., *A Theory of Personal Autonomy*, 86 ETHICS 30 (1975).

LAMON, LESTER C., BLACKS IN TENNESSEE 1791–1970 (1981).

LAPSLEY, ARTHUR B., THE WRITINGS OF ABRAHAM LINCOLN (1905).

LASCH, CHRISTOPHER, THE TRUE AND ONLY HEAVEN: PROGRESS AND ITS CRITICS (1991).

Lass, Andrew, *Romantic Documents and Political Monuments: The Meaning-Fulfillment of History in 19th-Century Czech Nationalism*, 15 AMERICAN ETHNOLOGIST 456 (1988).

LATHAM, FRANK B., THE GREAT DISSENTER: JOHN MARSHALL HARLAN 1833–1911 (1970).

LAWRENCE, FREDERICK, PUNISHING HATE: BIAS CRIMES UNDER AMERICAN LAW (1999).

LeFEVRE,ROBERT, THE FUNDAMENTAL OF LIBERTY (1988).

LeRoy, Michael H., *Farm Labor Contractors & Agricultural Producers as Joint Employers Under the Migrant & Seasonal Agricultural Worker Protection Act: An Empirical Public Policy Analysis*, 19 BERKELEY JOURNAL OF EMPLOYMENT AND LABOR LAW 175 (1998).

LES BENEDICT, MICHAEL, A COMPROMISE OF PRINCIPLE: CONGRESSIONAL REPUBLICANS AND RECONSTRUCTION, 1863–1869 (1974).

Lessig, Lawrence, *The Regulation of Social Meaning*, 62 UNIVERSITY OF CHICAGO LAW REVIEW 943 (1995).

Lessig, Lawrence and Cass R. Sunstein, *The President & the Administration*, 94 COLUMBIA LAW REVIEW 1 (1994).

LEUCHTENBERG, WILLIAM E., THE SUPREME COURT REBORN: THE CONSTITUTIONAL REVOLUTION IN THE AGE OF ROOSEVELT (1995).

LEVINSON, SANFORD, CONSTITUTIONAL FAITH (1988).

——, *They Whisper: Reflections on Flags, Monuments, & State Holidays, & the Construction of Social Meaning in a Multicultural Society*, 70 CHICAGO-KENT LAW REVIEW 1079 (1995).

LIBERTY (David Miller, ed., 1991).

THE LINCOLN ENIGMA (Gabor Boritt, ed., 2001).

LINCOLN, ABRAHAM, THE COLLECTED WORKS OF ABRAHAM LINCOLN (Roy P. Basler, *et al.* eds., 1953).

——, SPEECHES & WRITINGS, 1859–1865 (1989).

LINDLEY, RICHARD, AUTONOMY (1986).

LIPPMANN, WALTER, PUBLIC OPINION (1957).

LITWACK, LEON F., BEEN IN THE STORM SO LONG: THE AFTERMATH OF SLAVERY (1979).

Livingstone, John D., *Uniformity of Patent Law Following Florida Prepaid: Should the Eleventh Amendment Put Patent Owners Back in the Middle Again*, 50 EMORY LAW JOURNAL 323 (2001).

LOCKE, JOHN, TWO TREATISES OF GOVERNMENT (Peter Laslett ed., Mentor Press 1965) (1689).

——, THE WORKS OF JOHN LOCKE (1823).

LOFGREN, CHARLES A., THE PLESSY CASE: A LEGAL-HISTORICAL INTERPRETATION (1987).

LONG, DOUGLAS G., BENTHAM ON LIBERTY: JEREMY BENTHAM'S IDEA OF LIBERTY IN RELATION TO HIS UTILITARIANISM (1977).

LYND, S., CLASS CONFLICT, SLAVERY, AND THE UNITED STATES CONSTITUTION: TEN ESSAYS (1967).

LYSANDER SPOONER, THE UNCONSTITUTIONALITY OF SLAVERY (1853).

MACKAY, CHARLES, LIFE & LIBERTY IN AMERICA (1859).

MacKinnon, Catharine A., *Disputing Male Sovereignty: On* United States v. Morrison, 114 HARVARD LAW REVIEW 135 (2000).

MAINE, HENRY S., ANCIENT LAW (1861).

MALINOWSKI, BRONISLAW, FREEDOM: ITS HISTORY, NATURE, & VARIETIES (Robert E. Dewey and James A. Gould eds., 1970).

————, *The Group & The Individual in Functional Analysis*, 44 AMERICAN JOURNAL OF SOCIOLOGY 958 (1939).

Maltz, Earl A., *Fourteenth Amendment Concepts in Antebellum Era*, 32 AMERICAN JOURNAL OF LEGAL HISTORY 305 (1988).

MANDEL, BERNARD, LABOR: FREE AND SLAVE (1955).

MANELI, MIECZYSLAW, FREEDOM AND TOLERANCE (1984).

Marshall, Thurgood, *Commentary: Reflections on the Bicentennial of the United States Constitution*, 101 HARVARD LAW REVIEW 1 (1987).

Matsuda, Mary J., *Public Response to Racist Speech: Considering the Victim's Story*, 87 MICHIGAN LAW REVIEW 2320 (1989).

MAY, HENRY F., THE ENLIGHTENMENT IN AMERICA (1976).

McAdams, Richard H., *An Attitudinal Theory of Expressive Law*, 79 OREGON LAW REVIEW 339 (2000).

McCloskey, H. J., *Some Arguments for a Liberal Society*, 43 PHILOSOPHY 324 (1968).

McCLURE, ALEXANDER K., COLONEL ALEXANDER K. McCLURE'S RECOLLECTIONS OF HALF A CENTURY (1902).

McDONALD, FORREST, NOVUS ORDO SECLORUM: THE INTELLECTUAL ORIGINS OF THE CONSTITUTION (1985).

McDOUGALL, MARION G., FUGITIVE SLAVES (1969).

McGoldrick, James M., *Katzenbach v. McClung: The Abandonment of Federalism in the Name of Rational Basis*, 14 BRIGHAM YOUNG JOURNAL OF PUBLIC LAW 1 (1999).

McLEMORE, RICHARD A., ED., A HISTORY OF MISSISSIPPI (1973).

McMANUS, EDGAR J., THE NEGRO UNDER SLAVERY, IN BLACKS IN WHITE AMERICA: BEFORE 1865 (Robert V. Haynes ed., 1972).

McPHERSON, JAMES M., THE ABOLITIONIST LEGACY: FROM RECONSTRUCTION TO THE NAACP (2d ed. 1995).

————, BATTLE CRY OF FREEDOM: THE CIVIL WAR ERA (1988).

————, *Coercion or Conciliation? Abolitionists Debate President Hayes' Southern Policy*, 39 NEW ENGLAND QUARTERLY 474 (1966).

————, DRAWN WITH THE SWORD: REFLECTIONS ON THE AMERICAN CIVIL WAR (1996).

————, THE STRUGGLE FOR EQUALITY: ABOLITIONISTS & THE NEGRO IN THE CIVIL WAR & RECONSTRUCTION (2d ed. 1995).

Metz, Thaddeus, *Recent Work on the Meaning of Life*, 112 ETHICS 781 (2002).

MILL, JOHN STUART, ON SOCIAL FREEDOM (1941).

————, Three Essays (1975).

Miller, Loren, The Petitioners: The Story of the Supreme Court of the United states & the Negro (1966).

Miller, William Lee, Arguing about Slavery: The Great Battle in the United States Congress (1996).

Millis, Harry A., and Royal E. Montgornery, Organized Labor (1945).

Milner, David, Children and Race (1983).

Milton, George F., The Eve of Conflict: Stephen A. Douglas and the Needless War (1934).

Minogue, K. R., *Freedom as a Skill, in* Of Liberty (A. Phillips Griffiths ed., 1983).

Moore, Ambrose Y., The Life of Schuyler Colfax (1868).

Moore, Glover, The Missouri Controversy, 1819–1821 (1953).

Murphy, Walter F., *An Ordering of Constitutional Values*, 53 Southern California Law Review 703 (1980).

Myrdal, Gunnar, An American Dilemma: The Negro Problem & Modern Democracy (1944).

Nash, Gary B., Forging Freedom: The Formation of Philadelphia's Black Community 1720–1840 (1988).

Nash, Gary B., and Jean R. Sodelund, Freedom by Degrees: Emancipation in Pennsylvania & Its Aftermath (1991).

National Party Platforms, 1840–1960 (Donald B. Johnson and Kirk H. Porter eds., 1961).

Nevins, Allan, Ordeal of the Union 449–50 (1947).

The "New" Thirteenth Amendment: A Preliminary Analysis, 82 Harvard Law Review 1294 (1969).

Nieman, Donald G., Promises to Keep: African-Americans & the Constitutional Order, 1776 to the Present (1991).

————, To Set the Law in Motion: The Freedmen's Bureau & the Legal Rights of Blacks, 1865–1868 (1979).

Norton, Mary Beth, *Afro-American Family in the Age of Revolution, in* Slavery & Freedom in the Age of the American Revolution (Ira Berlin and Ronald Hoffman eds., 1983).

Novak, Daniel A., The Wheel of Servitude: Black Forced Labor after Slavery (1978).

Nozick, Robert, Anarchy, State, and Utopia (1974).

Nye, Russel B., Fettered Freedom: Civil Liberties & the Slavery Controversy, 1830–1860 (1949).

Oakes, James, Slavery & Freedom: An Interpretation of the Old South (1990).

Olmsted, Frederick L., The Cotton Kingdom: A Traveller's Observations of Cotton & Slavery in the American Slave States (1861).

OTIS, JAMES, PAMPHLETS OF THE AMERICAN REVOLUTION, 1750–1776 (Bernard Bailyn ed., 1965).

Paludan, Phillip S., *Law and the Failure of Reconstruction: The Case of Thomas Cooley*, 33 JOURNAL OF THE HISTORY OF IDEAS 597 (1972).

PARKER, THEODORE, A LETTER TO THE PEOPLE OF THE UNITED STATES TOUCHING THE MATTER OF SLAVERY (1848).

Pastore, Mariana Claridad, *Running from the Law: Federal Contractors Escape Bivens Liability*, 4 UNIVERSITY OF PENNSYLVANIA JOURNAL OF CONSTITUTIONAL LAW 850 (2002).

PETTIT, PHILIP, REPUBLICANISM: A THEORY OF FREEDOM AND GOVERNMENT (1997).

Pildes, Richard H., *Why Rights Are Not Trumps: Social Meanings, Expressive Harms, and Constitutionalism*, 27 JOURNAL OF LEGAL STUDIES 725 (1988).

Pildes, Richard H., and Richard G. Niemi, *Expressive Harms, "Bizarre Districts" and Voting Rights: Evaluating Election-District Appearances after Shaw v. Reno*, 92 MICHIGAN LAW REVIEW 483 (1993).

Pittman, Larry J., *Physician-Assisted Suicide in the Dark Ward: The Intersection of Thirteenth Amendment & Health Care Treatments Having Disproportionate Impacts*, 28 SETON HALL LAW REVIEW 774 (1998).

POORE, BEN PERLEY, PERLEY'S REMINISCENCES OF SIXTY YEARS IN THE NATIONAL METROPOLIS (1886).

Pope, James G., *The First Amendment, The Thirteenth Amendment, & the Right to Organize in the Twenty-First Century*, 51 RUTGERS LAW REVIEW 941 (1999).

———, *The Thirteenth Amendment versus the Commerce Clause: Labor & the Shaping of American Constitutional Law, 1921–1957*, 102 COLUMBIA LAW REVIEW 1 (2002).

POTTER, DAVID M., THE IMPENDING CRISIS, 1848–1861 (1976).

Pound, Roscoe, *Liberty of Contract*, 18 YALE LAW JOURNAL 454 (1909).

Powell, Gloria Johnson, *Self-Concept in White & Black Children, in* RACISM & MENTAL HEALTH (Charles V. Willie *et al.* eds., 1973).

PRICE, RICHARD, POLITICAL WRITINGS (D. O. Thomas ed., 1991).

Pushaw, Robert J., Jr., and Grant S. Nelson, *A Critique of the Narrow Interpretation of the Commerce Clause*, 96 NORTHWESTERN UNIVERSITY LAW REVIEW 695 (2002).

QUILLIN, FRANK U., THE COLOR LINE IN OHIO: A HISTORY OF RACE PREJUDICE IN A TYPICAL NORTHERN STATE (1913).

RAKOVE, JACK N., ORIGINAL MEANINGS: POLITICS AND IDEAS IN THE MAKING OF THE CONSTITUTION (1996).

RANDALL, JAMES G., CONSTITUTIONAL PROBLEMS UNDER LINCOLN (1926).

RAWLS, JOHN, COLLECTED PAPERS (Samuel Freeman ed., 1999).

———, POLITICAL LIBERALISM (1993).

————, A THEORY OF JUSTICE (1971).

RAZ, JOSEPH, THE MORALITY OF FREEDOM (1986).

————, *Rights & Individual Well-Being, in* ETHICS IN THE PUBLIC DOMAIN: ESSAYS IN THE MORALITY OF LAW & POLITICS (1994).

REID, WHITELAW, AFTER THE WAR: A TOUR OF THE SOUTHERN STATES, MAY 1, 1865–May 1, 1866 (1866).

Reinstein, Robert J., *Completing the Constitution: The Declaration of Independence, Bill of Rights & Fourteenth Amendment,* 66 TEMPLE LAW REVIEW 361 (1993).

REISS, OSCAR, BLACKS IN COLONIAL AMERICA (1997).

Rhodes, James F., *Antecedents of the American Civil War, in* THE CAUSES OF THE AMERICAN CIVIL WAR (Edwin C. Rozwenc 2d ed., 1972).

————, HISTORY OF THE UNITED STATES FROM THE COMPROMISE OF 1850 TO THE FINAL RESTORATION OF HOME RULE AT THE SOUTH IN 1877 (1892).

RICHARDS, DAVID A. J., CONSCIENCE & THE CONSTITUTION: HISTORY, THEORY, & LAW OF THE RECONSTRUCTION AMENDMENTS (1993).

RICHARDSON, JOE M., CHRISTIAN RECONSTRUCTION: THE AMERICAN MISSIONARY ASSOCIATION AND SOUTHERN BLACKS, 1861–1890 (1986).

RIDDLEBERGER, PATRICK W., GEORGE WASHINGTON JULIAN, RADICAL REPUBLICAN: A STUDY IN NINETEENTH-CENTURY POLITICS AND REFORM (1966).

RODGERS, DANIEL T., THE WORK ETHIC IN INDUSTRIAL AMERICA 1850–1920 (1978).

Ross, Thomas, *The Rhetorical Tapestry of Race: White Innocence & Black Abstraction,* 32 WILLIAM AND MARY LAW REVIEW 1 (1990).

ROZWENC, EDWIN C., SLAVERY AS A CAUSE OF THE CIVIL WAR (1963).

RUSSEL, ROBERT R., CRITICAL STUDIES IN ANTEBELLUM SECTIONALISM: ESSAYS IN AMERICAN POLITICAL AND ECONOMIC HISTORY (1972).

RUSSELL, JOHN H., THE FREE NEGRO IN VIRGINIA (1913).

SANDEL, MICHAEL J., LIBERALISM AND THE LIMITS OF JUSTICE (1982).

SANDIFER, DURWARD VALDIMIR, AND L. RONALD SCHEMAN, THE FOUNDATIONS OF FREEDOM: THE INTERRELATIONSHIP BETWEEN DEMOCRACY AND HUMAN RIGHTS (1966).

SAWYER, GEORGE S., SOUTHERN INSTITUTES: OR, AN INQUIRY INTO THE ORIGIN & EARLY PREVALENCE OF SLAVERY & THE SLAVE TRADE (1858).

Saxowsky, David M., *et al., Employing Migrant Agricultural Workers: Overcoming the Challenge of Complying with Employment Laws,* 69 NORTH DAKOTA LAW REVIEW 307 (1993).

Scanlon, Thomas, *A Theory of Freedom of Expression,* 1 PHILOSOPHY AND PUBLIC AFFAIRS 204 (1972).

Schauer, Frederick, *A Comment on the Structure of Rights,* 27 GEORGIA LAW REVIEW 415 (1993).

————, FREE SPEECH: A PHILOSOPHICAL ENQUIRY (1982).

———, *Is Government Speech a Problem?* 35 STANFORD LAW REVIEW 373 (1983).

SCHEDLER, GEORGE, RACIST SYMBOLS & REPARATIONS: PHILOSOPHICAL REFLECTIONS ON VESTIGES OF THE AMERICAN CIVIL WAR (1998).

SCHEINGOLD, STUART A., THE POLITICS OF RIGHTS: LAWYERS, PUBLIC POLICY, & POLITICAL CHANGE (1974).

SCOTT, WILLIAM B., IN PURSUIT OF HAPPINESS: AMERICAN CONCEPTIONS OF PROPERTY FROM THE SEVENTEENTH TO THE TWENTIETH CENTURY (1977).

SHIRER, WILLIAM L., THE RISE & FALL OF THE THIRD REICH: A HISTORY OF NAZI GERMANY (1960).

SIDGWICK, HENRY, THE ELEMENTS OF POLITICS (1919).

SIMMS, HENRY H., A DECADE OF SECTIONAL CONTROVERSY, 1851–1861 (1942).

SIMPSON, GEORGE E., AND J. MILTON YINGER, RACIAL & CULTURAL MINORITIES: AN ANALYSIS OF PREJUDICE & DISCRIMINATION (3d ed. 1972).

Singer, Joseph William, *No Right to Exclude: Public Accommodations and Private Property*, 90 NORTHWESTERN UNIVERSITY LAW REVIEW 1283 (1996).

SKINNER, QUENTIN, *The Paradoxes of Political Liberty, in* EQUAL FREEDOM (Stephen Darwell ed., 1995).

SLAVE TESTIMONY: TWO CENTURIES OF LETTERS, SPEECHES, INTERVIEWS, AND AUTOBIOGRAPHIES (John W. Blassingame ed. 1977).

SMITH, ELBERT B., THE DEATH OF SLAVERY: THE UNITED STATES, 1837–65 (1967).

SMITH, GERRIT, SPEECHES & LETTERS OF GERRIT SMITH . . . ON THE REBELLION . . . (1864–65).

SMITH, WILLIAM A., LECTURES ON THE PHILOSOPHY AND PRACTICE OF SLAVERY, AS EXHIBITED IN THE INSTITUTION OF DOMESTIC SLAVERY IN THE UNITED STATES (1856).

Smith, Roger M., *The Constitution and Autonomy*, 60 TEXAS LAW REVIEW 175 (1982).

Spain, Jr., Charles A., *The Flags & Seals of Texas*, 33 SOUTH TEXAS LAW REVIEW 215 (1992).

Springer, Chris, *The Troubled Resurgence of the Confederate Flag*, 43 HISTORY TODAY 7 (1993).

STAMPP, KENNETH M., THE ERA OF RECONSTRUCTION, 1865–1877 (1966).

———, THE IMPERILED UNION: ESSAYS ON THE BACKGROUND OF THE CIVIL WAR (1980).

———, THE PECULIAR INSTITUTION: SLAVERY IN THE ANTE-BELLUM SOUTH (1956).

Stanley, Amy Dru, *Beggars Can't Be Choosers: Compulsion & Contract in Postbellum America*, 78 JOURNAL OF AMERICAN HISTORY 1265 (1992).

Steinbock, Daniel J., *The Wrong Line between Freedom & Restraint: The Unre-*

ality, Obscurity, & Incivility of the Fourth Amendment Consensual Encounter Doctrine, 38 SAN DIEGO LAW REVIEW 507 (2001).

STEPHEN, JAMES F., LIBERTY, EQUALITY, FRATERNITY (R. J. White ed., 1967).

STEPHENS, ALEXANDER H., A CONSTITUTIONAL VIEW OF THE LATE WAR BETWEEN THE STATES: ITS CAUSES, CHARACTER, CONDUCT & RESULTS (1868).

Strauss, David A., *Common Law Constitutional Interpretation*, 63 UNIVERSITY OF CHICAGO LAW REVIEW 877 (1996).

———. *The Irrelevance of Constitutional Amendments*, 114 HARVARD LAW REVIEW 1457 (2001).

SULLIVAN, KATHLEEN M. AND GERALD GUNTHER, CONSTITUTIONAL LAW (2001).

Sunstein, Cass R., *Social Norms and Social Roles*, 96 COLUMBIA LAW REVIEW 903 (1996).

Sydnor, Charles S., *The Free Negro in Mississippi before the Civil War*, 32 AMERICAN HISTORICAL REVIEW 769 (1927).

Taslitz, Andrew E., *Condemning the Racist Personality: Why the Critics of Hate Crimes Legislation Are Wrong*, 40 BOSTON COLLEGE LAW REVIEW 739 (1999)

———, *Hate Crimes, Free Speech, & the Contract of Mutual Indifference*, 80 BOSTON UNIVERSITY LAW REVIEW 1283 (2000).

———, *Slaves No More! The Implications of the Informed Citizen Ideal for Discovery before Fourth Amendment Suppression Hearings*, 15 GEORGIA STATE UNIVERSITY LAW REVIEW 709 (1999).

TENBROEK, JACOBUS, EQUAL UNDER LAW (Collier Books 1965).

TENZER, LAWRENCE R., THE FORGOTTEN CAUSE OF THE CIVIL WAR: A NEW LOOK AT THE SLAVERY ISSUE (1997).

Thomas, Brook, *Plessy v. Ferguson & the Literary Imagination*, 9 CARDOZO STUDIES IN LAW AND LITERATURE 45 (1997).

THORPE, FRANCIS N., CONSTITUTIONAL HISTORY OF THE UNITED STATES (1901).

TINDALL, GEORGE B., AMERICA: A NARRATIVE HISTORY (1984).

Torok, John Hayakawa, *Reconstruction and Racial Nativism: Chinese Immigrants and the Debates on the Thirteenth, Fourteenth and Fifteenth Amendments and Civil Rights Laws*, 3 ASIAN LAW JOURNAL 55 (1996).

TRIBE, LAURENCE H., AMERICAN CONSTITUTIONAL LAW (1988).

———, *In Memoriam: William J. Brennan, Jr.*, 111 HARVARD LAW REVIEW 41 (1997).

———, *The Puzzling Persistence of Process-Based Constitutional Theories*, 89 YALE LAW JOURNAL 1063 (1980).

TROWBRIDGE, JOHN T., THE SOUTH: A TOUR OF ITS BATTLE-FIELDS & RUINED CITIES (1866).

Tsesis, Alexander, *Contextualizing Bias Crimes: A Social & Theoretical Perspective*, 27 LAW & SOCIAL INQUIRY 315 (2003).

————, DESTRUCTIVE MESSAGES: HOW HATE SPEECH PAVES THE WAY FOR HARMFUL SOCIAL MOVEMENTS (2002).

————, *Furthering American Freedom: Civil Rights & the Thirteenth Amendment*, 45 BOSTON COLLEGE LAW REVIEW 307 (2004).

————, *The Problem of Confederate Symbols: A Thirteenth Amendment Approach*, 75 TEMPLE LAW REVIEW 539 (2002).

TURLEY, DAVID, THE CULTURE OF ENGLISH ANTISLAVERY, 1780–1860 (1991).

TYLER, SAMUEL, MEMOIR OF ROGER BROOKE TANEY (1872).

UNDERKUFFLER, LAURA S., THE IDEA OF PROPERTY: ITS MEANING & POWER (2003).

Vandervelde, Lea S., *The Labor Vision of the Thirteenth Amendment*, 138 UNIVERSITY OF PENNSYLVANIA LAW REVIEW 437 (1989).

VAN DIJK, TEUN A., COMMUNICATING RACISM: ETHNIC PREJUDICE IN THOUGHT & TALK (1987).

Vassa, Gustavus, *The Life of Olaudah Equiano, the African, in* GREAT DOCUMENTS IN BLACK AMERICAN HISTORY (George Ducas and Charles Van Doren eds., 1970) (1789).

VAUGHN, WILLIAM PRESTON, SCHOOLS FOR ALL: THE BLACKS & PUBLIC EDUCATION IN THE SOUTH, 1865–1877 (1974).

VORENBERG, MICHAEL, FINAL FREEDOM: THE CIVIL WAR, THE ABOLITION OF SLAVERY, & THE THIRTEENTH AMENDMENT (2001).

A War Correspondent's View of St. Augustine and Fernandina: 1863, 41 FLORIDA HISTORICAL QUARTERLY 64(1962).

WARNER, RICHARD, FREEDOM, ENJOYMENT & HAPPINESS: AN ESSAY ON MORAL PSYCHOLOGY (1987).

Warren, Samuel D., and Louis D. Brandeis, *The Right to Privacy*, 4 HARVARD LAW REVIEW 193 (1890).

WE ARE YOUR SISTERS: BLACK WOMEN IN THE NINETEENTH CENTURY (Dorothy Sterling, ed., 1984).

WEEVILS IN THE WHEAT: INTERVIEWS WITH VIRGINIA EX-SLAVES (Charles L. Perdue, *et al* eds., 1976).

WELD, THEODORE, AMERICAN SLAVERY AS IT IS (1839).

————, Letter to Ray Potter (June 11, 1836) *in* LETTERS OF THEODORE DWIGHT WELD, ANGELINA GRIMKÉ WELD, & SARAH GRIMKÉ, 1822–1844 (Gilbert H. Barnes and Dwight L. Dumond eds., 1934).

WELLES, GIDEON, DIARY OF GIDEON WELLES (1911).

————, *The History of Emancipation*, 14 THE GALAXY 842 (1872).

Westin, Alan F., *John Marshall Harlan & the Constitutional Rights of Negroes: The Transformation of a Southerner*, 66 YALE LAW JOURNAL 637 (1957).

WHARTON, VERNON LANE, THE NEGRO IN MISSISSIPPI: 1865–1890 (1965).

WHEATLEY, PHYLLIS, A NATIVE AFRICAN AND A SLAVE (1995).

WHITE, JAMES B., WHEN WORDS LOSE THEIR MEANING: CONSTITUTIONS AND RECONSTITUTIONS OF LANGUAGE, CHARACTER, AND COMMUNITY (1984).

WIECEK, WILLIAM M., SOURCES OF ANTISLAVERY CONSTITUTIONALISM, 1760–1848 (1977).

WILLIAMSON, JOEL, AFTER SLAVERY: THE NEGRO IN SOUTH CAROLINA DURING RECONSTRUCTION, 1861–1877 (1965).

WILTSE, CHARLES M., JOHN C. CALHOUN: NULLIFIER, 1829–1839 (1949).

Wolff, Tobias B., *The Thirteenth Amendment & Slavery in the Global Economy*, 102 COLUMBIA LAW REVIEW 973, 1040 (2002).

WOOD, GORDON S., THE ROLE OF IDEOLOGY IN THE AMERICAN REVOLUTION (John R. Howe, Jr. ed., 1970).

YOUNG, JAMES P., RECONSIDERING AMERICAN LIBERALISM: THE TROUBLED ODYSSEY OF THE LIBERAL IDEA (1996).

YOUNG, ROBERT, PERSONAL AUTONOMY: BEYOND NEGATIVE AND POSITIVE LIBERTY (1986).

Index

About the Author

Alexander Tsesis, visiting Professor at University of Pittsburgh School of Law, is Visiting Assistant Professor at Chicago–Kent College of Law, and Visiting Scholar at the University of Wisconsin Law School, Institute for Legal Studies. He is the author of *Destructive Messages: How Hate Speech Paves the Way for Harmful Social Movements* (NYU Press, 2002). He has published on a variety of legal issues, including free speech, federally sponsored programs for the homeless, poverty issues surrounding domestic violence victims, and the over–institutionalization of troubled children.